CAMBRIDGE COMMENTARIES ON
WRITINGS OF THE JEWISH AND CHRISTIAN WORLD
200 BC TO AD 200
VOLUME 4

# Early Rabbinic Writings

CAMBRIDGE COMMENTARIES ON
WRITINGS OF THE JEWISH AND CHRISTIAN WORLD
200 BC TO AD 200

*General Editors:*
P. R. ACKROYD
A. R. C. LEANEY
J. W. PACKER

1 i *Jews in the Hellenistic World: Josephus, Aristeas, the Sibylline Oracles, Eupolemus* – John R. Bartlett
1 ii *Jews in the Hellenistic World: Philo* – R. Williamson
2 *The Qumran Community* – M. A. Knibb
3 *Early Rabbinic Writings* – H. Maccoby
4 *Outside the Old Testament* – M. de Jonge
5 *Outside the New Testament* – G. N. Stanton
6 *Jews and Christians: Graeco-Roman Views* – Molly Whittaker
7 *The Jewish and Christian World 200 BC to AD 200* – A. R. C. Leaney

# EARLY RABBINIC WRITINGS

HYAM MACCOBY
*Fellow of Leo Baeck College, London*



CAMBRIDGE UNIVERSITY PRESS

Cambridge
New York New Rochelle Melbourne Sydney

Published by the Press Syndicate of the University of Cambridge
The Pitt Building, Trumpington Street, Cambridge CB2 1RP
32 East 57th Street, New York, NY 10022, USA
10 Stamford Road, Oakleigh, Melbourne 3166, Australia



First published 1988

Printed in Great Britain at the University Press, Cambridge

*British Library cataloguing in publication data*

Maccoby, Hyam
Early rabbinic writings. – (Cambridge commentaries on writings of the Jewish and Christian world 200 BC to AD 200; v. 3).
1. Judaism 2. Rabbinical literature
I. Title
296.1'7 BM 496.5

*Library of Congress cataloguing in publication data*

Maccoby, Hyam, 1924–
Early rabbinic writings.
(Cambridge commentaries on writings of the Jewish and Christian world, 200 BC to AD 200; 3)
Bibliography.
Includes index.
1. Rabbinical literature – History and criticism.
2. Rabbinical literature – Translations into English.
I. Title. II. Series: Cambridge commentaries on writings of the Jewish and Christian world, 200 B.C. to A.D. 200; 3)
BM496.5.M23 1988 296.1'205'21 87-26793

ISBN 0 521 24248 7 hard covers
ISBN 0 521 28553 4 paperback



CE

*To my children,*
*David, Deborah and Melanie,*
*my son-in-law, Alan,*
*and my grandson, Daniel*

# Contents

# General editors' preface

The three general editors of the Cambridge Bible Commentary series have all, in their teaching, experienced a lack of readily usable texts of the literature which is often called pseudepigrapha but which is more accurately defined as extra-biblical or para-biblical literature. The aim of this new series is to help fill this gap.

The welcome accorded to the Cambridge Bible Commentary has encouraged the editors to follow the same pattern here, except that carefully chosen extracts from the texts, rather than complete books, have normally been provided for comment. The introductory material leads naturally into the text, which itself leads into alternating sections of commentary.

Within the severe limits imposed by the size and scope of the series, each contributor will attempt to provide for the student and general reader the results of modern scholarship, but has been asked to assume no specialized theological or linguistic knowledge.

The volumes already planned cover the writings of the Jewish and Christian World from about 200 BC to AD 200 and are being edited as follows:

1 i *Jews in the Hellenistic World: Josephus, Aristeas, the Sibylline Oracles, Eupolemus* – John R. Bartlett, Trinity College, Dublin
1 ii *Jews in the Hellenistic World: Philo* – R. Williamson, University of Leeds
2 *The Qumran Community* – M. A. Knibb, King's College, London
3 *Early Rabbinic Writings* – H. Maccoby, Leo Baeck College, London
4 *Outside the Old Testament* – M. de Jonge, University of Leiden
5 *Outside the New Testament* – G. N. Stanton, King's College, London
6 *Jews and Christians: Graeco-Roman Views* – Molly Whittaker, University of Nottingham

A seventh volume by one of the general editors, A. R. C. Leaney, *The Jewish and Christian World 200 BC to AD 200*, examines the wider historical and literary background to the period and includes tables of dates, relevant lists and maps. Although this companion volume will preface and augment the series, it may also be read as complete in itself and be used as a work of general reference.

P.R.A. A.R.C.L. J.W.P.

# Author's preface

Though it is the policy of this series to use the New English Bible (NEB) for biblical quotations, I have found that the older translations – which I have sometimes amended by my own translations – were often more suitable, because of their greater literalness, for the purposes of the present volume. Where it is important to know which particular translation is being employed, I have specified the version within the text (Authorized Version: AV, Jewish Publication Society: JPS).

I have adhered, in general, to a uniform system of transliteration of Hebrew terms and names, but I have retained those spellings that have become familiar in the English language, such as the Mishnah, Ishmael, and Gamaliel. It was sometimes difficult to decide, however, whether a given term or name had acquired sufficient general use for this treatment.

Rabbinic passages have all been translated newly by me, though, of course, I have consulted previous translations where available.

I wish to thank the editors of the series for their great patience and helpfulness.

My heartfelt thanks go to my wife, Cynthia, for her constant help and support, and for her searching and constructive criticism.

# Glossary

*'aggadah*: see *haggadah*.

*'Aḥer* ('another'): name given to Elisha ben Abuyah after his defection.

*ʿAlenu* ('It is our duty . . .'): the opening word and title of a prayer for the unification of mankind in the worship of God.

*ʿam ha-'areṣ* (literally, 'people of the land', but employed to mean 'person of the land'):

1. 'layman', in the sense of one not learned in the Torah (see *talmid ḥakam*);
2. 'layman', in the sense of one not a member of a ritual-purity society (see *ḥaber*).

*'Amora*, pl. *'Amora'im* ('speaker'): a teacher of the period AD 200 to AD 500, between the closure of the Mishnah and the closure of the Talmuds (see *Tanna* and *gemara*).

*'anšey maʿaseh* ('men of deed'): a name given to wonder-workers of the Pharisaic movement (see *Ḥasidim*).

*ʿAqedah* ('binding'): the incident of the Binding of Isaac by Abraham (Gen. 22:1–10).

*baraita* ('outside'): a Tannaitic pericope not included in the Mishnah.

*berakah*, pl. *berakot* ('blessing'): a liturgical form beginning with the words, 'Blessed are you, Lord . . .', expressing thanks for some benefit enjoyed.

*bet din* ('house of judgement'): a court of justice.

*bet din ha-gadol* ('the Great Court'): the supreme court, or Sanhedrin.

*bet ha-keneset* ('house of assembly'): synagogue.

*bet ha-midraš* ('house of study'): school or college.

*binyan 'ab* ('building a father'): induction, one of the hermeneutic methods (see p. 162).

*dabar ha-lamed meʿinyano* ('something that is understood through its context'): one of the rabbinic hermeneutic methods of explaining the Torah (see p. 177).

*dayo* ('it is sufficient for it'): a principle of the rabbinic theory of the *a fortiori* argument (*qal wa-ḥomer*), by which the conclusion cannot contain any term not contained in the premise.

*demai* (derivation not certainly known): produce about which there is doubt whether it has been tithed.
*de-rabbanan* ('of the rabbis' or 'rabbinical', Aramaic): descriptive of laws instituted by human authority (opposite: *de-'oraita*).
*deraša* ('interpretation', from the root *daraš*, 'to search', see *deruš* and *midrash*): an interpretation, using rabbinic hermeneutic methods, of a scriptural text, not necessarily in a work of the genre *midrash* (see *pešat*).
*derek 'ereṣ* ('the way of the world'): etiquette and courtesy, rules of which were collected in the late Talmudic tractate, *Derek 'Ereṣ*.
*deruš*: equivalent to *deraša*.
*de-'oraita* ('of the Torah', Aramaic): descriptive of laws, whether of the Written or of the Oral Torah, having Divine authority (opposite *de-rabbanan*).
*dibbur* ('word'): used in the Targums and elsewhere, to mean the Word of God (see *memra*).
*din* ('judgement'): used sometimes to mean 'logic' or 'reasoning'.
*dinar*: see *zuz*.
*'ebyon* ('poor'): one who is not just poor, but destitute.
*'erusin* ('betrothal'): preliminary stage of marriage (see *nissu'in*).
*gemara* ('learning by heart'): Gemara, the commentary on the Mishnah. This, together, with the Mishnah itself, comprises the Talmud. An authority of the Gemara is called an *'Amora*.
*gemilut ḥasadim* ('the performance of mercies'): deeds of charity to all in distress (see *ṣedaqah*).
*genizah* ('hiding place'): *Genizah*, store-room where Jewish documents of all kinds were preserved out of reverence for the name of God contained in them.
*ger tošab* ('resident stranger'): a Gentile living in the Land of Israel, who observes the Noachian Laws and some others, but is not a full convert to Judaism (cf. *ger ṣedeq*, 'righteous stranger', a full convert).
*gezerah šawah* ('similar expression'): a hermeneutic method by which a law is deduced from the occurrence of a distinctive biblical expression in different contexts (see p. 174).
*gilluy 'arayot* ('the uncovering of nakedness'): acts of sexual depravity, as listed in Lev. 18.
*ḥaber*, pl. *ḥaberim* ('associate' or 'fellow'):

1. a member of a society of those voluntarily undertaking to observe a supererogatory standard of ritual purity and tithing (see *'am ha-'areṣ*);

2. a member of any other religious society, e.g. a charitable organisation or a society for the decent burial of the dead;
3. a title of scholars (like 'fellow' in English).

*ḥaburah*, pl. *ḥaburot* ('fellowship'): a group formed for any religious purpose; especially for the supererogatory observance of ritual purity and tithing.

*haggadah* ('telling'): the non-legal, homiletic aspect of rabbinic activity, often found in the form *'aggadah* (see *halakah*).

*Haggadah*: the liturgy of the *Seder* service in the home on Passover evening.

*ḥakamim* ('Sages'):
1. the name, *Ḥakamim*, by which the Pharisaic leaders were known before AD 70;
2. used in the Mishnah to denote 'the majority of the rabbis'.

*halakah* ('going'):
1. the legal aspect of rabbinic activity (see *haggadah*);
2. a legal ruling.

*halakah le-Mošeh mi-Sinai* ('a law given to Moses from Sinai'): a law of the Oral Torah regarded as having divine authority.

*Halakic Midrashim*: an alternative name for the Tannaitic Midrashim.

*ḥaliṣah* ('loosening'): the divorce of the brother's widow in levirate law, so-called because of the rite of loosening the shoe (Deut. 25:9).

*Hallel* ('praise'): the liturgical recital of Ps. 113–18 at festivals and new moons.

*Ḥanukkah* ('dedication'): a minor festival commemorating the rededication of the Temple after the victory of Judas Maccabaeus over the Seleucid Greeks (164 BC).

*ḥaroset* ('clay-like'): a sweet, soft mixture of fruits and spices (Passover *Seder*).

*ḥasid* ('saint'): one who practised a standard of virtue higher than that required by the law.

*Ḥasidim*:
1. a religious movement of the second century BC, which supported the Maccabaean revolt against the Seleucid Greeks;
2. a group of the Pharisaic movement in the first century BC, which practised supererogatory virtue and included charismatics and wonder-workers (see *'anšey ma'aseh*);
3. a movement of ascetics and mystics in Germany in the thirteenth century AD;
4. a movement, beginning in the eighteenth century AD, which stressed religious emotion and charisma.

*ḥasid šoteh* ('foolish saint'): one who, in pursuing saintliness, fails to observe common-sense rules for the preservation of life.

*ḥerem* ('setting apart'):
1. form of excommunication (more serious than *nidduy*);
2. property dedicated for holy purposes.

*ḥesed* ('loving-kindness'):
1. the quality of benevolence;
2. an act of benevolence.

*heykal*, pl. *heykalot* ('palace'): one of the seven palaces of the Seventh Heaven, entered by the mystic in trance, on his journey to the throne-room of God.

*ḥol ha-moʿed* ('the non-holy part of the festival'): the intermediate days of Passover and Tabernacles, during which most kinds of work were permitted.

*ḥullin* ('non-holy things'): ordinary food, having no sanctity (see *terumah* and *qodašim*).

*karpas* ('celery' or 'parsley'): salad or vegetable dish which forms part of the Passover *Seder* service.

*kelal uperaṭ* ('the general and the particular'): one of the hermeneutic methods (see p. 176).

*ketubah* ('written deed'): the marriage contract, containing the settlement due to the wife in case of divorce or the husband's death.

*lewayah*, or *halwayah* ('escort'):
1. the courtesy of accompanying a parting guest;
2. the funeral procession.

*log*: a liquid measure, equal to the volume of six eggs (see *se'ah*).

*maʿamad* ('standing'): regional group of laymen, associated with one of the twenty-four courses (*mišmarot*) of the priests.

*maʿaseh berešit* ('the practice of, or connected with, the Creation'): mystical discipline directed towards attaining a vision of the secrets of Creation.

*maʿaseh merkabah* ('the work of the Chariot'): mystical discipline directed towards attaining a vision of the Divine Chariot (Ezek. 1).

*maʿaser*, pl. *maʿaserot* ('tenth'): tithe prescribed in the Bible (Num. 18:21; Deut. 14:22–9; 26:12). (See *terumah*.)

*malkut šamayim* ('the Kingdom of Heaven'):
1. the rule of God in the present. This is accepted by reciting the *Shemaʿ*;
2. the eschatological rule of God over all mankind.

*maqom* ('place'): a name of God signifying 'All-present' or 'Ever-present'.

*maror* ('bitter'): bitter herbs eaten as part of the Passover *Seder* service.

*maṣah*: unleavened bread, prescribed for Passover.

*memra* ('word'): used to mean the Word of God (see *dibbur*).

*menorah* ('lamp'): the Menorah, the seven-branched candlestick in the Sanctuary of the Temple.

*met miṣwah* ('corpse of commandment'): an abandoned corpse: all passers-by are required to engage themselves in giving it decent burial.

*meturgeman*, or *turgeman* ('interpreter'): a synagogue functionary who translated orally the weekly biblical lection into Aramaic for the better understanding of the people.

*middah*, pl. *middot* ('measure'):
1. measurement;
2. quality or attribute;
3. hermeneutic method.

*midras* ('pressure'): uncleanness caused to an object by pressure on it from certain sources of impurity (see Lev. 15:4, 9, 20, 23, referring to sitting, lying and riding).

*midrash* ('searching', see *deraša*):
1. the genre of rabbinic literature in which *haggadah* and *halakah* are displayed by means of continuous or ordered exposition of Scripture;
2. (pl. *midrashot*), a unit or pericope of a Midrashic work.

*Midrash*, pl. *Midrashim*: a rabbinic work of the genre *midrash*.

*minah*: a unit of money, equal to 100 *dinars*.

*minyan* ('number'): a quorum of ten required for public prayer.

*miqweh*, or *miqwah* ('gathering'): the ritual pool of forty *se'ahs*, used for the immersion of people or objects in order to remove ritual impurity.

*mishnah* ('repetition'):
1. the genre of halakic compilation arranged by topics, not in the order of exegesis of Scripture;
2. (pl. *mishnayot*), a subsection or pericope of a Mishnah.

*Mishnah*, a: any work in the *genre* of *mishnah*, e.g. the Mishnah of Rabbi Akiba.

*Mishnah*, the: the Mishnah of Rabbi Judah the Prince, accepted as the most authoritative collection of the halakic aspects of the Oral Torah.

*mišneh torah* ('copy of the law'): rabbinic designation of the book of Deuteronomy.

*Mishneh Torah*: work by Maimonides (1135–1204).
*miṣwah* ('commandment'):
1. A biblical commandment, whether positive or negative;
2. a religious act, or a welcome opportunity to perform one.

*Nasi* ('prince'): title of the President of the High Court.
*Nazirite* (Hebrew, *nazir*, 'abstinent'): one bound by a vow to abstain from wine, etc. (Num. 6:1–21).
*ne'eman* ('trusted'): a member of a society for the supererogatory observance of tithing.
*nešamah*:
1. breath;
2. soul.

*niddah* ('separation'): a menstruating woman, whose contact causes ritual impurity.
*nidduy* ('banishment'): form of excommunication (for thirty days).
*Nišmat* ('the breath of . . .'): first word and title of a Sabbath prayer, containing praise of God.
*nissu'in*: the final stage of marriage (see *'erusin*).
*Noachian Laws*: laws obligatory on Gentiles ('sons of Noah').
*noṣerim* ('Nazarenes'): Jewish–Christians.
*'omer* ('sheaf'):
1. a dry measure, the quantity of grain in one sheaf;
2. the *'Omer* of barley offered on the sixteenth of Nisan (Lev. 23:10–14).

*'oneg šabbat* ('Sabbath-delight', see Isa. 58:13): the duty of celebrating the Sabbath in a manner conducive to ease and pleasure.
*pardes* ('garden'): a name given to the ultimate experience of those practising mysticism.
*pe'ah* ('corner'): the duty of leaving a corner of a field, when reaping, for the poor (Lev. 19:9).
*peraṭ ukelal* ('the particular and the general'): one of the hermeneutic methods (see p. 176).
*perušim*, or *perušin* ('separated ones'):
1. the Pharisees (probably originally so-called by their opponents, the Sadducees);
2. sectarians, heretics;
3. observers of supererogatory ritual purity (equivalent to *ḥaberim*);
4. ascetics, abstaining from wine and meat (see p. 142).

*peruṭah*: a small coin, equal to one-sixteenth of a *pondion*.

*pesaḥ*:
1. the paschal sacrifice;
2. the Passover festival.

*pešat* ('plain'): the literal meaning of a biblical text (see *deraša*).

*pesuqey de-zimrah* ('verses of song'): the early part of the morning liturgy, consisting of psalms of praise.

*pondion* (from Latin *dupondium*): a coin, equal to sixteen *peruṭahs*, and worth one-twelfth of a *dinar* or *zuz*.

*prosbol*, or *prozbol* (from Greek *probole* or *pros boulei*): a document exempting a loan from the seventh-year cancellation instituted in Deut. 15:1–11.

*Purim* ('lots', see Esther 9:24–6): minor festival commemorating the events described in the Book of Esther.

*qal wa-ḥomer* ('light and heavy'): the *a fortiori* argument, one of the hermeneutic methods (see p. 173).

*qarqa'* ('land'): immovable property.

*Qedušah* ('declaration of holiness'): section of the liturgy in which the congregation pronounces, 'Holy, holy, holy' (Isa. 6:3).

*Qidduš* ('sanctification'): ceremony in the home with wine, inaugurating the Sabbath or festival meal with blessings.

*qidduš ha-šem* ('sanctification of the name'): martyrdom.

*qodašim* ('holinesses'): consecrated objects, sacrifices (see *terumah*).

*quppah* ('basket'): communal fund for weekly distribution to the poor of the locality (see *tamḥuy*).

*Rabban*: title of certain leading authorities.

*ruaḥ ha-qodeš* ('the holy spirit'): Divine inspiration.

*ša'aṭnez* (derivation uncertain): a mixture of wool and linen, forbidden as clothing (Deut. 22:11).

*Sanhedrin* (from Greek *synhedrion*):
1. supreme council and court of seventy-one members;
2. smaller court of twenty-three members.

*se'ah*: a measure of liquid or dry capacity, equal to six *qabs*, or twenty-four *logs*.

*ṣedaqah* ('righteousness'): charity, in the sense of almsgiving (see *gemilut ḥasadim*).

*seder* ('order'):
1. *Seder*, the order of service in the home on Passover night;
2. (pl. *sedarim*), an Order of the Mishnah, one of its six main divisions.

*šeḥiṭah* ('slaughtering'): the prescribed manner of slaughtering animals for food.

*šekinah* ('residence'): the special presence of God in a particular place. Sometimes equivalent to 'Divine inspiration'.
*sela'*: a coin, equal to two *šeqels*.
*semikah* ('leaning on'): the ordaining of a rabbi by laying on of hands.
*šemiṭṭah* ('release'): the Seventh Year, when debts were cancelled, and the land had to lie fallow.
*semukin* ('proximities'): a hermeneutical method based on the near proximity of biblical passages.
*šeney ketubim* ('two verses'): a hermeneutic method, by which contradictory verses were harmonised (see p. 175).
*šeqel*: a coin, equal to two *dinars*, and worth half a *sel'a*.
*Shema'* ('Hear . . .'): title and first word of the affirmation of God's unity (Deut. 6:4), the centre of the liturgy.
*simḥat ha-miṣwah* ('joy of the commandment'): sense of pleasure and privilege in having an opportunity to perform a biblical commandment.
*šomer sakar* ('guardian for pay'): one hired to watch over animals or property.
*šopar*: musical instrument made from an animal's horn, blown on New Year and other religious occasions.
*soper*, pl. *soperim* ('scribe'):
1. Scribe, title of religious leaders, especially those of the pre-Tannaitic period beginning with Ezra;
2. scribe, writer of documents and scrolls of the Torah.

*talmid ḥakam* ('scholar and sage'): one learned in the Written and Oral Torah (see *'am ha-'areṣ*).
*talmud torah* ('learning of Torah'): the duty of applying oneself to learning the Written and Oral Torah.
*tamḥuy* ('food-plate'): daily food distribution for all the poor indiscriminately (see *quppah*).
*tanna*, pl. *tanna'im* ('repeater' or 'teacher'):
1. a *Tanna*, an authority of the period AD 10 to AD 200 (see *'Amora*).
2. one who learnt the Mishnah by heart.

*targum* ('translation'): Aramaic translation of the Bible.
*tebul yom* ('he who immersed that day'): one who has taken a ritual bath to remove impurity but retains a minor degree of impurity until the evening (Lev. 11:25, etc.).
*tepillah* ('prayer'): the petitionary part of the liturgy, especially the Eighteen Benedictions.

*terumah*, pl. *terumot* ('offering'): the portion of the produce (from a sixtieth to a fortieth) given to the priests (Num. 18:8, 26–7). (See *ḥullin*, *maʿaser*, and *qodašim*.)
*tešubah* ('return'): repentance.
*torah še-be-ʿal peh* ('teaching that is by mouth'): the Oral Torah.
*torah še-bi-ketab* ('teaching that is by writing'): the Written Torah.
*yeṣer ha-raʿ*: the evil inclination.
*yešibah*: an academy.
*zab*: one who is ritually unclean through a sexual disease (Lev. 15:1–15).
*zakut*: merit acquired through the performance of good deeds.
*zuz*: a coin, also called *dinar*, worth half a *šeqel*, and equal to twelve *pondions*.

# Abbreviations

## *Tractates of the Mishnah, in alphabetical order.*

(For the tractates of the Mishnah in their proper order see p. 50.)

| | | | |
|---|---|---|---|
| 'Ab. | 'Abot | | |
| ʿA. Zar. | ʿAbodah Zarah | Naz. | Nazir |
| ʿArak. | ʿArakin | Ned. | Nedarim |
| B.B. | Baba Batra | Neg. | Negaʿim |
| Bek. | Bekorot | Nid. | Niddah |
| Ber. | Berakot | 'Oh. | 'Oholot |
| Beṣ. | Beṣah | ʿOrl. | ʿOrlah |
| Bikk. | Bikkurim | Par. | Parah |
| B.M. | Baba Meṣʿia | Pe'ah | Pe'ah |
| B.Q. | Baba Qamma | Pes. | Pesaḥim |
| Dem. | Demai | Qid. | Qiddušin |
| ʿEd. | ʿEduyyot | Qin. | Qinnim |
| ʿEr. | ʿErubin | R.Š. | Roš ha-Šanah |
| Giṭ. | Giṭṭin | Šab. | Šabbat |
| Ḥag. | Ḥagigah | Sanh. | Sanhedrin |
| Ḥal. | Ḥallah | Šeb. | Šebiit |
| Hor. | Horayot | Šebu. | Šebuʿot |
| Ḥul. | Ḥullin | Šeq. | Šeqalim |
| Kel. | Kelim | Soṭ. | Soṭah |
| Ker. | Keritot | Suk. | Sukkah |
| Ket. | Ketubot | Taʿan. | Taʿanit |
| Kil. | Kil'ayim | Teb. Y. | Tebul Yom |
| Maʿas. | Maʿaserot | Tam. | Tamid |
| Mak. | Makkot | Tem. | Temurah |
| Makš. | Makširin | Ter. | Terumot |
| Meg. | Megillah | Toh. | Tohorot |
| Meʿil. | Meʿilah | ʿUqṣ. | ʿUqṣin |
| Men. | Menaḥot | Yad. | Yadayim |
| Mid. | Middot | Yeb. | Yebamot |
| Miq. | Miqwa'ot | Yoma | Yoma |
| M. Qat. | Moʿed Qatan | Zab. | Zabim |
| M.Š. | Maʿaser Šeni | Zeb. | Zebaḥim |

## OTHER ABBREVIATIONS

| | |
|---|---|
| b. | Babylonian Talmud |
| M. | Mishnah |
| Mek. | Mekilta deRabbi Ishmael |
| Mek. SbY. | Mekilta deRabbi Simeon ben Yoḥai |
| Mid. | Midrash |
| Mid. Qoh. | Midrash Qohelet |
| Mid. Tan. | Midrash Tanna'im |
| R. | Rabbah |
| S. ʿOl.R. | Seder ʿOlam Rabbah |
| Targ. | Targum |
| Targ. Onq. | Targum Onqelos |
| Targ. Ps. J. | Targum Pseudo-Jonathan |
| Tos. | Tosephta |
| y. | Yerushalmi (Palestinian Talmud) |
| Yalq. Š. | Yalqut Šimoni |

## NOTE ON PRONUNCIATION

š is pronounced sh, as in 'shut'
ṣ is pronounced ts, as in 'shuts'
ḥ is pronounced ch, as in 'loch'
ṭ has a harder sound than t
q has a harder sound than k

# PART I

# The rabbinic literature

## INTRODUCTION

The literature with which we shall be dealing in this volume is that of the group known variously as the Pharisees, the *Ḥakamim* ('Sages'), or the rabbis, the religious group that proved to be the most significant for the development of Judaism up to modern times.

The literature is extensive and comprises a world-view of great nobility, unity and comprehensiveness. Yet hardly any of it is 'literary', in the sense of being the sustained composition of a single author presenting an individual vision. It is characteristic of this literature that it is presented as the work of an anonymous compiler, bringing together the views of a large number of named rabbis, sometimes reinforcing each other, but more often conflicting without rancour. The total impression is of a corporate literary effort, in which a large number of experts, belonging to successive generations, is engaged in a common enterprise: the clarification of Scripture and the application of it to everyday life. To find a similar type of literary activity in other cultures is not easy. The work of the Alexandrian scholars on Homer and other Greek classical writers is similar in some ways, but very different in others. The nearest analogy is probably the organization of scientific research in modern times: the feeling of comradeship in an enterprise of great theoretical and practical significance; the background of agreed assumptions, combined with great freedom for difference of opinion among qualified researchers; the submission of views to the criticism of the general body of experts; the acquisition of fame and reputation for individuals, but only within a framework of shared effort, so that no individual can become dominant, or acquire a type of authority different in kind from that of his fellows.

There is a great contrast between the rabbinical literature and that of the Bible itself. Each book of the Bible is presented as the work of an individual author, even when that author remains anonymous, and even though material from previously existing sources is incorporated or modified or transmuted through hidden exegesis. The same applies to the works of the Apocrypha, the Pseudepigrapha, and to the writings of the Qumran sect. None of these works presents itself as a compilation of exegeses, legal opinions or decisions, but as a unitary work of art, belonging to a recognizable genre, such as narrative, history, poetry or apocalypse. Even when such works are concerned with law (as in the Qumran *Manual of Discipline*), they are presented quite differently from the rabbinical legal writings: no individual authorities or differences of opinion are recorded, but categorical commands are issued, in the same style as the legal passages in the Bible itself. And even when such works actually arise from the exegesis of earlier works, they do not present themselves as exegetical works, but as independent compositions (e.g. Chronicles, Jubilees).

The genre of the rabbinical writings, then, is that of the compilation, and this may seem a very humble, journeyman type of literary composition if it can be called literary at all. Certainly, the use of this type of composition does express a lowering of literary objective which may be expressed in the formula that the rabbis did not claim inspiration. They denied that their works were informed by the holy spirit as they thought the Bible was; this may be otherwise expressed as the belief that the gift of prophecy had ceased, and would not be renewed until the coming of the Messiah. Yet it would be quite wrong to regard the rabbinical writings as mere jottings, or as handbooks of reference, or even as works of commentary such as those of the Alexandrian school of scholiasts. The rabbinical writings have a much more ambitious aim which is to embody the Oral Torah (p. 3), and this aim involves a complex patterning which raises the whole enterprise to the level of an art-form requiring assessment from a literary standpoint, as well as from a historical or religious standpoint.

The above remarks apply to the main body of rabbinical works, but it should be mentioned that there are some rabbinical compositions which are not compilatory in character, and require a different kind of literary assessment, more in accordance with that demanded by the Bible and Apocrypha. These works, however, are few in number, and will be given separate treatment in this book.

It will be seen, then, that what distinguishes the main rabbinic works from mere static compilations of previously existing materials is their character of being work-in-progress; each rabbinic work, such as the Mishnah, or the Halakic Midrashim, presents the state of the Oral Law at a particular moment in time, rather like a scientific progress-report in modern times, surveying the current state of progress in a particular scientific discipline, with accounts of controversies going on about disputed points or problematic areas. It is thus a defining characteristic of rabbinic literature that it is full of controversy. One rabbi's viewpoint is stated only to be contradicted by that of another rabbi. Decision-making procedures are not very much in evidence as far as the literature itself is concerned, even in legal matters, where decisions between rival views were of urgent practical importance. Such decision-making procedures did exist where demanded by practicality, as we know from later rabbinic literature, and also from discreet indications in the classical literature before us; but this is not the ostensible concern of the pre-Talmudic literature, which seems much more interested in giving us a full picture of the activity going on in the rabbinic schools, and of the range of possibilities envisaged in those schools in their work on the exegesis of Scripture.

## THE ORAL TORAH

To enter into the spirit of the rabbinic literature of our period, therefore, it is essential to grasp the concept of the Oral Torah (*torah še-be-ʿal peh*), the root concept of the whole literature. It was believed that God had given Moses the Written Torah (*torah še-bi-ketab*), comprising the Pentateuch, and that this was the perfect Word of God, containing not only the divine commandments by which the people of Israel were to live, but also the story of God's dealings with mankind, the election of Israel and the meaning of all history, past, present and to come. The other books of the Bible, comprising the Prophets and the Writings, were also regarded as inspired, but not as adding anything essential to the books of Moses, on which, however, they threw light, both in its legal and religio-historical aspects.

In addition to the Written Torah, there had existed since the time of Moses, it was believed, the Oral Torah, consisting of explications and expansions of the Written Torah. The Oral Torah was necessary not because of any imperfection in the Written Law, but because of the inescapable limitations of anything set down in writing: that it may require elucidation and cannot cover every possible practical contingency or every question that might be asked about it. Thus, for example, the Torah tells us to refrain from work on the Sabbath day, but it does not give any detailed definition of 'work', though it does give a few instances of the kind of activity forbidden under this category. It is the business of the Oral Torah, therefore, to fill in these gaps.

How, then, was it conceived that the authority of the Oral Torah differed from that of the Written Torah? The answer is somewhat complex. It was thought that the *nucleus* of the Oral Torah was given to Moses by God, and was therefore of equal authority to the Written Torah itself. This nucleus consisted of traditions of great antiquity, designated, in the legal sphere, as *halakot le-Mošeh mi-Sinai* ('laws of Moses from Sinai'). But these traditions formed only a small proportion of the Oral Torah. The bulk of the Oral Torah was of lesser authority, being attributed to the enactment or decision of figures in the post-Mosaic period, ranging from biblical personalities, such as King Solomon and Ezra to sages of the Pharisaic and rabbinic periods, the ascriptions becoming more numerous as the authorities concerned were more recent. Thus, while the Written Torah, simply by virtue of being written down, had a timeless quality, so that 'nothing could be added to it or taken away' (Deut. 4:2), the Oral Torah was a living, growing body of law and lore, responding to changing circumstances and becoming more comprehensive in scope as the unfolding of time posed new questions. This process of Oral Torah was conceived, with some justification, as being discernible in the Bible itself, for example, in the judiciary activity of the Judges and the explanatory role of Ezra (see Neh. 8:8).

The chief characteristic of the Oral Torah (apart from its Sinaitic nucleus) in point of authority, in contrast to the Written Torah, was thus its *fallibility*. This derived from the fallible status of its enactors and decision-makers; for it was considered that the Torah itself had given the religious authorities of each successive age a power of decision, or of enactment (within certain limits), which did *not* depend on the possession of inspiration ('the holy spirit', *ruaḥ ha-qodeš*), but was simply inherent in the office of sage or judge. This meant that, in principle, the enactments or decisions of the authorities of one generation could be reversed by the authorities of some succeeding generation, if they felt that there was good reason: for example, if the special circumstances leading to an enactment had ceased to hold, or even if the earlier authorities had made a mistake in their interpretation of the Written Torah, or of the traditions of the Oral Torah. There is, thus, in rabbinic Judaism, nothing corresponding to the Catholic doctrine of 'the infallibility of the Church' (though, of course, the Church achieved a measure of flexibility despite this doctrine).

The fallibility of the Oral Torah, considered as a process, rather than as fixed revelation, is stressed in many sayings and stories. One of the most famous of these is found in the Babylonian Talmud (b. B.M. 59b) in the form of a legend about two of the rabbis of our period, Joshua and Eliezer: it is related that once when these two rabbis were in dispute on a point of law, the majority decided in favour of Rabbi Joshua. Eliezer, however, would not accept this decision, being so sure that he was right; he therefore called on God to confirm his view by a 'voice from Heaven'. The voice duly came, saying 'Rabbi Eliezer is right', but the council of rabbis then ruled the 'voice from Heaven' out of order, on the ground that God, having given the rabbis the right of decision by majority vote, could not intervene to influence the discussions of the rabbis! It is then reported that God laughed, and said 'My children have defeated me'. This daring story declares the right of those who shape the Oral Torah to make mistakes. The human process of reaching truth, or provisional truth, by an effort of reasoning and discussion is thus sanctified. The watchword is 'It is not in heaven'. This is said about the Torah in Deut. 30:12, and was taken to mean that, while the Torah, in its written form, was given *from* Heaven, its practical implementation, the Oral Torah, was on earth and must partake of earthly imperfection.

## CANONICITY

Yet the chief embodiment of the Oral Torah is the Mishnah, which is a kind of canonical work. It is necessary to enquire, then, how the canonicity of the Mishnah differs from that of the Scripture, or Written Torah, and indeed how it is possible for the Oral Torah, with its inbuilt fallibility, to give rise to canonical works at all.

There are some commonly held misunderstandings about how the Mishnah was regarded. It is often said, for example, that it was believed that the Oral Torah given to Moses on Mount Sinai together with the Written Torah was nothing but the Mishnah itself, word for word. Such a belief, of course, would have been preposterous, since the Mishnah consists mainly of sayings attributed to rabbis of the first and second centuries AD about fifteen hundred years after the date assigned to Sinai. Moreover, many of the topics discussed in the Mishnah did not yet exist at the time of Moses; for example, the Mishnah's tractate, *Megillah*, discusses the rites of *Purim*, a festival, which, on the authority of the Bible itself, was set up in the time of Mordecai and Esther about 900 years after the time of Moses. The establishment of *Purim*, indeed, is a typical piece of Oral Law, dating from biblical but post-Mosaic times, showing how new rites and laws could arise from the powers of Jewish authorities responding to the needs of their period; another such innovation was the festival of *Ḥanukkah*, instituted during the Hasmonean period in the second century BC, and also mentioned in the Mishnah. It is safe to say, therefore, that no one ever explained the canonicity of the Mishnah by saying that it was revealed on Mount Sinai alongside the Written Torah; the most that one can say is that in some poetic Midrashic passages (e.g. Mid. Qoh. 1:10) it is envisaged that the whole of the Oral Torah, in its manifold later development, lay in the mind of Moses *in potentia*, a thought that emphasizes the organic unity of the Oral Torah throughout its centuries of accumulation.

The canonicity of the Mishnah must be quite differently understood. It was canonized from below, rather than from above. It was by a decision 'of all Israel' (to use a term from a later date) that the Mishnah was elected to be the official summary of the Oral Torah at a certain cross-section of history, chosen, one might say, to act as a platform or launching-pad for the further development of the Oral Torah. The Mishnah of Rabbi Judah the Prince was not the only candidate for this honour. We hear of other compilations that might have been elected; the Mishnah of Rabbi Akiba, for example, which has not survived, but was apparently organized under the same main headings as the version of the Mishnah that eventually won the day. Rabbi Meir, too, made his compilation; but it was the more comprehensive version presented by Rabbi Judah that gained the vote, though where and by what agency the vote was taken, or whether it was by an unspoken consensus, we do not know. This is not to say that Rabbi Judah's Mishnah was the perfect embodiment of the Oral Torah; on the contrary, it is in some respects defective, as we shall see. Its lacunae are supplied by a penumbra of subsidiary collections, one of which, the Tosephta, survives *in toto*, others only in fragments, and others, being organized on an entirely different plan, provide a different perspective.

At a later stage of the Oral Law, a similar choice presented itself in relation to the two Talmuds, the Babylonian Talmud and the

Palestinian Talmud. It was the Babylonian Talmud that was elected to canonical status, though the rejected candidate, the Palestinian Talmud, retained a semi-canonical status, just as had been the case with the rejected candidates for the position of the Mishnah. But it is clear that when the Mishnah, and later the Babylonian Talmud, were given this special position, they did not acquire canonicity in the sense of being regarded as works directly inspired by the holy spirit of God, like the books of the Bible. If a parallel is sought in the history of Christianity, something rather similar can be found in the official status given to the works of St Thomas Aquinas in the Catholic Church.

The above considerations explain how it is that the term 'Oral Torah' is applicable to what is in fact a huge body of written literature. The explanation usually given is that it was forbidden, at first, to write down the oral traditions, and that this was only permitted under pressure of circumstances, after the destruction of the Jewish state, when otherwise many traditions might have been lost. This is certainly part of the truth of the matter. There was a strong inhibition against the *publication* (though not really against the mere writing-down for mnemonic purposes) of religious material which might be thought to be bidding for canonical status equal to that of the Bible. It should be remembered that, for the greater part of our period, the canon of the Bible was not yet completely fixed. Many books were still being written, as the corpus of Apocrypha, Pseudepigrapha and Qumran writings shows, claiming Divine inspiration and thus claiming a place in the Bible. Even in the Pharisaic movement, the status of certain books, such as Ecclesiastes and the Song of Songs and Ben Sira, was still being debated (see M. Yad. 3:5). In general, however, the Pharisees were agreed about the biblical canon, and it was, therefore, important for them, at this stage of recent agreement, to watch out for possible intruders, and to disclaim unwarranted pretensions in anything that they themselves might put into writing. Thus in this period of the final settling of the canon, the term 'Oral Torah', with the significance of non-scriptural but valid teachings, became a valuable safeguard against infringement of the biblical canon.

As the canon of the Bible became more firmly accepted, it became easier to relax this inhibition and to allow the widespread publication of collections of the traditions of the Oral Torah, and even, finally, to confer on some of these collections the kind of canonicity that would not rival the canonicity of Scripture.

## THE STYLE OF THE RABBINIC WRITINGS

It should be noted that the *style* of the rabbinic writings is very much in accordance with the conception of Oral Torah outlined above. The atmosphere conveyed is one of *discussion* rather than promulgation, and this, in the last resort, is the meaning of the word 'oral' in the expression 'Oral Torah'. It is not so much that this kind of teaching was handed down by word of mouth for countless generations with a mystic embargo on reduction to writing, but that, even when put into writing, it remained a record of oral discussions going on among multiple personalities in the academies and also in the law-courts. Thus, one more qualification is necessary to our definition of rabbinic writing as *compilation*: that the compiler of a rabbinic work such as the Mishnah is not like the composer of an anthology, each item of which comes from an individual *author*. In a rabbinic work, each contribution quoted comes originally from an *oral context* (the law-court or the academy discussion-room), and even if there are intermediate written sources, none of these sources has lost its oral atmosphere or its character as a record of oral discussions. Thus the typical way of building up units of thought in a rabbinic work is by some such formula as 'Rabbi So-and-so says . . .' or 'The Sages say . . .'. Never once do we find the formula 'It is written . . .' except in relation to Scripture.

An important and characteristic feature of rabbinic writings is thus the uncategorical way in which commands are issued. Much has been written about the rabbinic use of participles as imperatives, but much of this has been beside the point. It is not that the participle in Mishnaic Hebrew is the grammatical equivalent of the imperative in classical Hebrew, but that the Mishnah and other rabbinic writings are seeking a less authoritative way of issuing commands than is found in the Bible. Thus the force of the frequent participles in the rabbinic writings (expressing a present tense, not an imperative) is 'This is the way of behaving, or *halakah*, that has been arrived at after our discussions'. The upshot is not 'Do this' but 'This is what one does'. Thus right at the beginning of the Mishnah, we find:

From when do they read the *Shema'* in the evening? From the time that the priests enter to eat their *terumah* until the end of the first watch: (these are) the words of Rabbi Eliezer. But the Sages say: Until midnight. (See p. 53.)

It is not too much to say that this quiet opening of the Mishnah contains the whole atmosphere of the Oral Torah.

## PHARISEES AND SADDUCEES

The above discussion leaves us with certain questions that demand an answer. When, in fact, did the concept of an Oral Torah first arise? How did the Sadducees differ from the Pharisees in their attitude to Oral Torah? What different genres exist in the literature of the Oral Torah, and what is the history of these genres? What is the meaning of the distinction between *halakah* and *haggadah* – a distinction that, to a large extent, determines the development of genres in this literature?

We are told by Josephus that the Pharisees were the authors of 'decrees' which they 'had imposed on the people', and also that they 'have delivered to the people a great many observances by succession from their fathers, which are not written in the laws of Moses; and for that reason it is that the Sadducees reject them, and say, that we are to esteem those observances to be obligatory which are in the written word, but are not to observe what are derived from the tradition of our forefathers. And concerning these things it is that great disputes and differences have arisen among them, while the Sadducees are able to persuade none but the rich, and have not the populace obsequious to them, but the Pharisees have the multitude on their side' (*Ant.* XIII. 10.6 (297)). This testimony is very important, and, properly understood, disposes of many dubious theories about the Pharisees, and their relationship to the Sadducees.

Josephus is telling us that the Pharisees had a double role: to 'make decrees', and to preserve traditions. These two roles might seem contradictory, for one is innovative and the other conservative; but in the light of the characterization of the Oral Torah above, we can see that there is no real contradiction, for the Oral Torah was a dynamic process, in which the conservation of precedents was combined with a continual flow of new decisions, which were then in turn conserved, or, occasionally, overturned in the light of new circumstances. The Sadducees, on the other hand, opposed the Oral Torah, and we can see from Josephus that the common characterization of the Sadducees as conservatives and of the Pharisees as innovators is a very inadequate account of the differences between the two groups. In one important respect, it was the Sadducees who were the innovators. For Josephus' account makes plain that the Sadducees did not deny the antiquity of the Pharisees' traditional observances; they rejected them only because they were not to be found written in the Bible. Josephus' picture thus confirms what is found in the rabbinic writings: that the Pharisees were the protectors of the observances of the *people*, observances endeared to them by long usage, while the Sadducees wished to abolish these customs on theoretical grounds, namely that no justification could be found for them in Scripture. An interesting example is the water-libation ceremony observed during the Tabernacles feast (see M. Suk. 4:9). This was a highly popular rite involving much jollification, including dancing and juggling with torches, and its affinity with pagan rain-making rites shows its great antiquity. The Pharisees supported it, and the Sadducees wished to abolish it; here, undoubtedly, the Sadducees were the innovators.

Yet the above consideration ought not to deprive the Pharisees of their well-deserved reputation as a reforming party, combating the *status quo*. The Sadducees were the party in possession of political power. The *status quo* which they were defending derived from the time of the Ptolemaic suzerainty, which had made the High Priest ruler of Judaea and given him a central authority which he had never had in biblical times. The Pharisaic party (earlier called *Ḥasidim*, see I Macc. 2:42) arose during the period of the corruption of the High Priesthood, in the period *c.* 170 BC, and their aim was to assert the ancient right of the laity to call authority, whether royal or priestly, to account. This movement was both revolutionary and traditional, thus following in the footsteps of the biblical lay prophets who had rebuked the kings and priests of their time. The rejection of the Oral Torah by the Sadducees, therefore, had a political significance: it meant a rejection of the movement of lay leaders, whether *Ḥasidim* or *Ḥakamim* or rabbis, who claimed superior authority to that of the priests, and exalted the traditions of the people above the priestly exegesis of Scripture.

The anti-priest bias of the Pharisaic movement can be seen throughout the rabbinic literature. It can be seen, for example, in the saying of the Mishnah 'A learned bastard takes precedence over an ignorant High Priest' (M. Hor. 3:8). Here 'learned' means particularly 'learned in the Oral Torah'. This does not mean that the Pharisees, or their successors the rabbis, wished to abolish the priesthood, but they wished to keep the priests in their place as ceremonial functionaries without teaching authority. This valuation of the priesthood was actually shared by the majority of the priests themselves, for most of them were supporters of the Pharisees. It was only the richer and more politically influential priests, those from whom the High Priest would normally be chosen by ruling secular authorities such as Herod I or later the Romans, who were Sadducees. The lower-ranking priests repudiated Sadducaism; some of them, indeed, became Pharisee sages, and thus qualified for teaching authority through mastery of the Pharisaic educational system and of the Oral Torah – for in Pharisaism no qualifications of birth were required to become a sage, and even a priest could qualify! Thus, in Pharisaic eyes, the hereditary priesthood, proud of its descent from Aaron the brother of Moses, had inherited the pomp of the Temple worship, but nothing else. Even in the conduct of the Temple service, they were to act under the direction of the Pharisee sages; and, in practice, they did so. Even the Sadducee High Priests bowed to the will of the people, as both Josephus and the rabbinic writings testify, and conducted the Day of Atonement and Tabernacles services in accordance with Pharisaic law even where it differed from Sadducean doctrine. Thus the physical descendants of Aaron had to defer to the spiritual descendants of Moses, who, it should be noted, kept the teaching role for himself, but handed over the sacerdotal role to Aaron. In its opposition to the pretensions of the High Priesthood to teaching authority, Pharisaism thus felt itself to be in the true, ancient tradition of biblical Judaism. This division, in Pharisaism, between the teaching and the sacerdotal role, so different from the pattern of Christianity, has given rise to much misunderstanding of Jewish history: for example, the role of Caiaphas in the condemnation of Jesus has been misconstrued as an expression of hostility by the central authority of Jewish religion (corresponding to the Pope in Christianity), whereas in fact Caiaphas, a quisling appointee of the Romans and regarded by the vast majority of the people as a Sadducean heretic, was entirely unrepresentative of the Jewish religion and was in any case motivated by the political terms of his appointment.

## PHARISEES AND RABBIS

This then was the nature of the movement for whom the concept of the Oral Torah was so important, and which gave rise to the rabbinic literature. It must be asked, however, how strong the historical link actually was between the Pharisaic movement, which existed before the political and religious disaster, the destruction of the Temple (AD 70), and the rabbinic movement which arose after that destruction. The literature which we have is, after all, entirely from the post-Destruction period, and is therefore called 'rabbinic', not 'Pharisaic'. The question is whether there is any real historical continuity between the Pharisees and the creators of the rabbinic literature, and how much of that literature can be assigned a pre-Destruction origin, in the sense of consisting of traditions, transmitted orally or in private memoranda, over the gap of the Destruction, and finally incorporated, whether word-for-word or in an edited form, in the rabbinic writings.

The rabbis certainly *claimed* to be the direct heirs of the Pharisees (though the actual name Pharisees, or *perušim*, appears rather rarely in the rabbinic literature, being probably a name mostly used by people outside the movement). Hillel and Shammai, in particular, are regarded as the 'fathers' of the rabbinic world and the two schools which they founded, called the House of Hillel and the House of Shammai are quite frequently mentioned and quoted as the source of views. Other famous Pharisaic teachers quoted in the rabbinic literature include Gamaliel I (mentioned in the New Testament, in Acts 5:34–9 as a prominent Pharisee), his son Simeon ben Gamaliel, mentioned in Josephus (*Life* 38 (190–3)) as taking a prominent role in the conduct of the war against Rome, the charismatic Ḥanina ben Dosa, and Joḥanan ben Zakkai, who, by surviving the war and founding his academy at Jabneh (Jamnia), provided the link between the old régime of Pharisees and the new régime of rabbis.

Nevertheless, the vast majority of the views cited in the Mishnah and other rabbinic writings are given in the names of post-Destruction figures such as Rabbi Eliezer and Rabbi Joshua and their younger contemporaries, Rabbi Akiba and Rabbi Ishmael, both of whom founded influential schools. This fact has led some scholars (prominent among whom is Jacob Neusner) to regard the rabbinic movement as basically a new departure, owing far less to the Pharisees than it liked to claim, and as the real originators, in the post-Destruction era, of the whole concept of Oral Torah, by which they sought to give their teachings an aura of antiquity and tradition.

The Pharisees, according to this view, did not have the wide range of interests found in the rabbinic literature, but were a small and uninfluential group of pietists, who concentrated their energies on the observance of laws of ritual purity in table-fellowships (*ḥaburot*). The stricture of the New Testament that the Pharisees were more interested in 'tithing mint and dill' than in 'the weightier matters of the Law, justice, mercy and good faith' (Matt. 23:23) is thus supported by this school of opinion, though without the coloration of hostility and derogation found in the New Testament and in much of the earlier school of German scholarship; for have not modern studies taught us a new respect for ritual and purity-observances as a feature of religion?

This conception, if accepted, would profoundly affect our view of the rabbinic literature treated in this volume, for it would force us to regard the main attitudes of this literature as originating in the post-Destruction period, and, therefore, as irrelevant to the study of the time of Jesus. The Pharisees would have to be regarded as having little influence on the development of the Mishnah and other rabbinic works, except that they contributed some ideas on ritual purity. In particular, it is urged that the rabbinic concepts, relating to covenant, repentance, the Messianic age, the mission of Israel, charity and good deeds, should not be attributed to the Pharisees. According to one extreme view these ideas are not to be found even in the Mishnah, but only in later rabbinic works, reacting *against* the Mishnah.

There is little reason, however, to accept such findings in view of the strong contrary evidence from Josephus, the New Testament, the Targums and the rabbinic writings themselves. Josephus, as we have seen, stresses that the Pharisees claimed to be the guardians of a mass of traditions and that they were regarded by the majority of the people as authorities on Jewish religion. Josephus also stresses that the main point of difference between the Sadducees and the Pharisees was on the issue of Oral Torah versus Scripture. Further, Josephus tells us that the Pharisees had a more lenient attitude than the Sadducees as regards penalties, and that they were critical of ruling powers, whether Jewish kings or occupying foreign forces; also that they were of such political importance that they were strongly represented in the counsels of the nation, both before and during the war against Rome. None of this is consonant with the picture of the Pharisees as a retiring society of ritualists.

The New Testament, too, is far from assigning a tiny, unassuming role to the Pharisees. Though critical of Pharisaic attention to tithing, it ascribes a very wide range of authority to the Pharisees, saying that 'they sit in Moses' seat' (Matt. 23:2), and, though it makes some reference to ritual-purity observances, such as hand-washing and vessel-washing, it nowhere identifies the Pharisees with the 'table-fellowships', which, indeed, are not even mentioned in the New Testament. (It is only a modern scholarly theory, based on nothing in the texts, that relates Jesus' association with sinners to the question of ritual purity and 'table-fellowship'.) The impression of the Pharisees given by the New Testament, though hostile, is certainly not one of an insignificant group, taking no part in the general life of the nation.

The Targums (the Aramaic translations of the Bible, made for the benefit of the Aramaic-speaking populace) also provide important evidence of the continuity between the Pharisees and the post-Destruction rabbis. Recent scholarship has shown that the Targums, though they continued to receive accretions until a late period, have a substantial stratum dating from the period of Jesus or even earlier. This stratum contains material, both of a *halakic* ('legal') and *haggadic* ('homiletic') kind, which shows continuity, both in its similarities and its differences, with the later rabbinic literature. The Targums, therefore, should be regarded as, at least in part, an early form of rabbinic literature stemming from the Pharisees themselves, showing that the range of interests and breadth of concepts of the Pharisees was the same as that of the rabbinic movement.

The later rabbinic literature, including the Mishnah, Midrashim and Talmuds, also contains much evidence of continuity between the Pharisees and the rabbinic movement, though we have to take into account the suggested possibility that this continuity may have been exaggerated for purposes of authority. Some sayings may have been attributed pseudepigraphically to pre-Destruction figures such as Hillel or Joḥanan ben Zakkai, but equally, a number of sayings attributed to post-Destruction figures may have originated in a Pharisaic milieu. An interesting example of this is the saying 'The Sabbath was handed over to man, not man to the Sabbath', which is attributed in the Babylonian Talmud to Rabbi Jonathan ben Joseph, but is also found in almost identical form in the mouth of a pre-Destruction figure, Jesus himself (see p. 170). What is beyond doubt is that a great deal of unattributed (i.e. anonymous) material in the Mishnah and Tosephta comes from the pre-Destruction period, since it describes the practical functioning of a Jewish state, with its judiciary, high and low, its system of penalties, litigation and regional administration. The theory that this was taken over from non-Pharisaic sources (e.g. from the Scribes, regarded as a body quite separate from the Pharisees) faces the difficulty that the Scribes are always closely associated with the Pharisees in the New Testament, and also that it is hard to understand in this case why the rabbis were so insistent that they derived it all from the Pharisees.

The sayings ascribed to pre-Destruction teachers (i.e. Pharisees) in the Mishnah cover many topics other than ritual purity, for example, laws of charity, laws relating to marriage, the institution of the *prosbol* (see p. 75) and the law of the bailee. Yet the proportion of ritual-purity sayings ascribed to them is noticeably higher than the proportion of pronouncements on this topic in the Mishnah as a whole. To conclude from this, however, that the Pharisees were interested primarily in ritual purity is very unsafe. There may be many reasons why the Mishnah tends to quote the Pharisees on ritual-purity more frequently than on other topics; this is an idiosyncrasy of the Mishnah rather than an indication of the actual range of interests of the Pharisees. Such statistical considerations in the study of the Mishnah should not be allowed to outweigh the evidence of Josephus, the New Testament and the Targums.

On the whole, then, the strong likelihood is that the rabbinic literature is, as its creators claimed, the culmination of a long process of Oral Torah. It arose out of an orally transmitted culture centred on the exposition of the Bible, and found its setting in three institutions, all created by the Pharisaic movement: the synagogue, the house of study, and the 'house of judgement' (*bet din*) or rabbinical law-court. The synagogue, or 'house of assembly' (*bet ha-keneset*), gave rise to three sources of rabbinical literature: the Targum (based on the originally oral exposition of the Bible in Aramaic), the Midrash (based on the sermon, or homily, with its ingredients of Bible stories and parables, applied to exhortation, comfort and rebuke), and the liturgy (in which the poetic and devotional sides of the rabbinical character were developed). The 'house of study' (*bet ha-midraš* or *yešibah*), together with the *bet din*, gave rise to the corpus of legal discussion and decisions which were reduced to writing in the Mishnah and its associated writings. None of these genres, however, is found in an insulated form, since they are all the product of a unitary outlook. Legal argument is always liable to shade into homily, or vice versa. The function of the rabbi was never to be a specialist, but to combine in his repertoire all possible ways of studying or putting into practice the many-stranded religio-historical complex of the Bible.

The oral culture arising from the centrality of the Bible in Jewish society should thus not be confused with the kind of oral culture found in primitive tribes, where tribal lays are memorized and transmitted by word of mouth in a pre-literate stage. Jewish society was highly literate, and indeed had an ideal of universal literacy that foreshadowed modern European educational patterns. The oral culture arose out of this very literacy; for it comprised the day-to-day discussion of study groups of various kinds all focusing their attention on the written word, the Bible. The unfinished quality of the Oral Torah, the feeling that it was never quite at the stage of being definitively put into writing, and that every attempt to embody it required further attempts, supplements and supplements of supplements, arose from the sense of the inexhaustibility of the Bible, the conviction that discussion of it could never be brought to completion because each new generation was able to discover new insights or to apply it in previously unforeseen ways.

Such a concerted effort of commentary, appreciation and application to life certainly had an inhibiting effect on original composition. In the rabbinical literature there are very few individual efforts to compose in a particular genre (one exception is the *Seder ʿOlam Rabbah* by Rabbi Yose ben Ḥalafta, a historical work, see p. 220). We look in vain, in the rabbinical movement, for dramatists, novelists or writers of epic poetry, such as were the glory of Greek literature, or of previous ages of Jewish literature in the Bible itself and in the intertestamental literature. But to compensate for this lack of cultivation of individual talent, we have something unique: a communal endeavour of enormous energy. So far from showing exhaustion and rigidity, as has often been asserted in the interests of the theory that the advent of Christianity made Judaism obsolete, rabbinical Judaism produced a literature of unexampled vigour and sense of direction.

## THE HISTORICAL BACKGROUND

It may be asked, from a historical standpoint, how far this great burst of literary activity was connected with the conditions of national disaster, following the destruction of the Temple and the Second Commonwealth. There certainly seems to be a parallel between the conditions which brought about the compilation and canonization of the Bible itself and those that brought the rabbinical writings into being. If the Bible, as a central literary institution, was the product of the first Destruction, the rabbinical literature was the product of the second Destruction. In both cases, national disaster necessitated the consolidation and centralization of a diffused tradition which had previously existed in variegated regional forms without an urgent need for standardization. When the Pharisaic teachers who had survived the disaster assembled at Jabneh under the leadership of Joḥanan ben Zakkai, they pooled their knowledge of Oral Torah and formed a common treasury. There are indications that many of the differences of opinion between which the Mishnah adjudicates were not so much clashes of individuals as variations of regional practice, reported in the name of individual rabbis, rather than created by them. Otherwise, it would often be difficult to account for the proliferation of opinions, by which one rabbi has only to state something for some other rabbi to contradict him. The breakdown of the organic functioning of the Jewish state, in which community practice rather than resort to rule books or manuals was the guide to living, necessitated a more conscious formulation of the whole corpus of Oral Torah; and the drawing together of survivors made imperative an adjudication between the various strands of tradition. But at the same time, as in the case of the consolidation of the biblical canon, the focusing and unification of the tradition released new energies and sharpened the communal consciousness of the values which had sustained the community.

## HALAKAH AND HAGGADAH

We may now go on to survey more closely the works and genres to which the urge for consolidation gave rise, working on the abundant material of the biblical canon and the Oral Torah. But before we embark on this survey, it is necessary to consider with some care the two basic categories informing all the rabbinic literature, *halakah* and *haggadah*.

The Bible itself includes two categories: commandments, whether moral or legal; and narrative, contributing to a historical perspective in which the Jewish religious community sees itself as having a special role in the story of God's relations with humanity. These are certainly not the only categories of material in the Bible: for example, neither the Psalms nor the wisdom literature can be covered by these descriptions. For that matter, by no means all the rabbinical material is adequately covered by the categories of *halakah* and *haggadah*, but the two terms serve as a useful broad distinction with which to approach the problem of determining the various genres within the rabbinic literature.

*Halakah* means literally 'going' or 'way', and it means the way in which a biblical commandment has been translated into customary practice by the decisions of the Oral Law. The word applies to the field of law, and especially to the settlement of disputed questions. It can refer to the whole field of such questions or to some individual question or decision; for example, 'Rabbi A says such-and-such, Rabbi B disagrees, and the *halakah* is . . .'. The word *halakah* thus partakes of the provisional and uncategorical character of the Oral Torah; it does not have the emotional charge of the word *miṣwah* ('commandment'), which refers to the biblical injunctions themselves, the implementation of which in practical life is the business of the *halakah*. Thus the Bible gives the commandment, 'Thou shalt not murder', which no rabbi will call into question; but the *halakah* is concerned with the settlement of difficult questions on the topic of murder: whether one may kill in self-defence, for example, or to save the life of another in variously postulated circumstances (see p. 183). *Halakah* is thus a matter of the recording of opinions and precedents and the discussion of the new questions which life is continually throwing up, while *miṣwah* is the eternal, unchanging principle which acts as the starting-point of discussion.

It would be wrong to say, however, that *halakah* simply means rabbinical thinking about the biblical commandments, for there are important areas of rabbinical thought on human behaviour which are not covered by the term *halakah*. The rabbinical wisdom literature, such as the Mishnah tractate *'Abot*, recommends attitudes (such as 'a good heart') which cannot be formulated in terms of *halakah*, and there is also the whole area of supererogatory virtue ('the measure of saintliness') which goes 'beyond the line of the law' (see p. 134). Thus the aim of *halakah* is to define a minimum standard of good behaviour and decency, rather than to comprehend the entirety of the moral life.

However, because, in rabbinical thought, the main aim of human life is to achieve a satisfactory state of morality in the community, rather than to cultivate the graces of life, such as saintliness, mystical experience or courtliness in social relations (*derek 'ereṣ*, literally, 'the way of the world'), the way of *halakah* is central to Judaism. Though mysticism, saintliness and courtliness form part of the rabbinical conspectus, they are always kept firmly in the periphery, a fact that should be borne in mind when considering aspects of rabbinical literature that seem to invite comparison with religions, say, of centrally mystical orientation. To study the *halakah* and thus work towards the kind of society envisaged by the *halakah* is, to the rabbis, to pursue the specifically human task, and also the task especially entrusted to the Jews who understood themselves as deputed by God to lead humanity, not in the acquisition of spiritual or artistic gifts of an unusual kind, but in the development of a just and kindly community life as the essential basis without which the cultivation of special gifts is mere selfishness.

The place of *halakah* in rabbinic Judaism must therefore be related to its general outlook and guiding myth, and here we must have recourse to the category of *haggadah*. Just as *halakah* is a refinement of the legal aspects of the Bible (the commandments), so the *haggadah* consists of reflection on and systematization of the non-legal, narrative parts of the Bible. The Bible sets the Torah in a context of world history, moving towards a climax in the 'End of Days', with the people of Israel as leading actors in the drama, in the role of 'the first-born son of God' (Exod. 4:22). The *haggadah* takes up and sifts out the various themes composing this drama, incorporating material from contemporary life and also accumulated orally transmitted material from the folklore which comprised a perennial strand in the Oral Torah.

*Haggadah* means literally 'telling' (the word is just as often found in the Aramaized form *'aggadah*). In a specialized sense, the word *haggadah* means the telling of the story of the Exodus from Egypt every Passover, as enjoined in Exod. 13:8; and this sanctification of story-telling, as the means of inculcating thankfulness to God and awareness of his dealings with mankind, has become so pervasive in rabbinic Judaism that it has become the main method of homiletics. Every religion begins with a story; and the effort of theologians is to distil the meaning of the story in abstract terms: to turn a story into a system. In rabbinic Judaism, the story-telling element never disappears into abstract creeds or theology, but there is some systematic development, half-way between story and theology, in which overlapping concepts, such as 'Covenant', 'Kingdom of God', 'deeds of loving-kindness', and 'the world to come', crystallize out of the circumambient myth, and comprise a loose patterning and orientation for further developments of the narrative tradition. The *haggadah* thus gives the rationale for the practice of the *halakah*. While the *halakah* is subject-matter for teaching in the schoolhouse, the *haggadah* is subject-matter for preaching in the synagogue, giving scope for enthusiasm, emotion and the inspiriting of flagging hopes of the fulfilment of God's promises and the coming of a better world, in accordance with the scheme of history initiated by the deliverance from Egypt and the election of Israel as God's chief instrument in history. The haggadic compilations which we have are thus mainly homiletic material organized round the main preaching occasions in the Jewish year; while the halakic compilations are the product of the academies, formed out of lecture notes and records of teaching sessions.

The Oral Torah, therefore, has a double aspect, consisting of both *halakah* and *haggadah*. It is thus mistaken to translate Oral Torah as 'Oral Law', just as it is misleading to translate the Written Torah as 'Law' (the word actually means 'teaching' or 'directive'). There is, however, a distinction to be drawn between *halakah* and *haggadah* as regards the kind of authority assigned to each. The *halakah* has a kind of authority not granted to the *haggadah* but, on the other hand, the *haggadah* has a kind of authority not granted to the *halakah*.

The authority of the *halakah* resides in its binding quality. It issues in propositions that have legal force. This entails, however, that a great many *halakic* propositions do *not* have legal force, since they are the minority opinions that have been overruled. The *halakah* consists of discussions, issuing in decisions about what is forbidden and what is permitted (or, in rabbinic terminology, what is 'bound' and what is 'loosed', see Matt. 16:19). On the other hand, the very fact that decisions are reached by a process of discussion means, as pointed out above, that decisions, even when reached, do not have canonical authority in the sense of being regarded as divinely inspired utterances, and are subject, in principle, to revision in the light of further information. The authority of halakic decisions is that of 'the rule of law', by which society confers on its legislature the right to make binding decisions, which are enforceable until revoked by a similar process. Nevertheless, this whole process of legislation is regarded in rabbinic Judaism (which differs here from modern democratic legislatures) as having divine sanction. This means that it is a religious, not merely a societal, duty to obey the decisions of the lawfully constituted legislature (*bet din*, or, in earlier times, *Sanhedrin*), as long as they are in force, even when one has reason to disagree with them. Further, it is at all times a religious duty to *study* the whole legislative process, from its inception in biblical principles to its implementation in rabbinic decisions, including the minority opinions which were overruled, but which retain some legal force in that they may one day become the basis for a new decision. This duty of study (*talmud torah*) is incumbent on every Jew, not merely on those taking a leading role in the legislative process; so that the legislature, ideally, comprises the whole Jewish community, and any and every Jew may be called on at some time to make or participate in a halakic decision. The authority of the *halakah* is thus not merely a demand for obedience from those under its authority, but a call to every Jew to participate in a continuous process of legislation.

The authority of the *haggadah* is very different. Here too, conflicts of opinion may occur, but they take place on a plane that does not require a process of decision. Every haggadic remark has an aura of poetry and imagination, and it is impossible for one poem to contradict another, even if, on a strictly logical interpretation, it appears to do so; such apparent contradictions merely illustrate the dialectical character of poetic thinking, in which opposites do not annihilate each other but interact and produce a synthesis. For example, several second-century rabbis provide interpretations of the biblical verse, 'And the spirit of God hovered over the face of the waters' (Gen. 1:2). One interprets the word 'spirit' very literally to mean 'wind', another says that the 'spirit of God' means 'the Messiah', another says that 'the spirit of God' means Adam. No one attempts to adjudicate between these comments, and they are all regarded as valid; each is a response of an individual rabbi to the verse in question, by which he expresses a particular mood, or relates it to one of the complexes of ideas that exist in the *haggadah*, whether historical or epochal, theological or anthropological, or folkloristic. The test of a haggadic idea is simply its poetic force. Thus we find the notion, in the rabbinic literature, that the creation of *haggadah* requires not intellectual power, but a special kind of talent. The great Rabbi Akiba, the giant of the *halakah*, was reproved when he ventured into the field of *haggadah*, and told to go back to the *halakah* where he belonged.

The special kind of religious expression found in the *haggadah*, halfway between exegesis and poetic creation, a personal response to Scripture, yet disciplined within societally formed concepts or clusters of concepts, is unique to rabbinic Judaism. It is sometimes argued by scholars that the *haggadah* is unimportant in rabbinic Judaism compared with the *halakah*, since it lacks the kind of authority attaching to the latter, and does not achieve the credal definition found in Christianity. On this view, rabbinic Judaism is essentially a system of orthopraxis, with a mere penumbra of hazily formed doctrinal concepts comprising suggestions towards a theology, but not taken seriously enough to be systematized. This is to misunderstand the nature of the *haggadah* by regarding it as crudely performing the function of what in Christianity is called 'theology'. This is a caricature of rabbinic Judaism because it applies to Judaism a Christian framework and system of valuation. In Christianity, there is a drive towards systematization of theology and creed because the central myth is one of belief and faith as the mode of salvation. The way a Christian *believes* is crucial to his salvation; so it is into the definition of the *creed* that the main effort of analysis and codification goes; it is here, paradoxically, that the poetry tends to be driven out in the search for certainty, clarity and unanimity. In Judaism, there is not this anxiety about salvation. Being in the Covenant guarantees salvation, which does not require any uniquely defined attitude of belief. The emphasis is not on achieving salvation, but on carrying out the terms of the Covenant by maintaining and improving the society of which the Torah is the blueprint. It is in the details of communal living, *halakah*, that the drive for certainty, clarity and unanimity exists, while the realm of creed, *haggadah*, is regarded as a powerhouse of inspiration and vitality, rather than as an urgent lifeline of rescue from damnation. It can thus retain its poetic ambivalence and fertility and does not have to be reduced to agreed formulas. This does not mean that it is unimportant; on the contrary, the place of the *haggadah* in Judaism in vitalizing the *halakah*, and giving it an ambience of myth, mystery and cosmic feeling, has been constant.

## HAGGADAH AND MIDRASH

It is necessary here to discuss the relationship between the term *haggadah* and the term *midrash*. This is necessary because the term *midrash* has acquired a number of meanings, in the course of time, so that a full history of its evolution would have to take into account developments in the ancient, medieval and even modern world. Since the term has become so laden with meanings, the best course here is to define it very simply in relation to the period with which we are concerned, while giving some indication of later usages with which this definition should not be confused.

With regard to our period, a *midrash* means any kind of statement of Oral Torah, whether halakic or haggadic, found in the works called Midrashim. A rabbinic work which consists of the teachings of Oral Torah tied to the systematic exegesis of Scripture is called a Midrash (e.g. the Mekilta of Rabbi Ishmael, a consecutive exposition of Exodus). The distinction which we convey in English by the use of a capital letter is expressed differently in Hebrew which has no capital letters: a 'Midrash', meaning a work, is treated as a masculine noun with the plural 'Midrashim', while a *midrash*, meaning a passage or pericope, is treated as a feminine noun having the plural *midrashot*. The word *midrash* can also be used to mean the *genre* to which the Midrashim belong.

The Midrashim of our period contain both halakic and haggadic material, and have therefore been called 'the Halakic Midrashim' (to distinguish them from Midrashim of a later period which are almost entirely haggadic.) Since this designation is somewhat misleading (because it seems at first sight to connote entirely halakic Midrashim), the better term has been devised, 'Tannaitic Midrashim', indicating that the rabbis quoted in them were of the earlier generations known as *Tanna'im*, not of the later generations known as *'Amora'im* (see p. 42). The Midrashim concerned are the Mekilta, Sifra and Sifre and some smaller works (see p. 147).

As opposed to these Midrashim, there are other works, also of our period, which also contain teachings of the Oral Torah, but *not* arranged in the form of exegeses of Scripture; instead, they are in the form of teachings arranged under *topics*, such as the Liturgy, Agricultural Laws, Festivals or Damages. These are the Mishnah and Tosephta, and some smaller works. Consequently, they are not called Midrashim. Their method is not exegesis, but codification, though incidental exegeses are not rigidly excluded. The rabbis cited in them are also *Tanna'im*.

This gives us a very clear definition of a *midrash* for our period, which will be adhered to in this volume. It means simply a passage in one of the Tannaitic Midrashim, and such a passage would consist of an exegesis of Scripture in the rabbinical style (which will be discussed later, see p. 172) issuing in an item of Oral Torah, whether haggadic or halakic. We shall never refer to a passage in the Mishnah, or Tosephta as a *midrash*, much less to a passage in the Qumran writings or Josephus.

This, however, may puzzle some readers who have seen, in other books, references to *midrash* not only in the Qumran writings and Josephus, but even in the New Testament and the later books of the

Old Testament. This usage arises from some developments in the meaning of the word *midrash* after our period.

The method of codification by topics was applied in the Mishnah and Tosephta to *halakah*, and so successful did this method of presenting *halakah* prove, that it put an end to the Midrashic style as far as *halakah* was concerned. Consequently, later applications of the Midrashic method, after the Tannaitic period, were entirely (or almost entirely) in the field of *haggadah*. Consequently, the term *midrash* became more and more identified with *haggadah*, and in Jewish medieval commentaries on the Bible (by Rashi and others), the *midrash* of a biblical verse often seems to signify its haggadic meaning (as opposed to the plain, literal meaning which these commentators increasingly sought). In fact, Rashi and the other commentators, if carefully examined, will be found never to have used the term *midrash* to refer to haggadic passages in works such as the Talmud outside the Midrashim (though they did use other terms for such passages derived from the same root *daraš*, meaning 'to search', e.g. *deraša*, *deruš*). In modern times, however, many scholars have extended the term *midrash* to mean any *haggadah*-type exegesis or even re-working of Scripture, characterized by a free elaboration of the text. In this sense, it has become quite usual to speak of *midrash* in Josephus or the New Testament, especially where the narrative context of the Bible text is elaborated. A further extension of the term *midrash* is found in modern literary critics, who have become aware of the subjective, creative element in all exegesis, and have used the word *midrash* to refer even to the exegesis of Shakespeare.

These later modifications of the word *midrash* have made it a somewhat slippery term, and it is therefore best for our purposes to ignore them and adhere to the simple and historically accurate definition given above, which is in accordance with traditional Jewish usage. There is no objection, however, to speaking of *halakah* or *haggadah* in non-rabbinic works, since these terms are not tied to any specific genre. It is the authentic Jewish usage, however, to treat the term *midrash* as denoting a passage in a Midrash, in a way that is strictly parallel to the use of the term *mishnah* to mean a passage in the Mishnah, and to adopt this usage is the best way to avoid an awkward overlapping between the words *midrash* and *haggadah*.

A comment may be helpful here on the history of the word *midrash*. There were non-technical usages of the term *midrash*, both before and during the era of rabbinic literary activity. Thus the word *midraš* is found in the Bible (2 Chron. 13:22; 24:27) with the generalized meaning, 'exposition'. It is also found in rabbinic literature in non-technical senses: for example, *bet ha-midraš* means 'house of learning', not 'house for the study of Midrashim'. We find in *'Abot*: 'Not study (*midraš*) but doing is the main thing' (M. 'Ab. 1:17); see also M. Ket. 4:6, where the word is used of the interpretation of a non-scriptural text. These are survivals of early (before the second century AD) usage, in which the term had not yet been appropriated to a particular genre of rabbinic literature. Similar non-specialized usages of the word *mishnah* can also be found, for example, M.'Ab. 3:7. All these usages are irrelevant here, since we are concerned with the rabbinic technical use of *midrash* and *mishnah*.

## MISHNAH AND MIDRASH

Dating rabbinic writings is always difficult. It is of the nature of a rabbinic work that it develops by a process of accretion, so that the final date of redaction should be regarded as the end of the process of composition, rather than as the 'date' of composition. Thus the Mishnah is often said to have been 'composed' by its 'author', Rabbi Judah the Prince, at about AD 200, which would put it at the very end of our period. Yet the evidence is that the plan of the Mishnah was invented by Rabbi Akiba at about AD 120. Rabbi Akiba composed a first version of the Mishnah, which was developed by Rabbi Meir, and received its final elaboration from Rabbi Judah the Prince. The Tannaitic Midrashim, on the other hand, received their final redaction in the third century, which might seem to make them too late to be included in our period; but since their main development was during the second century, they can be regarded legitimately as second-century literature, and extracts from them are accordingly included in this book (though care has been taken to exclude passages traceable to the third century). The same considerations apply to the halakic codification, the Tosephta, second in importance only to the Mishnah, which received its final redaction in the third century, but the body of which belongs to the second century.

The question has been raised by certain scholars whether a tension exists between the codificatory works and the Bible-commentary works. Do these two modes of literature reflect a conflict between two schools of thought in the rabbinic movement?

The codificatory method seems to imply that the Oral Torah has a degree of autonomy: its laws may be listed under convenient headings without requiring to be grounded in Scripture. The Bible-commentary method, on the other hand, seems to imply that the independence of the Oral Torah is only apparent, for its laws and concepts can all be derived from Scripture.

An extreme view has been proposed by Jacob Neusner: that the Tannaitic Midrashim were written as a counterblast to the Mishnah, and reflect a strongly conflicting standpoint. The Mishnah stands for the view that the Oral Torah has separate independent authority: consequently, the Mishnah does not cite scriptural authority for its statements. It is written in a purposely unbiblical style to show that it has its own authority as the 'Bible' of the Oral Torah, of equal standing to the Written Bible. The Tannaitic Midrashim, however (followed by the Talmud), seek to reassert the paramount position of Scripture, regarded as the fount of all Torah teaching.

This view is implausible. The Mishnah, though its plan precludes the derivation of the bulk of its laws from Scripture, does contain a sufficient number of scriptural derivations, incidentally introduced, to show that it has no objection to such derivations in principle. It is merely the codificatory aim itself that reduces the number of scriptural derivations. If we want to study the laws as a system, reflecting the different departments of human activity, then the needs of system and classification take precedence over the desire to find scriptural sanction. The same phenomenon is noticeable in all later codifications of Jewish law. Moreover, the unbiblical style of the Mishnah, so far from suggesting a claim to status as a separate 'Bible', evinces its tentative, unpretentious status as a compendium of the fallible Oral *halakah* (see above, p. 8).

It may be asked, however, why it should have been felt necessary at all to derive the propositions of the Oral Torah from the Written Torah. The Midrashim and the Talmud show a strong propensity to do this, even though the plan of the Mishnah reduces such derivations to a minimum. If all the Oral Torah can be found in the Written Torah, does not this seem to be a capitulation to the position of the Sadducees, for whom Written Torah was everything? Indeed, some scholars have seen the scriptural derivations as an attempt to counter Sadducean charges that the Pharisees slighted the authority of Scripture by instituting their own unscriptural rulings. (These charges seem to be reflected in the New Testament accusation, probably derived from a Sadducean source, that the Pharisees, by their 'tradition', 'make God's word (i.e the Bible) null and void' (Mark 7:13).)

To give an illustrative example, the Mishnah gives a list of thirty-nine principal categories of work which are forbidden on the Sabbath. The Mishnah does not attempt to give scriptural support for this list, which, on the Mishnah's treatment, we might suppose to be derived from an oral tradition independent of Scripture. The Talmud (b. Šab. 49b), however, tells us that all these categories of work can be deduced from Scripture, since the injunction to observe the Sabbath is placed next to the description of the building of the Tabernacle (Exod. 35), which, as the details of its construction show, required all these kinds of work: by the principle of exegesis called *semukin* (deduction from the juxtaposition of passages), we learn that all modes of work required to build the Tabernacle are forbidden on the Sabbath.

It is clear that the list of forbidden categories of work *was* in fact derived from tradition, and that the *tour de force* by which they are derived from Scripture was a secondary exercise. This can be proved from the Mishnah, which admits, in another context, that 'the laws of the Sabbath are like mountains hanging on a hair' (M. Ḥag. 1:8), i.e. have very little scriptural support. Why, then, were such exercises of exegesis undertaken? Why not rest content with the idea that the Oral Torah fills out the gaps in the Written Torah?

The answer is that it was never Pharisaic doctrine that the Oral Torah was necessary because of imperfections in the Written Torah. The imperfection, as they thought, lay in the human intellect, which was unable to understand the perfect Word of God fully, and therefore needed an Oral Torah to interpret Scripture. God, in pity for the imperfection of the human intellect, gave an Oral Torah, or the nucleus of one, in order to help man to understand his perfect Written Torah. Even the hermeneutics, by which the Written Torah was to be interpreted, were part of the Oral Torah given to Moses on Mount Sinai: this would include the principle of *semukin* mentioned above. Yet so perfect is the Written Torah, that, rightly understood, it even contains the principles of its own interpretation. Thus, the logical method known as *qal wa-ḥomer* (the *a fortiori* argument) was part of the Oral Torah, but it can also be learnt from certain passages in Scripture: even the refinement of it known as *dayo* (the principle that the conclusion of an *a fortiori* argument must not contain any term not present in the premise) can be learnt from a biblical passage, the punishment of Miriam by leprosy (see p. 174). Thus the efforts of Midrash and Talmud to find biblical justification for items known from the Oral Law should be understood as religious exercises. These constant renewals of the links between the Oral Torah and the Written Torah, overcoming the gap necessitated by human imperfection, are explorations into the mind of God, as revealed in his Word.

Thus the method of codification and the method of Bible interpretation are not in conflict, but complement each other. One proof of this is that Rabbi Akiba, the great pioneer of codification, was also a leader in the field of Bible interpretation. Codification was necessary in order to achieve a conspectus of the whole Oral *halakah*, so that urgent practical decisions could be facilitated by the existence of a manual of law arranged for systematic understanding and memorization. Bible interpretation was necessary so that contact should not be lost with the Word of God, which underlay, informed and inspired all developments in Oral Torah.

This did not mean that scriptural support had to be found for those enactments of the Oral Torah that were admittedly human (or rabbinical), but only for those which were regarded as part of the nucleus of Oral Torah given to Moses by God on Sinai. The thirty-nine categories of work, for example, were regarded as in this latter class. Enactments such as 'the washing of hands', which were fully admitted to be rabbinical (see p. 122), would not require a 'searching' of Scripture to find support for them.

It should be noted that, for the most part, the authority of the nuclear *halakah* did *not* derive from any exegetical support that might be found for it, but from its status as traditional law. To search for scriptural support for a law *known* to be binding by tradition was an extra exercise of piety, which came into the category of *talmud torah* (the duty of learning Torah). Scholars outside the Jewish milieu have often derided the tortuous arguments by which the rabbis allegedly derived laws from Scripture. But this is to misunderstand the process. The rabbis, on the whole, did not operate a bizarre system of exegesis in order to produce new laws, although they sometimes produced bizarre arguments in order to add scriptural support to laws they already knew to be valid. In fact (a point generally overlooked), the more bizarre the argument, the more likely it is that the law in question was regarded as unquestionable by reason of its antiquity, and therefore required scriptural derivation by hook or crook. An example of this is the argument by which the rabbis, in controversy with the Sadducees, defended the immemorial custom of offering the *'omer* ('barley-sheaf') on the second day of Passover despite the plain text supporting the view of the Sadducees that this offering should be made on the Sunday after the beginning of the festival (Lev. 23:11). (See p. 130.)

On the other hand, there are *some* examples of rabbis using the exegetical apparatus to create changes in the law, but this is almost always in cases when some urgent *reform* was felt to be necessary. An example is the abolition by Rabbi Joḥanan ben Zakkai of the ordeal, sanctioned by the Bible, for 'the woman suspected of adultery'. When a rabbi occasionally tried to use the exegetical apparatus to make the law more severe, he was generally overruled.

The actual exegetical methods, by which the rabbis derived *halakah* or *haggadah* from the text of the Bible, are a mixture of common sense, logic, stylistic analysis and legal structuralism, all of which would have some validity if applied to any text, but which are given an air of unreality, to modern eyes, by the assumption that the Bible is a perfectly composed work in which every peculiarity is full of meaning. The rapt attention thus given by the rabbis to every nuance of the biblical text is only rivalled by the approach of some modern literary critics to the analysis of poetry. For further remarks on the rabbinical exegetical methods, see p. 162 and p. 172.

We may now consider the individual works that form the corpus of rabbinical literature in our period.

## THE TARGUMS (see also p. 185)

These are the translations of the Bible, or parts of the Bible, into Aramaic. They must be reckoned as belonging to the rabbinic literature because, where they offer interpretation (as every translation, even the most literal, must do to some extent), they do so within the rabbinic tradition. The Targums, like other rabbinic literature, began orally and were gradually reduced to writing, with many revisions, before reaching a final form. The original context of the Targum was the synagogue, where the reading from the Torah and Prophets, on Sabbaths and festivals, was orally translated into Aramaic by an interpreter (*meturgeman*), every three verses, for the benefit of the people, who mostly did not understand Hebrew. This practice began probably in the first century BC. As the translations became standardized, under the supervision of the rabbis, they began to take shape in writing. The Targums fall into two main categories: the official Targums, known as 'Onqelos on the Torah', and 'Jonathan on the Prophets'; and the Unofficial Targums, written in a Galilean dialect of Aramaic, known as the 'Palestinian Targums'. The Official Targums are much more literal than the Palestinian Targums. Much controversy has raged about which of these two categories is of the earlier date. The influential view of Kahle that the Palestinian Targums are earlier, and that the Official Targums are later and Babylonian in origin, has become doubtful because of the work of Kutscher, Kaufman and Tal. It seems probable now that the Official Targums are the earlier, and are also Palestinian, with only superficial Babylonian colouring later. Accordingly, in this volume, the extracts given are primarily from the Official Targums, with reference to the Palestinian Targums where relevant.

The Targums give very valuable evidence of rabbinic Judaism in the first century AD, especially where they retain vestiges of earlier *halakah* and *haggadah*. The main influence on them, however, has been that of the rabbis of the second century AD, whose views were later collected in the Mishnah and Midrashim.

## THE MISHNAH

This is the most important halakic work of our period. It is the culmination of an effort, beginning at Jabneh after the destruction of the Temple in AD 70, to collate the laws by pooling all existing customs and traditions. Thus, for example, laws relating to the administration of the Temple and its sacrifices were contributed by surviving priests who had taken part in the Temple service, laws relating to the administration of justice were contributed by judges, and laws relating to the practices of the table-fellowships by members of them. There were probably some written collections of laws even at this time. As time went on, a plan for the classification of all laws under six main headings emerged, and collections were made attempting to include all laws under these six titles: these finally became the six 'Orders' (*sedarim*) of the Mishnah, the collection which subsumed and superseded all the previous collections. The orders of the Mishnah are: Seeds, Appointed Time, Women, Damages, Holinesses and Purities (see p. 49). The final editor of the Mishnah, in these orders, is regarded by tradition as Rabbi Judah the Prince, who completed his work of editorship *c.* AD 200. The text of the Mishnah as we have it, however, has been affected by later editors, especially the *'Amora'im*, or authorities of the Talmud, who sometimes inserted emendations into the text.

The earliest manuscripts of the Mishnah (including the Parma Manuscript) are no earlier than the thirteenth century, since the systematic destruction of Jewish holy writings formed part of Christian persecution. Earlier than this, however, are the texts of the Mishnah embedded in manuscripts of the Palestinian and Babylonian Talmuds, dated to the twelfth century. Some much earlier readings have been obtained from fragments found in the Cairo Genizah (see Glossary).

It is clear that the Mishnah sets out to be a law manual, thus excluding, as far as possible, non-legal material (*haggadah*) or devotional material. Yet it was found impossible to exclude such material completely. Sometimes *haggadah* creeps in as illustration of a legal topic (see, for example, the story about Honi the Circle-maker, p. 92). Sometimes it is used to round off a topic, at the end of a chapter, tractate or Order. The most conspicuous intrusion of *haggadah*, however, is the presence of a whole haggadic tractate, that of *'Abot*, which is included in the Order of Damages. This is a collection of ethical sayings, belonging to the genre of wisdom literature rather than to *halakah*. It was evidently felt that even though the Mishnah was primarily a law manual, it was necessary to include within it something of the background of religious and ethical emotion which informed rabbinic Judaism and gave rise to the proliferation of laws by which the Covenant community could be implemented on earth. Even *'Abot*, however, is far from encompassing the full range of concepts found in the *haggadah* of the Midrash and Talmud. *'Abot* restricts itself mainly to the ethic surrounding the rabbinic emphasis on the religious duty of study and education. This is the ethic appropriate to the Mishnah, which comprises that aspect of rabbinic Judaism demanding hard intellectual application. *'Abot* is unique in that it is a treatise on education which not only enjoins study and teaching as a feature of the religious life, but seeks to isolate the moral and spiritual characteristics necessary for good teaching and good studying.

Another apparently anomalous tractate of the Mishnah is *'Eduyyot* ('Testimonies'). This seems to be the only surviving example of a halakic genre in which the laws are arranged not under topics, but under the names of teachers who 'testified' to them. The laws in *'Eduyyot* are found elsewhere in the Mishnah under topics, so it is a problem why this tractate was included. The tractate does not appear to be earlier than the rest of the Mishnah.

Other anomalies can be observed in the system of classification itself. Thus it is a little difficult to see why the tractate *Berakot* ('Blessings'), which deals with the liturgy, is included in the Order of *Zera'im* ('Seeds'), which deals with agricultural laws. Some classifications are tenuous: for example, the tractate *Nedarim* ('Vows') is included in the Order *Našim* ('Women') only because certain vows made by women can be annulled by their husbands; and this leads also to the inclusion of the tractate *Nazir* ('The Nazirite'). The inclusion of *'Abot* in the Order *Neziqin* ('Damages') is hard to explain. Such anomalies, however, can be found in every code of law, because of the difficulties of categorization.

The term *mishnah* itself means literally 'repetition', an allusion to the practice of learning the laws and memorizing them by a process of repetition. This brings out the point made earlier that the field of *halakah* was the main focus of the duty of *talmud torah*; and it was here that efforts were directed to ensure that the student had a complete grasp and total recall of the whole body of learning, so that he could give quick decisions if required (the ethic here is similar to that required of medical practitioners today, whose training is directed towards memorization of all vital information, so that time will not be lost in an emergency by consulting books). In the field of *haggadah* such memorization was not required, since here the need was not for practical mastery, but for the imbibing of inspiration and edification. The Mishnah of Rabbi Judah the Prince became known as the Mishnah *par excellence*, but in fact the name 'Mishnah' was given to all compilations of a similar kind, except the Tosephta, which means 'Addition', i.e. 'Addition to the Mishnah of Rabbi Judah the Prince'. We know of other compilations called Mishnah (such as the Mishnah of Rabbi Akiba), but none of them has survived. So the position of nomenclature is similar to the case of the term *midrash*: the genre of collections of *halakah* in classified form is called *mishnah*; a work exemplifying this form is called a Mishnah; and a pericope from such a work is called a *mishnah*. There is no such thing as oral *mishnah* because *mishnah* by definition is one of the modes by which Oral Torah was put into writing (a point somewhat obscured by the fact that even though the Mishnah was in writing, it was the practice to learn it by heart, a practice common in Jewish academies (*yešibot*) down to the present day).

The question may be asked, What exactly was the purpose of the

Mishnah? Why does it include certain things, and omit others? Is it intended as a practical guide to conduct for Jews living in the period following the two national disasters (the destruction of the Temple and the failure of the Bar Kokhba revolt)? Or is it, on the contrary, intended to provide a nostalgic picture of the Jewish religious polity that had ceased to exist?

On the whole, we have to reply that the Mishnah is a picture of a functioning Jewish state, rather than a guide to living in a world where the Jewish state has ceased to operate. In a world of disintegration, the Mishnah gathers together the pieces and provides a blueprint for reconstruction. Thus the Mishnah comprises a tremendous act of faith in the eventual restoration of the Jewish commonwealth, and, in preparation for this event, makes ready the entire constitution by which it will be set up. There is certainly an element of nostalgia here, but much more evident is a calm confidence that this is the true state of affairs which has only been temporarily interrupted.

Thus the Mishnah, in the tractate *Sanhedrin*, describes the rights, duties and limits of power of the Jewish monarchy, or of the supreme judiciary body, the Sanhedrin, completely ignoring the fact that these arms of the state had ceased to exist. Moreover, the detailed procedure of the Temple, which actually lay in ruins, is described, even down to the casting of lots by priests for the performing of sacrifices, or the description of the various chambers, such as the Wood Chamber, the Wheel Chamber and the Chamber of Hewn Stone. The tractate *Yoma*, about the ritual of the Day of Atonement, says nothing about how this solemn day was observed in the synagogues in the days of the rabbis of Mishnaic times; instead it describes the full ritual of the Temple. One whole tractate, *Qinnim*, is devoted to curious mathematical problems arising from bird-sacrifices; to study such a tractate was an academic exercise, but one which focused the mind on the messianic hope, for with the restoration of the Temple these problems would become practical.

On the other hand, much of the Mishnah was of practical importance even in conditions of political powerlessness. Jewish courts were given certain powers even by alien rulers, and the laws outlined in the Order of Damages, including laws of compensation for injuries to persons or property, were administered and applied not only in the Mishnaic period but throughout the Middle Ages. Laws concerning charity or other 'deeds of loving-kindness' did not require a functioning state or courts of law for their continuance, but only personal piety, fostered by the study of the Mishnah. Most of the laws of the Sabbaths and festivals could be observed in the home or the synagogue even in the absence of a Temple, and the Mishnah tractates on these topics continued to be of practical importance.

We conclude, then, that the Mishnah was not intended primarily as a practical manual of Jewish law and practice (though parts of it certainly served this function). The Mishnah's main aim was political: to prevent the Jews from sinking into the mentality of a defeated people, with horizons bounded by the position assigned to them in the Roman Empire. Jews studying the Mishnah were continually reminded that they were the heirs of a great polity, with a legal system of its own, and that their subjection to the polity and law of Rome was merely temporary. The Mishnah, indeed, has nothing to say about day-to-day politics or even great contemporary events, but takes a long-term view, thus removing itself not only from contemporary politics, but also from short-term apocalyptic hopes. It quietly outlines a polity that had never quite existed in the past (for all attempts to implement it had fallen short), but would come into existence in the indefinite future; meanwhile, life was to be lived as best a subject people might live it in the Roman Empire. Again, it would be wrong to say that the Mishnah is *merely* political. In Judaism, politics and religion were inextricably entwined. Political liberation had been one of the great religious themes of Judaism ever since the liberation from Egypt.

However, the Mishnah does not state its own aims, and all attempts to see it as a whole have to go beyond what is on the printed page. The reticence of the Mishnah arises from the fact that, whether concerned with the past, the present or the future, it is primarily a book of law. It does not attempt to comprehend the full range of rabbinic thought and feeling. It gives an account of the current state of the *halakah* (even on matters beyond practical implementation), but it eschews, as far as it can, the *haggadah*, which defies codification. Yet the Mishnah assumes the full range of haggadic ideas, and makes no sense without them.

The Mishnah is written in a very succinct and technical style, so that a literal translation is very often unintelligible. Its style is full of mnemonic features, and is best characterized by saying that it is written in such a way as to facilitate memorization by the kind of reader who is familiar with its technical vocabulary and does not need elementary explanations. There is evidence that there was a class of persons called *tanna'im*, or 'repeaters' (not to be confused with the more familiar use of the word *Tanna'im* meaning 'authorities of the Mishnaic period'), who made it their business, either professionally or as a service to the community, to memorize the whole Mishnah, and would assist the discourses of the rabbi by acting as a kind of human concordance.

## THE TOSEPHTA

The Mishnah, despite its comprehensiveness, was still only a selection of the vast amount of halakic material in existence in the second century AD in the form of collections or individual traditions. Once the Mishnah was composed, and accepted as authoritative, the materials that had been left out of it did not all sink into oblivion; much was preserved in various ways as a complement to the Mishnah. A pericope of such extra-Mishnaic material is called a *baraita* ('something outside', i.e. outside the Mishnah of Rabbi Judah the Prince). Many *baraitas* are to be found in the two Talmuds, where they are often adduced in discussion of the Mishnah. To discuss the Mishnah is indeed the main business of the Talmuds, and a knotty point in the Mishnah may often be illuminated by reference to a *baraita* dealing with the same point. Often a *baraita* is discovered to be in contradiction to the Mishnah, and the elucidation of the point of contention helps to unravel the complexities of the topic. The Talmuds regard the *baraitas* as contemporary with the Mishnah and as having a similar kind of authority (i.e. as having Tannaitic authority), though, in the final analysis, the Mishnah is usually given preference. In fact, a considerable number of the *baraitas* cited in the Talmuds are post-Tannaitic (i.e. 'Amoraic) and are therefore not within the purview of the present volume. Those Talmudic *baraitas* that can be shown to be genuinely Tannaitic are part of early rabbinic literature, and some examples of them have been included in this volume.

The Tosephta ('supplement') is a great repository of *baraitas*. It is a compendium of material relevant to the Mishnah, and should be regarded as an enormous appendix to that work. The material is arranged under topics having similar headings to those of the Mishnah (with the omission of a few tractates). Since the Tosephta is ancillary to the Mishnah, it lacks many of the qualities that make the Mishnah a unitary work, such as unity of style, full subordination of topics within a general design, and unity of aim. While it includes many *baraitas* contemporary with the Mishnah (many of which throw light on the Mishnah itself by their more expansive style), it also contains much material that is irrelevant to our present purpose, being subsequent to the Mishnah and presupposing it as a basis for discussion. Many of the *baraitas* found in the Tosephta are identical to *baraitas* cited in the Talmuds, and their form in the Tosephta is less liable to textual corruption. It seems, however, that the Tosephta as we have it was not known to the authorities of the Talmuds. They do refer at times to a work called 'Tosephta', but this was a different work. Our Tosephta may have been compiled from previous works also called 'Tosephta' as late as the fourth or fifth centuries AD; but it is still an important witness to early rabbinic literature.

In addition to the huge Tosephta (which is four times longer than the Mishnah), there are extant some examples of shorter *baraita* literature in the form of monographs dealing with a particular topic. For historical purposes, the most important *baraita* of this kind is *Megillat Ta'anit*, probably the earliest extant rabbinic work, which, in the course of giving laws about days that are too joyous for rites of mourning or fasting, throws light on events in the Hasmonean period (see p. 218).

## THE LITURGY

A very important aspect of the creative activity of the rabbis was the liturgy. While there are many problems in dating the various components of the liturgy, it is clear that the main outline was complete during our period. This comprised the recitation of the *Shema'*, the affirmation of the unity of God, with its accompanying blessing, which stress God's role as Creator, and loving Father, and also the *Tepillah*, or 'prayer', consisting of blessings and petitions. In the 'blessings' (*berakot*), the innermost feelings and religious concepts of the rabbis are particularly to be found. At the same time, the rabbis showed their system of values in the selection they made from the biblical Psalms and other biblical works for inclusion in the liturgy, particularly the succession of psalms which was called the *Hallel* and which was recited on festivals (Pss. 113–18). They themselves also composed many moving hymns and prayers, both for public and private worship. An important feature of the liturgy was the lectionary of readings from the Torah and the Prophets on the Sabbaths and festivals, by which the entire Torah was read in the course of a three-year cycle (later, in Babylonia, reduced to a one-year cycle). The liturgy thus contained an educational element, which was reinforced by the institution of the sermon, and by the accompanying translation of the readings (*targum*).

The locus of the above forms of worship was the synagogue, but the rabbis also created a pattern of worship for the home. They composed the blessings of the *Qidduš* ('sanctification') ceremony performed by the head of the household with wine and bread at the beginning of a Sabbath or festival meal, and also the blessings of the Grace, recited after every meal containing bread, even during weekdays. Many other ceremonies, with appropriate blessings, were performed in the home, but the most impressive domestic rite was the Passover *Seder*, with its special rubric, the *Haggadah*, a characteristic rabbinic composition. Certain features of the rabbinic liturgy, whether public or private, were regarded as symbolic substitutes for the Temple ritual, which ceased when the Temple was destroyed in AD 70. The elaborate liturgy of the Day of Atonement is especially patterned in this way. In general, however, the rabbinic liturgy is not primarily expiatory or even petitionary, but rather an expression of praise and thanksgiving.

## THE MIDRASHIM

The main Midrashim with which we are concerned are the Tannaitic Midrashim (or Halakic Midrashim), as explained above (p. 23). (For further details of the Tannaitic Midrashim, see p. 147.) The later haggadic Midrashim, however, are not entirely irrelevant, for some of their material (especially in Genesis Rabbah and Leviticus Rabbah) can be traced to the period of the early rabbinic literature. Accordingly, some of their content is included. Some of the later Midrashim are not continuous commentary in the same sense as the Tannaitic Midrashim. Their principle of continuity is based on the lectionary cycle, and they aim to provide sermons or sermonic material for the Sabbaths and festivals of the year in their order, without attempting to provide a full commentary on each reading. Midrashim of this kind are thus called Homiletic Midrashim. The post-classical Midrashim, many of which should be called more properly 'haggadic works' rather than Midrashim, are not represented here at all.

## MISCELLANEOUS WORKS

Some rabbinic works of our period do not fall into any of the categories discussed above. These are:

1. *Seder ʿOlam* ('Order of the World'). This is a historical work, ascribed to the second-century rabbi, Yose ben Ḥalafta, often mentioned in the Mishnah as simply Rabbi Yose. There is no reason to doubt the authorship of Yose ben Ḥalafta, but the work, as we have it, is not quite the same as when the author wrote it, since it omits certain passages found cited in the Talmud, and contains certain additions. The work is remarkable in that it is a 'book' in the modern sense, not a compilation of rabbinical opinions. It sets itself a theme or problem, namely the chronology of biblical and post-biblical events in Jewish history, and works out this problem in monographic style. The work cannot be called either *halakah* or *haggadah*, as it has no legal or homiletic purpose, but simply the solution of its historical problem. Verses from the Bible are often quoted, and are often interpreted by the rabbinical hermeneutic methods; but the work is not a commentary on the Bible, and therefore cannot be called a Midrash. This is the first work to put a date for the creation of the world; and it is interesting both on account of its errors of chronology (for example, getting the dates of the Persian domination very wrong), and also on account of its accuracy, which can be explained by Rabbi Yose's access to ancient traditions, and possibly to the work of the Jewish hellenistic chronographer Demetrius (third century BC). In order to distinguish *Seder ʿOlam* from an early medieval chronological work with the same name, our work is usually called *Seder ʿOlam Rabbah* ('The Great *Seder ʿOlam*').

2. *The mystical literature*. Despite the fundamental rationalism and this-worldly emphasis of rabbinic Judaism, there was also a rabbinic form of mysticism which gave rise to a considerable literature. This literature cannot be regarded as belonging to the genre of *midrash*. 'These texts', writes Gershom Scholem in *Major Trends in Jewish Mysticism*, p. 46, 'are not Midrashim, i.e.: expositions of biblical passages, but a literature *sui generis* with a purpose of its own. They are essentially descriptions of a genuine religious experience for which no sanction is sought in the Bible. In short, they belong in one class with the Apocrypha and the apocalyptic writings rather than with the traditional Midrash'. Nevertheless, these

writings differ very considerably from the apocalyptic writings in that they occupy a peripheral role in the Judaism to which they belong. Mysticism was regarded as the perquisite of a few gifted souls, not as the main business of life.

The mystical literature mostly belongs to a later time, but it has its roots in our period, and certain passages in the literature have been dated, with good reason, to the second century AD. The earliest mystical work, *Šiʿur Qomah* ('The Measure of the Body'), a description of the Heavenly Man, or *Adam Qadmon*, should probably be dated before AD 200, except for certain additions; and chapters of later works, particularly *The Lesser Heykalot* and *The Greater Heykalot*, probably have the same early date. Consequently, extracts from some of these works are included in this volume, together with certain passages from the Mishnah, Tosephta and Talmud which throw light on the phenomenon of rabbinic mysticism. The connection between this mysticism and hellenistic forms of mysticism, especially Gnosticism, is one of the most vexed questions of rabbinic scholarship.

3. *The wisdom literature.* The tractate *'Abot*, mentioned above (p. 31), is included in the Mishnah, yet it really belongs to a different genre. Like the other works discussed in this section, it is not tied to the exposition of Scripture, but consists of observations on life culled by the rabbis from their own experience and thought. It belongs, therefore, to the *genre* of 'wisdom literature', of which the book of Proverbs is a biblical example. The Tosephta does not contain a work analogous to *'Abot*, but there does exist a separate work which has the same relation to *'Abot* as the Tosephta in general has to the Mishnah: this is called *'Abot deRabbi Nathan*, which re-works the material of *'Abot* in a more expansive manner, adding some earlier and some later material.

## THE MAIN RABBINIC FIGURES (For this section, see also Leaney, *The Jewish And Christian World*, pp. 187–95)

It will be seen from the above account of the early rabbinic literature that, with very few exceptions, authors in the usual sense are not to be found. Nevertheless, all the rabbis cited in the rabbinic literature are contributors to that literature in as much as the rabbinic works are a tapestry of their opinions and traditions. In studying the Mishnah, Tosephta and Midrashim, together with the *baraitas* of the Talmuds, we gain a picture of a teeming intellectual and religious life, covering many generations, with a great many rabbis, some well-delineated, some rather shadowy figures, in the relation to each other of colleagues, pupils or teachers. We know that Rabbi Judah ha-Nasi (the 'Prince' or 'Chief') was the 'author' of the Mishnah, but nothing of his individual personality appears in that work, of which he is the unobtrusive editor; yet, like the other rabbis, his personality is known to us from his opinions, his style of controversy, and various stories told about him in the literature. Thus when we speak of the 'main figures of the early rabbinic literature', we are referring to the heroes of that literature, rather than its creators, in the sense usual in the discussion of other forms of literature.

This does not mean that we possess any actual biographies of the rabbis of this period, since biography was not a mode of writing practised. Instead, we have to glean details of the lives of the great figures from legal and haggadic contexts in which stories of the rabbis often embellish some halakic or homiletic point. These details, moreover, are often of a legendary character, especially when they concern the earlier figures, who lived before the destruction of the Temple. Often a story tells us more about the world-outlook of the rabbinic movement than about the actual life of the main figure featured in the story. Yet this legendary aura never becomes pure myth; there is always a sense of realism in the rabbinic narratives, since they depict not saviour figures or even prophets, but a movement of colleagues, collaborating in a common enterprise, to which no single figure is essential, though each is regarded with honour. Discounting the legendary, we may arrive at a fairly detailed picture of the history of the movement, from its beginning in Hasmonean times, and of its leading figures.

## *Before* AD *70*

('pre-Tannaitic' generations and first generation of *Tanna'im*)

According to the Mishnah tractate *'Abot*, chapter 1 (which gives a fragmentary account of the succession of Pharisaic authorities), the first Sages after the cessation of prophecy were an anonymous body called 'the men of the Great Assembly', regarded as existing at about 350 BC. The first Sage to emerge from anonymity was Simeon the Just. The rabbinic stories about him are almost entirely legendary; he is regarded as contemporary with Alexander the Great, but may perhaps be identified with the historical figure, Simeon II, who receives high praise in the book of Ben Sira (Ecclus. 50), in which case his date is *c.* 200 BC. Some further names were preserved about whom little was known. Of these, Joshua ben Peraḥiah is of interest because later Jewish tradition regarded him as the teacher of Jesus. His date (*c.* 120 BC) makes this impossible, but he had a rebellious pupil, perhaps also called Jesus, and this was enough to cause the identification at a time when rabbinic tradition preserved no genuine memory of Jesus of Nazareth. The first Pharisaic leader with some historical substance is Simeon ben Shetaḥ (*c.* 80 BC), who, after vicissitudes in the reign of Alexander Jannaeus, led the Pharisees to a position of power and influence during the reign of Salome Alexandra, afterwards regarded by the rabbinic movement as a golden age of peace and prosperity. He was followed by the 'pair', Shemaiah and Abtalion, of whom little is known. Next, however, came another 'pair', Hillel and Shammai, who figure considerably in the rabbinic literature, and who were evidently regarded by the rabbis as their chief spiritual ancestors, since they gave them the title 'Fathers of the World' (M. 'Ed. 1:4). These leaders flourished from about 30 BC to AD 10, and their names must have been well known to Jesus. Hillel is credited with having drawn up the first list of hermeneutical methods (*middot*). His list contained seven, but Rabbi Ishmael later extended the list to thirteen, while later still, the list was extended to thirty-two (see p. 172).

The stories about Hillel tell us that he was a Babylonian, who came to Judaea to learn Torah, endured great privation in pursuing this aim, but eventually achieved eminence. He was a man of great patience, unlike his colleague Shammai. The stories of Hillel's superiority to Shammai, however, may arise from the rivalry between the later disciples of Hillel (called 'the House of Hillel') and those of Shammai (called 'the House of Shammai'), though the generally more lenient and tolerant outlook of the House of Hillel must have owed something to the personality of Hillel himself. Some of the stories about Hillel, and some of the sayings attributed to him, are similar to stories and sayings about 'wise men' current throughout the hellenistic world; for example, his version of the 'golden rule' 'Do not do unto others what is hateful to you', has many hellenistic parallels, including the version attributed to Jesus in the Gospels (Matt. 7:12; Luke 6:31). We must conclude that Hillel and Shammai belonged to a somewhat legendary age, as far as the compilers of the rabbinic literature were concerned, and their teachings have come to us in fragmentary form. The strong tradition that

Hillel was the promulgator of the far-reaching social reform known as the *prosbol*, by which business loans were facilitated in spite of the biblical seventh-year restrictions (see p. 75), is probably historically correct.

The two Houses succeeded Hillel and Shammai (*c.* AD 10) in the work of the Oral Torah and are reckoned as the first *Tanna'im*. Later accounts show the House of Hillel as dominant even in this pre-70 period, and portray the relations between the two Houses as mostly amicable. Modern scholars have doubted this representation, which they regarded as coloured by the post-70 triumph of the Hillelites. Certainly, some rabbinic stories show that the Shammaiites were sometimes dominant in the pre-70 period, but there is little justification for the view that the latter were always dominant. The probable truth is that dominance swayed from one group to the other. The New Testament's account of Gamaliel, who was a Hillelite (Acts 5:34–9), gives independent evidence of the Hillelite leadership of the Pharisees at one point, at least, during the pre-70 period. Relations between the two groups were sometimes strained, but they never degenerated into schism, and, on the whole, they settled their differences by majority vote.

The discussions between the two Houses were preserved in a very incomplete form. A leading figure was Gamaliel I, Hillel's son or grandson. He was given the title 'Rabban' ('chief' or 'teacher'), a title reserved for the chief figure of the Pharisaic movement. The expression '*rabbi*' ('my master' or 'my teacher') was not used as a title in the pre-70 period, but only as a form of respectful address (Matt. 23:7; John 1:38). Certain traditions show that Gamaliel's authority extended widely over the Diaspora; this militates against the view that the Pharisees during this period were a retiring, non-political group. Nor is it true that they shunned political or military office, for Gamaliel's son, Rabban Simeon ben Gamaliel, took a prominent part in the conduct of the war against Rome, as attested by Josephus (*War* IV.3.9 (158), *Life* 38 (191–92)), who also attests that a leading Zealot, Ẓadoq, was a Pharisee (*Ant.* XVIII.1.1 (4)). On the whole, however, the Pharisees adopted a cautious political role.

The contemporary and successor of Rabban Simeon ben Gamaliel I was Rabban Joḥanan ben Zakkai, whose main activity came after the war against Rome.

A group of the pre-70 Pharisees that stood somewhat apart from the others were those called *Ḥasidim* ('saints'), who were charismatic wonder-workers (see Glossary, *Ḥasidim*, 2). They were sometimes called 'the men of deed' (*'anšey ma'aseh*), because of their feats of healing and rain-making, and their supererogatory works of saintliness. Figures of this type were Ḥanina ben Dosa, Ḥoni the Circle-maker, and Abba Ḥilqiah. The Pharisaic movement was broad enough to encompass many religious types, and these charismatic figures (who, however, were not regarded as prophets) were highly respected by the more rationalistic teachers. This is shown by the friendship between Rabban Joḥanan ben Zakkai and Ḥanina ben Dosa, though a certain tension can be discerned in their relationship. To exaggerate this tension into a state of conflict is, however, a mistake (see p. 78). Jesus can perhaps be best understood as belonging to the Ḥasidic wing of the Pharisaic party, but this cannot be urged as an explanation of his alleged conflict with the mainstream Pharisees.

## *After 70* AD

After the Roman defeat of the Jewish revolt, Rabban Joḥanan ben Zakkai was allowed to set up an academy and Sanhedrin in Jabneh. Here the Oral Torah was taught and developed, and the future of Judaism secured. Joḥanan ben Zakkai himself enacted important reforms. He was regarded also as an adept in the mysticism of the heavenly Chariot (*ma'aseh merkabah*) (see Ezek. 1).

His successor was Rabban Gamaliel II (*c.* AD 80), of the Hillelite dynasty (which was preferred when it afforded a suitable candidate). His generation is regarded as the second generation of the *Tanna'im*. The second generation thus consisted entirely of post-Destruction figures, who are much more vivid and real in the literature than their predecessors, since their teachings and personalities were still alive in memory when the literature began to take final shape: indeed some of this generation provided the first written materials that formed the nucleus of the Mishnah and Midrashim.

Rabban Gamaliel II was a strong personality, but he had some equally strong personalities to contend with, and his period of office had some stormy episodes. It seems from the stories of this period that Gamaliel was concerned to curb the independence of those rabbis who regarded themselves as centres of authority, and to set up a system of consensus and decision for the entire Jewish people, whether in the Land of Israel or in the Diaspora. In this aim, he came into conflict (though never into schism) with his great contemporaries Joshua ben Ḥananiah and Eliezer ben Hyrkanus. He had the support, however, of the greatest rabbi of the age, Akiba ben Joseph, who, though belonging to a younger group of scholars, took a key role in reconciliation, sympathizing both with Gamaliel's centralizing aim and with the desire of the latter's antagonists for greater freedom. After one clash between Gamaliel and Joshua, the general body of rabbis actually deposed Gamaliel from his position as leader, or *Nasi*, and appointed Rabbi Eleazar ben Azariah in his place, but after a reconciliation in which Akiba took his usual role of peacemaker, Gamaliel was restored to his position, but with Eleazar as his associate or joint-president. Another clash led to the disciplining of Rabbi Eliezer, who, nevertheless, continued to be reverenced both by his own and by later generations (p. 5).

Rabbi Akiba's contemporary in the younger group, which comprised the third Tannaitic generation (120–139 AD), was Rabbi Ishmael ben Elisha, to whom the list of thirteen exegetical principles (*middot*) is attributed. Some of the Tannaitic Midrashim stemmed from Ishmael's school, while the others originated with Akiba (see p. 147). Ishmael favoured a more natural mode of interpretation ('The Torah speaks the language of men'), while Akiba introduced more artificial methods, by which laws or lessons could be deduced from insignificant particles in the text. Akiba travelled widely, visiting many Diaspora communities, probably in order to further Gamaliel's aim of centralizing religious authority. It is unlikely, however, that he became involved in anti-Roman politics, though when the messianic figure Bar Kokhba appeared, Akiba was impressed by his claims, and declared him to be indeed the Messiah. Akiba was martyred during the Hadrianic persecution that followed the failure of Bar Kokhba's revolt, not because of his support of Bar Kokhba, but because he persisted in teaching the Torah after such teaching had been banned.

Among the contemporaries of Akiba were Rabbi Tarpon, a hearty and argumentative scholar; Aqilas (Aquila), a proselyte, who translated the Bible into Greek; Ben Azzai and Ben Zoma, two unordained scholars who suffered from incautious practice of mysticism (see p. 136); and the picturesque figure of Elisha ben Abuyah, the renegade rabbi, who defected from Judaism and was known as *Aḥer* ('Another').

The fourth generation of *Tanna'im* (*c.*139–165), was led by

Rabben Simeon ben Gamaliel II, a less considerable scholar than his father, Gamaliel. His court, or *bet din*, was moved from Jabneh to Usha, in Galilee, some time before the Bar Kokhba revolt. Great personalities of this generation were Rabbi Josiah and Rabbi Jonathan (pupils of Rabbi Ishmael, who are often mentioned in the Ishmaelic literature (see p. 147), but not in the Mishnah), and the pupils of Akiba, Rabbi Meir, Rabbi Simeon ben Yoḥai, Rabbi Yose ben Ḥalafta (author of *Seder ʿOlam*) and Rabbi Judah ben Ilʿai. Also prominent was Rabbi Nathan of Babylon, who was active in the next generation as well. Rabbi Meir was regarded as the most brilliant scholar of his generation. He contributed to the development of the Mishnah, as did Rabbi Nathan. Meir was of tolerant disposition, and associated with the outcast Aḥer, in the hope of reclaiming him. Meir's wife, Beruriah, was regarded as a scholar of high standing. Meir and Nathan came into conflict with the Patriarch Simeon, whom they sought to depose, but failed. Accommodation with Rome was painfully achieved by this generation, though some, including the great Simeon ben Yoḥai, did not become reconciled to Rome easily.

With the fifth generation of *Tanna'im* (AD 165–200), we come to the end of our period. The leader of the rabbis in this generation was the illustrious Rabbi Judah the Prince, the compiler of the Mishnah (135–219). He moved his court from Usha to Beth Sheʿarim, also in Galilee, and later to Sepphoris. His relations with Rome were good, and he acquired wealth and power. His domination over the scholars of his age was unchallenged. Many stories of his friendship with a Roman Emperor called Antoninus are told (perhaps Marcus Aurelius Antoninus). Such was Rabbi Judah's eminence that he was known as simply 'Rabbi'. He was revered for his saintliness as well as for his scholarship. Among his contemporaries were Eleazar ben Simeon, the son of Simeon ben Yoḥai, who, unlike his father, had close relations with Rome, and Pinḥas ben Yair, a saintly ascetic. Only Nathan the Babylonian, however, a survivor from the previous generation, rivalled Rabbi Judah in learning or authority. A brilliant pupil of Rabbi Judah was Abba Arika, who returned to his home, Babylonia, and founded there the famous academy of Sura, from which sprang the great rabbinic culture culminating in the Babylonian Talmud. Abba Arika became known as 'Rab', the Babylonian equivalent to 'Rabbi', and his status was considered that of a *Tanna*, not an *'Amora*. Another important disciple was Rabbi Ḥiyya bar Abba, also Babylonian in origin, who played a great part in the development of the Tosephta, and is also reckoned as a

*Tanna*. These younger contemporaries of Rabbi Judah are sometimes reckoned as a sixth generation of *Tanna'im* (AD 200–20).

## THE MAIN IDEAS OF THE EARLY RABBINIC LITERATURE

The ideas of the rabbinic movement arise from reflection on the Bible. They comprise a certain development towards systematization and even abstraction, without, however, ever becoming independent abstract thinking, i.e. a system in which ideas are derived from postulates of pure reason.

To the rabbis, religious ideas came not from philosophical contemplation, but from a stupendous event – the intervention of God in human history at the time of the Exodus. This event meant not only deliverance from slavery and oppression, but also the establishment of Israel as a religio-political entity through the revelation on Mount Sinai which took the form of a Covenant between God and Israel, the promise of a land, and the promise of a transformed world. A narrative pattern of tremendous resonance produced ideas about the nature of God, about the purpose of human history, about the mission of Israel, and about love of one's fellow man:

1. *The nature of God*. The display of God's power in the Exodus shows him to be a transcendent Deity, superior to all the forces of nature; yet it also shows his nearness to humanity, since he hears the cry of the oppressed and intervenes in human history.
2. *The Covenant-people*. The choice of the Israelites to be the Covenant-people was not due to any merit, but was part of God's plan for the world which he created – a plan which he had partially divulged to the Patriarchs, Abraham, Isaac and Jacob. The Covenant was a personal bond between God and every Israelite; a relation of love by which God's commands would be obeyed not out of servile fear or hope of reward, but as an expression of free choice and partnership between God and man. The immediacy of the relationship between Israel and God meant that every other form of subservience was abolished or weakened. For example, the Babylonian authority Rab, declaring the right of workers to strike, based this right on the Exodus, by which the Israelites became the servants of God and were thus freed from subservience to man.
3. *The Land*. The Land of Israel was given to the Israelites as part of the Covenant, and could be retained only under the terms of the

Covenant. Having the Temple at its centre, it was to act as a Temple–land for the whole world, administered by the Israelites as a nation of priests. The Torah, in its holiness provisions, such as the dietary laws, the calendar of Sabbaths and festivals and the tithes and purities, was a priestly code intended for the Israelites alone; but its central core of love of God and man was intended for all humanity. The Land, therefore, and its Temple, was instituted for the benefit of the whole world.

4. *The promise of a transformed world.* The culmination of history would be the conversion of the whole world to the worship of the one God (see p. 210). At that time, Israelite sovereignty would be restored under its king, the Messiah, and the ideal of the Temple as a centre of worship for all mankind would be realised, with the people of Israel as the recognized priest–nation. Military empires would come to an end, and war would be abolished, though nations would continue to exist in their God-ordained territories.

The above brief sketch of rabbinic Judaism will be given substance in the extracts from the rabbinic literature translated in this volume. It will be seen that the rabbis based their world-view entirely on the Hebrew Bible, but they developed their own characteristic vocabulary, some of which was entirely their own, and some of which employed words or expressions taken from the Bible but given a particular nuance. For example, the word *miṣwah* appears very frequently in the Hebrew Bible to mean simply 'commandment'. In rabbinic usage, however, the word acquired a wealth of meaning derived from the associations of performing God's commandment in a condition of Covenant. The word came to mean a privilege by which one was enabled to express the Covenant relationship. In this spirit it was said 'The reward of a *miṣwah* is another *miṣwah*' (M. 'Ab. 4:11). Another example is the rabbinic expression *malkut šamayim* ('the Kingdom of Heaven'), a concept based on the vocabulary of Scripture, but full of meaning in relation to the whole family of rabbinical concepts. The rabbinical concepts, indeed, form a family rather than a hierarchy. There is no rigid demarcation between them, but each of them overlaps with all the others. They are, therefore, not scientific or philosophical concepts; each takes off directly, though from a slightly different angle, from the underlying myth of God's epiphany in the Exodus and its consequences for human history and man's self-image. Other examples of rabbinical concepts are *berakah* ('blessing'), *gemilut ḥasadim* ('performance of deeds of loving-kindness'), *qidduš ha-šem* ('sanctification of the Name'), *ṣedaqah* ('charity'), *derek 'ereṣ* ('courtesy'), *šekinah* ('God's indwelling presence'), *zakut* ('merit', but also 'privilege').

Thus the rabbinical literature, though wholly subordinating itself to Scripture, which it endeavours to 'search' and explicate, in fact contains great originality arising from the struggle to make biblical values actual in the times in which the rabbis found themselves – times, mostly, of adversity and national disaster in which biblical promises for the Jewish people as the most significant community in human history were hard to maintain. In this difficult atmosphere, a tremendous effort of conservation was necessary to prevent the traditions from being lost; but this very effort endowed the traditions with new life and development, producing a unique literature which became the basis for the further survival and growth of Judaism.

# PART II

# Selected Passages

## THE MISHNAH

See Part I, pp. 30 to 35, for a general characterization of the Mishnah.

The six Orders (*seder*, pl. *sedarim*) of the Mishnah are: *Zera'im* ('Seeds'), *Mo'ed* ('Appointed Time' or 'Festival'), *Našim* ('Women'), *Neziqin* ('Damages'), *Qodašim* ('Holinesses'), and *Tohorot* ('Purities'). The Orders are divided into tractates (*maseket*, pl. *masektot*), and the tractates are divided into chapters (*pereq*, pl. *peraqim*), which are again divided into pericopes (*mishnah*, pl. *mishnayot*).

*Zera'im* is concerned mainly with the agricultural aspects of the Torah. Its subject-matter includes: the liturgy (included probably because many of the blessings contained in it are pronounced when partaking of the fruits of the land); 'the corner of the field' and other rights of the poor (Lev. 19:9–10; Deut. 24:19–21); tithes of various kinds; 'forbidden mixtures' in plants, animals and garments (Lev. 19:19; Deut. 22:9–11); the sabbatical year (Exod. 23:11; Lev. 25:2–7; Deut. 15:1–11); forbidden fruits (Lev. 19:23–5); and First-fruits (Deut. 26:1–11).

*Mo'ed* is concerned with the religious calendar. It deals with the Sabbath; the pilgrim-festivals, Passover, Pentecost and Tabernacles; the High Festivals, the New Year and the Day of Atonement; the minor festivals; and public fasts.

*Našim* concerns marriage and divorce. It deals with levirate marriage (Deut. 25:5–10); marriage deeds; 'the Suspected Adulteress' (Num. 5:11–31); weddings; divorces; and vows of various kinds.

*Neziqin* (the more colloquial, or Aramaized, plural *–in* rather than *–im* is traditional) is concerned mainly with civil and criminal law, and its administration. It deals with damages, injuries, thefts and compensation for them (Exod. 21:28–36; 22:1–5); lost property; guardianship; buying and selling; lending, hiring and renting; commerce and land-dealing; inheritance; courts and their sanctions;

oaths; and erroneous decisions by courts. This Order also contains three tractates which do not seem relevant to the civil or criminal law: *ʿEduyyot* (see p. 31), *ʾAbot* (see p. 00) and *ʿAboda Zara* (on idolatry).

*Qodašim* is concerned mainly with the Temple service. It deals with sacrifices of animals; grain-offerings; the slaughtering of animals for ordinary use; the first-born; dedications of persons or things to the Temple; exchanges for dedicated things (Lev. 27:10–27); expiatory sacrifices; profanation of sacred things; the daily morning and evening sacrifice; the measurements and design of the Temple; the service of the priestly guards; and bird-sacrifices.

*Tohorot* is concerned with ritual purity and impurity. It deals with impurity of vessels and garments; impurity conveyed by a corpse; leprosy of persons, garments and houses (Lev. 13; 14); 'the Red Cow' (Num. 19); lesser impurities; ritual pools; impurity of a menstruating woman; the moistening of foodstuffs as a prerequisite of susceptibility to impurity (Lev. 11:34, 38); impurity of a sexually diseased person; the state of a person between immersion in the ritual pool and sunset; impurity of hands; and the various parts of plants in relation to impurity.

## *The tractates of the Mishnah, in their Orders*

### The Order of *Zeraʿim* ('Seeds')

| | *Biblical reference* |
|---|---|
| *Berakot* ('blessings') | Deut. 6:4; 8:10 |
| *Pe'ah* ('corner of the field') | Lev. 19:9; 23:22 |
| *Demai* ('produce doubtfully tithed') | |
| *Kil'ayim* ('Two Kinds') | Lev. 19:19; Deut. 22:11 |
| *Šebiit* ('The Seventh Year') | Exod. 23:10–11; Lev. 25:2–7 |
| *Terumot* ('Priestly portions') | Num. 18:11 |
| *Maʿaserot* ('Tithes') | Num. 18:21 |
| *Maʿaser Šeni* ('Second Tithe') | Deut. 14:22–6, 28f |
| *Ḥallah* ('Dough-offering') | Num. 15:18–21 |
| *ʿOrlah* ('Fruit of young trees') | Lev. 19:23f |
| *Bikkurim* ('First-fruits') | Deut. 26:1–11 |

## The Order of *Moʿed* ('Appointed time')

| | |
|---|---|
| *Šabbat* ('Sabbath') | Exod. 20:8–11 |
| *ʿErubin* ('Extension of Sabbath limits') | Exod. 16:29 |
| *Pesaḥim* ('Passover offerings') | Lev. 23:5–8 |
| *Šeqalim* ('Dues to the Temple') | Exod. 30:13–16 |
| *Yoma* ('The Day of Atonement') | Lev. 16:1–34; Num. 29:7–11 |
| *Sukkah* ('The Feast of Tabernacles') | Lev. 23:39–43 |
| *Beṣah* ('Egg', from its first word; the alternative descriptive title is *Yom Tob*, 'Festival') | Exod. 12:16 |
| *Roš ha-Šanah* ('The New Year') | Lev. 23:24f |
| *Taʿanit* ('Fast-days') | |
| *Megillah* ('Scroll of Esther') | Esther 9:28 |
| *Moʿed Qatan* ('Mid-festival days') | |
| *Ḥagigah* ('The festival offering') | Deut. 16:16 |

## The Order of *Našim* ('Women')

| | |
|---|---|
| *Yebamot* ('Sisters-in-law') | Deut. 25:5–10 |
| *Ketubot* ('Marriage-deeds') | |
| *Nedarim* ('Vows') | Num. 30:1–15 |
| *Nazir* ('The Nazirite') | Num. 6:1–21 |
| *Soṭah* ('The Suspected Adulteress') | Num. 5:11–31 |
| *Giṭṭin* ('Bills of divorce') | Deut. 24:1 |
| *Qiddušin* ('Marriages') | |

## The Order of *Neziqin* ('Damages')

| | |
|---|---|
| *Baba Qamma* ('The First Gate') | Exod. 21:1–36; 22:1–6 |
| *Baba Meṣʿia* ('The Middle Gate') | Exod. 22:7–15; Deut. 22:1–3 |
| *Baba Batra* ('The Last Gate') | |
| *Sanhedrin* ('The Sanhedrin') | Num. 11:16; Lev. 5:1 |
| *Makkot* ('Floggings') | Deut. 19:19; 25:2–3; Num. 35:11 |

| | |
|---|---|
| *Šebu'ot* ('Oaths') | Lev. 6:2–3; Exod. 22:11 |
| *'Eduyyot* ('Testimonies') | |
| *'Abodah Zarah* ('Idolatry') | Exod. 20:4–5 |
| *'Abot* ('The Fathers') | |
| *Horayot* ('Decisions') | Lev. 4:1–21 |

The Order of *Qodašim* ('Holinesses')

| | |
|---|---|
| *Zebaḥim* ('Animal-offerings') | Lev. 1; 3; 5; 6; 7 |
| *Menaḥot* ('Grain-offerings') | Lev. 2 |
| *Ḥullin* ('Non-holy meat') | Deut. 12:21 |
| *Bekorot* ('First-born animals') | Exod. 13:2, 12–13 |
| *'Arakin* ('Valuations') | Lev. 27:1–25 |
| *Temurah* ('The Substituted Offering') | Lev. 27:10 |
| *Keritot* ('Excisions') | Num. 15:30–1 |
| *Me'ilah* ('Sacrilege') | Lev. 5:15–16 |
| *Tamid* ('The Daily Offering') | Exod. 29:38–42 |
| *Middot* ('Measurements of the Temple') | |
| *Qinnim* ('The Bird-offerings') | Lev. 5:7; 12:8; 14:22; 15:14; Num. 6:9–10 |

The Order of *Tohorot* ('Purities')

| | |
|---|---|
| *Kelim* ('Vessels') | Lev. 11:32; 15:12 |
| *'Oholot* ('Overshadowings') | Num. 19:14 |
| *Nega'im* ('Kinds of leprosy') | Lev. 13–14 |
| *Parah* ('The Red Cow') | Num. 19:1–22 |
| *Tohorot* ('Purities') | Lev. 11:34 |
| *Miqwa'ot* ('Immersion-pools') | Lev. 11:36 |
| *Niddah* ('The Menstruant') | Lev. 15:19–24 |
| *Makširin* ('Means of susceptibility') | Lev. 11:38 |
| *Zabim* ('Gonorrhoea-sufferers') | Lev. 15:1–15, 25–30 |
| *Ṭebul Yom* ('He that immersed himself that day') | Lev. 11:25, etc. |
| *Yadayim* ('Hands') | |
| *'Uqṣin* ('Stalks') | |

## The beginning of the Mishnah

*Mishnah Berakot 1:1*

From when do they read the *Shemaʿ* in the evening? From the time that the priests enter to eat their *terumah* until the end of the first watch: the words of Rabbi Eliezer. But the Sages say: Until midnight. Rabban Gamaliel says: Until the shaft of dawn goes up. It happened that his (Rabban Gamaliel's) sons came from a house of feasting. They said to him: We have not read the *Shemaʿ*. He said to them: If the shaft of dawn has not gone up, you are obliged to read it. And not this alone, but wherever the Sages have said 'until midnight', their commandment is until the shaft of dawn goes up. The burning of the fats and limbs – their commandment is until the shaft of dawn goes up; and all things that must be eaten 'the same day' – their commandment is until the shaft of dawn goes up. If so, why have the Sages said 'until midnight'? In order to set a man far from transgression.

¶ This is the opening passage of the Mishnah, which immediately sets its tone (see p. 8). A knowledge of the liturgy is taken for granted, and discussion is limited to disputed points. But out of the discussion, an important principle of rabbinical legislation emerges.

*read the Shemaʿ*: 'read' means to recite aloud, not necessarily out of a written text. The *Shemaʿ* means the declaration of the unity of God; 'Hear, Israel, the Lord our God, the Lord is One', together with other prescribed passages (see p. 205). The *Shemaʿ* was to be read twice a day, in accordance with the precept, 'on thy lying down and on thy rising up' (Deut. 6:7). The question here is, How is the time of lying down to be defined?

*From the time that the priests enter to eat their terumah*: this means the time of the coming out of the stars. Priests who had become unclean through contact with some impurity such as a dead 'creeping thing' were forbidden to touch or eat the priestly food, or *terumah* (given from the harvests to the priests by Israelites, see Num. 18:8–11), though they were permitted to touch or eat non-priestly food. Priests who had immersed themselves in the ritual pool (*miqweh*) in the morning in order to cleanse themselves of their impurity, still had to wait until the evening before eating *terumah* (Lev. 22:6).

During the period from the morning immersion to the coming out of the stars, a person is termed a *tebul yom* ('he who immersed that day'). In this state, a person is regarded as having a mild degree of impurity, sufficient to transfer impurity to holy food but not to ordinary food. Thus a *ḥaber*, or member of a table-fellowship, may eat his food even when he is a *tebul yom*, for, although his vow or 'undertaking' compels him to eat even ordinary food 'in purity' (i.e. without conveying impurity to it), the mild degree of impurity adhering to a *tebul yom* is insufficient to convey impurity to ordinary food. For further explanation of ritual-purity matters, see pp. 67, 94–100. It should be remembered that ordinary Israelites (non-priests) were not much concerned about ritual purity, since being in a state of impurity, or conveying it to ordinary food, was not sinful in law. Only priests, or those laymen who made the special voluntary vow of the table-fellowships, had daily concern in the matter; and the seriousness involved was much greater for the priest than for the *ḥaber*, since the priest had to worry about committing sacrilege, while the *ḥaber* only had to worry about a possible breach of his vow. Moreover, as we have just seen, the task of the *ḥaber* was less arduous than that of the priest, ordinary food being less susceptible to impurity than holy food.

*until the end of the first watch*: there is disagreement in the Talmuds whether the night is regarded as divided into three watches or four. In any case, this way of dividing time is different from our method of reckoning by the clock, for a 'watch', whether a third or a quarter of the time between star-rise and dawn, would not be the same clock-time at different seasons of the year. The division into three watches seems to have been the older (see Judg. 7:19). The New Testament gives evidence of a division into four watches (Mark 6:48; Matt. 14:25); but also of a division into three watches (Luke 12:38).

*the words of Rabbi Eliezer*: his view is that after the end of the first watch, it is too late to recite the *Shema'*, since it is no longer the time of 'lying down' – the end of the first watch, is the latest time for going to bed.

*But the Sages say: Until midnight*: it becomes clear that the Sages actually agree with Rabban Gamaliel that the *Shema'* may be read until dawn, and that the limit of 'midnight' is merely precautionary. They understand the time of 'lying down' not to be the time of going to bed, but the time of sleeping.

*wherever the Sages have said 'until midnight'*: by setting the limit earlier than biblical law required, they ensured that people would not wait until dangerously near the deadline before reciting the *Shema'*: but this precautionary measure carried with it the danger that someone, having overstepped the midnight limit, might think that it was now too late to recite the *Shema'* and thus fail to observe a biblical precept. A tension between biblical law and the rabbinical legislation designed to protect it is thus noted right at the beginning of the Mishnah. The rabbinical efforts to ensure that the biblical law was observed might lead to a breach of it! It is thus enjoined that rabbinical law should always be distinguished from biblical law and never be regarded as having the same authority, but rather as being its minister.

*The burning of the fats and limbs*: see Lev. 6:9, '. . . the whole offering shall remain on the altar-hearth all night till morning'. This is not, in fact, an instance of a rabbinical precautionary enactment, for there was no rabbinical injunction to burn these portions before midnight. They are cited here merely to show that when something was to be done during the night, this meant not later than dawn.

*all things that must be eaten 'the same day'*: see Lev. 7:15, 'The flesh shall be eaten on the day of its presentation; none of it shall be put aside till morning'. In this instance, the rabbis did enact that this should be done before midnight (see M. Zeb. 5:5).

## The Sabbath meal

*Mishnah Berakot 8:1–2*

These are the things that are between the House of Shammai and the House of Hillel in the meal. The House of Shammai say: One makes a blessing over the day and afterwards one makes a blessing over the wine. And the House of Hillel say: One makes a blessing over the wine, and afterwards one makes a blessing over the day. The House of Shammai say: They wash the hands and afterwards mix the cup. And the House of Hillel say: They mix the cup and afterwards wash the hands. The House of Shammai say: One wipes one's hands with a napkin and puts it on the table. And the House of Hillel say: On the cushion. The House of Shammai say: They sweep the room and afterwards wash the hands. And the House of Hillel say: They wash the hands and afterwards sweep the room.

¶ At the opening of the Sabbath, the *qidduš* ('sanctification') service was performed in the home by the master of the house in the presence of family, friends and guests. Then followed the Sabbath meal, which had its own etiquette; and the finale was the service known as *birkat ha-mazon* ('grace after the meal'), which was preceded by a washing of the hands. The precise order of these proceedings was worked out during the first century AD, and our passage shows that certain details were a matter of dispute between the two main groups of the Pharisees, the followers of Hillel and the followers of Shammai. In the second century, elaborate reasons were given for these differences of opinion between the Hillelites and the Shammaites, but the real reasons were probably much simpler, being based on common-sense considerations, and on variations in Graeco–Roman etiquette. There was a reluctance among the second-century rabbis to admit that Jewish table etiquette was partly derived from Graeco–Roman practice (see also p. 84).

*a blessing over the day*: the wording was 'Blessed are you, Lord, who make the Sabbath holy'. For the full text of the *qidduš*, see p. 211.

*a blessing over the wine*: 'Blessed are you, Lord our God, King of the Universe, who create the fruit of the vine.' The reason for the difference of opinion (or, possibly, regional practice) about the order of these two blessings is that, on the one hand, it was felt that the wine blessing should immediately precede the drinking of the wine; while, on the other hand, it was felt that the climax of the *qidduš* service should be a celebration of the holiness of the Sabbath.

*They wash the hands and afterwards mix the cup*: wine was usually mixed with water in the proportions of one-third of wine to two-thirds of water; it was considered boorish to drink wine in neat form. To 'mix the cup' means, therefore, simply to 'fill the cup'. The disagreement is whether to wash the hands before the *qidduš*, or to wait until the *qidduš* is over, and wash the hands just before the blessing over bread which signalized the beginning of the meal. On normal weekdays, hands were washed before any meal containing bread; and it was normal to wash the hands and then commence the meal by 'breaking bread' (see Acts 2:42, 46). The question was whether to break this normal pattern on Sabbath, when *qidduš* preceded the meal, by washing hands before the *qidduš*. It should be noted that in the first century, this 'washing of hands' before a meal was probably a matter of hygiene only, as in contemporary Graeco–Roman practice; it was only in the second century that hand-washing began to be given a ritual-purity interpretation. Accordingly, the present dispute between the Houses was then given an elaborate ritual-purity interpretation, which is found in the Tosephta and Talmuds, but is not in the Mishnah. It is interesting that the Talmudic discussion of our passage in terms of ritual purity is so artificial that it is ignored by Maimonides in his classic codification of ritual-purity law.

*One wipes one's hands with a napkin and puts it on the table*: again this controversy was later given an elaborate ritual-purity explanation, but, in a first-century context, it represents a mere difference in etiquette. It was normal to wipe grease from the hands during the course of the meal, and no doubt in some circles it was considered seemly to keep the napkin used for this purpose away from general view by putting it on a cushion, instead of on the table.

*They sweep the room and afterwards wash the hands*: the hand-washing referred to here is the second hand-washing (*mayyim 'aḥaronim*), which took place just before the reciting of Grace. This second hand-washing was never given a ritual-purity interpretation, and the Talmuds agree that its purpose was hygienic (see b. Ḥul. 105 a–b). Consequently, the Talmuds do not attempt to give a ritual-purity connotation to this dispute about sweeping the room, but instead give a common-sense reason about possible damage to food. Ancient meals tended to leave food on the floor because of the reclining posture adopted, and therefore it was seemly to tidy up before proceeding to Grace. The dispute is probably a matter of etiquette: is the hand-washing preliminary to the Grace, or part of the Grace itself?

*Note that all this meticulousness about the conduct of the meal arose from the fact that the Sabbath meal, like the *qidduš* preceding it, was considered to be a religious obligation and ceremony, by which the holiness of the Sabbath was celebrated and its connotations of rest and delight were translated into action. Consequently, an atmosphere of dignity and ritual was associated with every detail of the meal.

**For the relevance of hand-washing incidents in the Gospels, see p. 122.

## The blessings and the rabbis

*Mishnah Berakot 9:5*

A person is obliged to bless (God) for evil just as he blesses him for good; as it is written, 'And thou shalt love the Lord thy God with all thy heart and with all thy soul and with all thy might' (Deut. 6:5,

AV). 'With all thy heart' – with thy two inclinations, with the good inclination and the evil inclination. 'And with all thy soul' – even if he takes away thy life. 'And with all thy might' – with all thy wealth. Another explanation of 'with all thy might' – for whatever measure he measures out to you, give thanks to him exceedingly.

A person should not behave frivolously while opposite the Eastern Gate, for it is directly in line with the Holy of Holies. He may not enter the Temple Mount with his staff or his shoes or his purse or with the dust upon his feet and he must not make it into a short-cut, and it goes without saying that he must not spit there.

All who closed the blessings that were in the Temple used to say 'from eternity'. After the heretics disgraced themselves and said that there is no world but one, they enacted that they should say 'from eternity to eternity'. And they enacted that a person should greet his fellow with the Name; as it is said, 'And behold Boaz came from Bethlehem, and said to the reapers, The Lord be with you'. And they said to him, 'May the Lord bless you' (Ruth 2:4). And it is said, 'May the Lord be with thee, thou mighty man of valour' (Judg. 6:12). And it is written, 'And despise not thy mother when she is old' (Prov. 23:22). And it is written, 'It is time to work for the Lord: they have made void thy law' (Ps. 119:126). Rabbi Nathan says: They have made void thy law because it is time to work for the Lord.

¶ This is the concluding *mishnah* of the tractate *Berakot*. It seems to be a rather miscellaneous group of remarks and *halakot*, but perhaps has more logical sequence, and validity as closure, than appears at first sight.

The first paragraph alone would seem to be a fitting closure to a tractate on 'blessings', since it universalizes the concept of 'blessing God' to an acceptance of everything, whether good or bad, that he sends us. What, then, is the relevance of the two paragraphs that follow?

We saw (p. 55) that the tractate opens with the tension between the commands of the Torah and the enactments of the rabbis. It is perhaps significant, then, that the tractate also closes with this tension. The final thought of the tractate is that there can even be times when the rabbis are called on to override the words of the

Torah, if the higher aims of the Torah demand such action. Rabbi Nathan's interpretation of the text is: It is time to work for the Lord, so the rabbis (not the wicked) have overridden thy law. In this context, the relevance of the penultimate paragraph is perhaps this: Not only the Temple itself is sacred, but also its environs. Similarly, do not let your reverence for the Torah blind you to the need to heed the words of the rabbis, whose words form an outer courtyard to the Temple which is the Torah itself.

*'With all thy heart' – with thy two inclinations*: the real point is not reached until the arrival of the exegesis of the phrase 'with all thy might', but it is typical of rabbinic style to provide incidental exegesis while on the way to the part of the biblical verse illustrating the main thesis. Probably, the exegesis of the whole verse circulated as a unit, independently of the purpose for which it is adduced here, and once quoted, it is quoted in full. This is even more probable in view of the fact that the relevant exegesis, when reached, does not even constitute part of the main exposition, but is 'another explanation'.

*with the good inclination and the evil inclination*: it is rabbinic doctrine that the human psyche contains two 'inclinations' or 'formations', one for good and the other for evil. Thus moral evil is based firmly in the human psyche, and not attributed to an evil cosmic power working against humanity (Satan being regarded as merely an angel, who performs tasks in obedience to God). Moreover, even the 'evil inclination' (*yeṣer ha-ra*ʿ) was regarded as a form of energy that could be harnessed for good. This is the point of the present remark, which, exegetically, is based on the form *lebab*, used in the text, instead of the more usual *leb*, for 'heart': the doubling of the consonant is held to refer to the double nature of the human heart. A similar comment is found in Sifre on Deut. 6:5.

*'And with thy soul' – even if he takes away thy life*: the Hebrew word translated by AV as 'soul' (*nepeš*) can also mean 'life', and this is taken to be its meaning here. This was the verse quoted by Rabbi Akiba, on the occasion of his martyrdom (see b. Ber. 61b).

*for whatever measure he measures out to you, give thanks to him exceedingly*: this interpretation depends on a three-fold pun on the Hebrew word for 'might' (*me'od*). The three punning words are *middah* ('measure'), *modeh* ('thankful') and *me'od* ('exceedingly'). Such punning interpretations were hardly taken seriously as exegesis of the biblical text, but as being part of a penumbra of meaning hovering around the text, and as being a way of attaching some salutary ethical teaching, however tenuously, to biblical authority. Yet it is for the sake of this interpretation, actually an afterthought in its original setting, that Deut. 6:5 was adduced in our present context.

*make it into a short-cut*: use it as a short-cut between two places outside the Temple Mount. The word used for 'short-cut' is *qapandaria*, derived from the Latin *(via) compendaria*.

*'from eternity to eternity'*: this expression is found in Neh. 9:5, in a context of blessing God. Our passage asserts that the formula of blessing in the Temple originally contained the expression 'from eternity', but that this was changed, by a rabbinical ordinance, to 'from eternity to eternity', in order to counteract heresy. The word for 'eternity' and for 'world' is the same in Hebrew (*'olam*). It seems that the rabbinical authorities referred to here, who enacted this change, must be those of the time of Nehemiah. Similarly, the rabbinical authorities referred to in the next instance cited, who enacted that the name of God should be used in greetings, must be those of the time of Boaz, who is regarded as having lived in the days of the Great Assembly, of which he was thought to have been a member (i.e. in the time of Nehemiah, about 450 BC). The quotation from Judges, however, is from a speech made by an angel, and cannot be regarded as evidence of a rabbinical enactment. Perhaps this is a later insertion in our text.

*'And despise not thy mother when she is old'*: this text is often quoted to mean 'Do not neglect rabbinical tradition'. The 'mother' here is the personified people of Israel, whose ancient traditions are guarded by the Pharisaic and rabbinic movement.

*'It is time to work for the Lord: they have made void thy law'*: this text, together with its rather startling interpretation by Rabbi Nathan (interpreting 'they' as the rabbis), is often quoted in the Talmuds to justify the temporary suspension of a law of the Torah for some great purpose ('time to work for the Lord'). The archetypal case of this was held to have been Elijah's performance of a sacrifice outside the Temple (I Kings 18:32ff) despite the prohibitions of Deuteronomy. The alleged enactment to use the name of God in greetings hardly comes into this category, but is rather intended merely as an example of age-old custom, for which the authority is human, not divine. The final quotation of Rabbi Nathan's saying then extends the authority of the rabbis even to the occasional temporary abrogation of biblical law, when circumstances demand. This balances

the warning given in the opening passage of the tractate not to overestimate the words of the rabbis in such a way as to nullify biblical commandments (p. 53). As a general rule, the rabbis' enactments must be subservient to Scripture; but occasionally they can temporarily override the letter in order to preserve the spirit.

## Things that have no measure

*Mishnah Pe'ah 1:1–2*

These are things that have no measure: *pe'ah*, First-fruits, the festival offering, deeds of loving-kindness and the study of the Torah. These are things whose fruits a person eats in this world, and the capital endures for him for the world to come: honouring one's father and mother, deeds of loving-kindness, bringing peace between one person and another; and the study of the Torah is over against them all.

¶ This is the opening of the tractate *Pe'ah*, which is concerned with the rights of the poor to certain portions of the agricultural yield. The opening and closing of tractates are sometimes occasions for relaxing of the strictly halakic orientation of the Mishnah and the introduction of haggadic or ethical matter.

*no measure*: no upper limit, though in some of the cases mentioned, the rabbis did institute a minimum.
*pe'ah*: 'corner'. The owner of a field is required to leave one corner unharvested, for the benefit of the poor (Lev. 19:9; 23:22). This is one of the poor-gifts prescribed by the Torah, the others being gleanings (*leqet*) that fall from the reaping, and any sheaf that is forgotten (*šikeḥah*); also there is the poor-tithe (Deut. 14:28–9).
*First-fruits*: see Exod. 23:19; Deut. 26:1–11, where no measure is prescribed; nor did the rabbis prescribe any measure in this instance.
*the festival offering*: at the three pilgrim festivals, Israelites were to 'appear before the Lord' in the Temple, and they were not to appear 'empty-handed'; but the amount of their gift was left to the individual, 'in proportion to the blessing which the Lord your God has given you' (Deut. 16:16–17).
*deeds of loving-kindness*: literally, 'the performance of mercies' (*gemilut ḥasadim*), a phrase difficult to render in English, because of the many-faceted meaning of the word *ḥesed*. This is one of the basic

rabbinic concepts, and it covers all deeds of charity, not merely to the poor, but to all in distress, such as visiting the sick, redeeming captives, or comforting mourners. When the Mishnah tells us, however, that there is no upper limit to deeds of loving-kindness, this applies to acts of personal kindness, not to financial charity, for it is a rabbinic principle that a person should not impoverish himself through charity: consequently, the limit was set that a person should not give more than a fifth of his income in charity (b. Ket. 50a). 'lest he should need to call upon his fellow creatures', i.e. lest he should merely add one to the number of the poor, and neglect his duty to his own family. Jesus' injunction, 'Sell everything you have, and give to the poor' (Mark 10:21), appears to contradict this rabbinic principle, but Jesus probably thought the Last Days were just about to start, and that therefore ordinary ethical and prudential considerations did not apply; or perhaps his demand was not a general principle but *ad hominem*.

*the study of the Torah*: no limit is set to this, for it is said, '. . . thou shalt meditate therein day and night' (Josh. 1:8). This does not mean that a person should neglect other duties in order to study, but that this is a duty that he can never regard himself as having completely fulfilled.

*things whose fruits a person eats in this world*: in his commentary on the Mishnah, Maimonides finely explains that deeds of humanity produce benefits in this world by helping to produce a humane, kindly society, but that all these deeds also have an other-worldly dimension, since they are performed in accordance with the will of God.

*the study of the Torah is over against them all*: or 'equal to them all'; not that it can take their place, but that it makes them all possible. The importance of study as a moral imperative is the most distinctive feature of rabbinic Judaism.

## The corner of the field

*Mishnah Pe'ah 2:5–6*

He who sows his field with one kind, even though he uses two threshing-floors on it, gives one *pe'ah*. If he sowed it with two kinds, even if he used one threshing-floor for them, he gives two *pe'ahs*. He who sows his field with two kinds of wheat, if he used one threshing-floor for them, gives one *pe'ah*; if two threshing-floors, two *pe'ahs*.

It happened that Rabbi Simeon of Miṣpah sowed (thus) and came before Rabban Gamaliel, and they went up to the Chamber of Hewn Stone and enquired. Said Nahum the Copyist: I am the recipient of a tradition from Rabbi Me'asha, who received it from his father, who received it from the Pairs, who received it from the Prophets as a *halakah* (given) to Moses from Sinai concerning one who sows his field with two kinds of wheat, that if he uses one threshing-floor for them, he gives one *pe'ah*; if two threshing-floors, two *pe'ahs*.

¶ The Torah says, 'Thou shalt not wholly reap the corners of thy field' (Lev. 19:9). The question here is 'What is the definition of a field?' Does it mean an area served by one threshing-floor? Or an area containing one crop? (The question of what kind of boundaries constitute a field has been dealt with earlier in the Mishnah.) The answer given is that if an area constituting one field, by virtue of its boundaries, nevertheless contains two different crops (i.e. of two species, such as wheat and barley), then it is regarded as two fields in relation to the giving of *pe'ah*, and two 'corners' must be left for the poor. So far, the number of threshing-floors used for the crop is irrelevant; but in the more delicate case of a field sowed with two kinds of wheat (the Tosephta adds 'or two kinds of barley'), the number of threshing-floors decides the issue. This ruling is reinforced by an anecdote showing that the Pharisees of Temple times regarded this point as settled by ancient tradition. Here, by the way, we have an important instance of Pharisaic interest in matters other than ritual purity. The rights of the poor were at least equally important to them, and these rights were interpreted in generous fashion, but without neglecting the rights of the farmers.
*Rabbi Simeon of Miṣpah*: little is known about this figure. The title 'Rabbi' is attributed to him anachronistically, since this title became current only after the destruction of the Temple (though it was used in earlier times as a respectful form of address). One tradition (b. Yoma 14b) attributes to Simeon of Miṣpah the first version of the Mishnah tractates *Tamid* and *Yoma*.
*Rabban Gamaliel*: he was the son, or possibly grandson of Hillel. His title 'Rabban' (literally, 'our teacher') was given to the successors of Hillel up to Rabban Simeon ben Gamaliel II. Gamaliel is mentioned in the New Testament as the Pharisee who spoke in defence of Peter and his companions (Acts 5:34–9), though that passage fails to

indicate that Gamaliel was actually the leader of the Pharisees. It is very unlikely that Gamaliel was the teacher of Paul, as claimed in Acts 22:3, though not by Paul himself in his Epistles.
*the Chamber of Hewn Stone*: this was the seat of the Sanhedrin, or Great Bet Din, which was the ultimate Pharisaic authority on matters of *halakah* (see Mantel, *History of the Sanhedrin*, pp. 54–102, for discussion of the constitution and membership of the Sanhedrin). 'Chamber' (*liškah*) was the name given to the offices situated in the Temple.
*Nahum the Copyist*: the word used is *liblar*, which is derived from the Latin *librarius*. The word has less august associations than the word *soper* ('scribe'), which was the sobriquet of Ezra, and later of the Sages.
*the Pairs*: Hebrew, *zugot*. These are the pairs of Pharisaic leaders mentioned in M. 'Ab. 1:4–12, as forming part of the chain of tradition stretching back to the Great Assembly, and before them, the Prophets.
*a halakah (given) to Moses from Sinai*: this was the designation of non-biblical laws regarded as so ancient that they belonged to the nucleus of the Oral Torah given to Moses on Sinai (see Part I, p. 4).

## Poor-relief

*Mishnah Pe'ah 8:7–9*

They do not give less to a poor man who is journeying from place to place than a loaf worth a *pondion* when four *se'ahs* go for a *sela'*. If he stayed the night, they give him support for staying the night. If he stayed over Sabbath they give him food for three meals. He who has food for two meals should not take from the charity-plate; for fourteen meals, should not take from the *quppah*. And the *quppah* is collected by two and distributed by three.

He who has two hundred *zuz* may not take Gleanings, the Forgotten Sheaf, *pe'ah* or Poor Man's Tithe. If he had two hundred less one *dinar*, and even as many as a thousand people give to him at one time, he may take. If his goods were pledged to a creditor or to cover his wife's *ketubah*, he may take. They may not compel him to sell his house or articles for essential use.

He who has fifty *zuz* with which he trades, should not take. And anyone who does not need to take, but takes, does not depart from the world before he comes to need the help of his fellow creatures; and anyone who needs to take, but does not take, does not die of old age until he is able to feed others from his own goods.

¶ Provision for the poor was one of the most important injunctions of the Torah (Deut. 15:11, etc.). In addition to private charity, sources of public support for the poor existed: some instituted by the Torah, and some by the rabbis. The present passage gives insight into the way in which these modes of poor relief were administered. Definitions of 'poor man' are given, but it is left to the individual to decide his own status and whether he is eligible to take the same benefits allotted to the poor. Only a moral injunction and warning against abusing these arrangements is appended as a restraint.

*a poor man who is journeying from place to place*: even a well-off person who finds himself stranded without money on a journey counts as a 'poor man' and must be succoured. Special consideration was given to the plight of a journeying poor person because his poverty forced him to leave his home and look for work.
*a loaf worth a pondion when four se'ahs go for a sela*ʿ: this is a formula found in other contexts where it is necessary to define 'a meal' (see M. ʿEr. 8:2). It means that if the price of wheat is one *sela*ʿ for four *se'ahs*, then a loaf costing not less than one *pondion* must be provided. A *pondion* is a forty-eighth part of a *sela*ʿ, while a *qab* is a twenty-fourth part of four *se'ahs*, so a *pondion* should buy half a *qab* of wheat. Allowing for the costs of manufacture of a loaf, a *pondion* would buy a quarter-*qab* loaf, which is the equivalent of the volume of six eggs (see b. ʿEr. 82b.) The word *pondion* (or *pundion*) is derived from the Latin *dupondium* (or *dipondium*), a Roman coin equal to two *asses*. A *sela*ʿ is equal to two *šeqels*.
*If he stayed over Sabbath they give him food for three meals*: it was considered a religious duty to have not less than three meals on the Sabbath, in fulfilment of *ʿoneg šabbat* ('Sabbath-delight'), so this was the minimum for a poor person supported over the Sabbath.
*the charity-plate*: Hebrew, *tamḥuy*, derived from *miḥyah* ('provision'). This was a collection plate from which were provided daily distributions of food for the poor, like the modern 'soup-kitchen'.
*the quppah*: literally, 'basket'. This was the substantial communal fund for giving a whole week's sustenance to the poor, a distri-

bution being made every Friday. This was available only to the poor of the locality, while the *tamḥuy* was available for 'all poor people wherever they may come from' (b. B.B. 8b and Tos. Pe'ah 4:9–10, see p. 134).

*collected by two and distributed by three*: the collection was done by two people, because 'no office for communal money affairs may be set up with less than two officers'. The collectors were voluntary communal workers, but temptation must not be put in their way, and scope for slander against them must be minimized. The distribution, however, was by three people, since the status of the distributors was that of a court or tribunal in money matters: such a tribunal had a minimum of three, and could consist of lay people. The *tamḥuy*, on the other hand, was both collected and distributed by three, since this was more convenient for a fund collected and distributed on the same day (b. B.B. 8b).

*He who has two hundred zuz*: a *zuz* is a half of a *šeqel*, and is the same as a silver *dinar* (a gold *dinar* being worth twenty-five times as much). It was reckoned that two hundred *zuz* would be enough to buy food and clothing for a person for one year. Anyone whose possessions amount to less than this comes under the definition of 'poor', and is entitled to the biblical provisions for the poor.

*and even as many as a thousand people give to him at one time, he may take*: if he has slipped below the poverty-line, receipts from charity are not to be reckoned as changing his status, and he may take the biblical entitlements of the poor, i.e. Gleanings, the Forgotten Sheaf, *pe'ah*, and Poor Man's Tithe.

*if his goods were pledged to a creditor*: mortgaged goods do not count towards the total of two hundred *zuz*.

*to cover his wife's ketubah*: the *ketubah* is the marriage contract, by which, in the event of divorce, the husband is bound to pay the wife a stipulated sum, in addition to returning to her any money or property that she brought into the marriage (see p. 100). Any sums which the husband is liable to pay in the event of divorce are not to be reckoned as his property for purposes of poor-benefit, even though he is happily married.

*They may not compel him to sell his house*: the value of his house is not reckoned in the figure of two hundred *zuz*, since to realise its value he would become homeless.

*or articles for essential use*: this is the probable meaning, but later interpretation, in the Palestinian Talmud, took it to mean articles of special decorative use, for Sabbaths and festivals.

*fifty zuz with which he trades*: in accordance with the proverb 'Fifty that are working are better than two hundred that are idle'. If he is able to do active trade with his fifty *zuz*, he is not reckoned among the poor.
*anyone who needs to take, but does not take*: The Palestinian Talmud, however, comments that he who needs to take, but does not take, is regarded as a 'spiller of blood', since he puts his own life in jeopardy. Later commentators reconcile the two views by saying that the Mishnah is referring only to someone who is able, by extraordinary efforts, to earn enough to avoid taking his entitlement under the poor-laws.

*The 'distribution' to widows mentioned in Acts 6:1–2 seems to have been a distribution of money, or possibly, food. It does not seem to come into the civic category of *quppah* or *tamḥuy*, but rather under the category of community-charity administered to members by those who, for any reason, have formed a separate group. *Quppah* and *tamḥuy* would not be confined to widows, nor to members of a single group. Each community or synagogue would take especial care of its own widows and orphans (who would be eligible also for the *quppah* and *tamḥuy* administered by the town or city for all categories of the poor). The Jerusalem Church probably regarded itself as having the status of a synagogue community, with special responsibility for the poor among its members. Widows are singled out (together with orphans and strangers) in the Torah as deserving objects of charity (Deut. 14:29; 16:11; 24:17, etc.).

There were thus three levels among donors of poor-relief or charity: civic, synagogal, and individual, while the biblical gifts to the poor were not regarded as charity but as the rights of the poor.

## The *Ne'eman* and the *Ḥaber*

*Mishnah Demai 2:2–3*

He who undertakes to be a *ne'eman*, tithes that which he eats and that which he sells and that which he buys; and he does not accept an invitation to a meal with an *'am ha-'areṣ*. Rabbi Judah says: Even if he accepts an invitation to a meal with an *'am ha-'areṣ*, he is a *ne'eman*. They said to him: He is not trustworthy about himself; how can be be trustworthy about what belongs to others?

He that undertakes to be a *ḥaber* does not sell to an *'am ha-'areṣ* either wet or dry, and does not buy from him wet, and does not accept an invitation to a meal with him and does not invite him to a meal in his own garment. Rabbi Judah says: Also he does not raise small cattle, and he is not free with vows or with merriment, and he does not allow himself to become unclean through a corpse, and he frequents the House of Study. They said to him: These things do not come under this heading.

¶ There are many misapprehensions, found even in scholarly books, about the 'table-fellowships' and their aims. The present passage is important for a true understanding of these voluntary groups.

*ne'eman*: literally, 'one who is trusted'. The *ne'eman* groups were not essentially attached to the 'table-fellowships' as a kind of apprentice stage, though some individuals might graduate from being a *ne'eman* to joining a *ḥaburah* ('table-fellowship'). The *ne'eman* was one who had made an 'undertaking' in relation to tithes only, while the 'undertaking' of a *ḥaber* concerned both tithes and ritual purity, primarily the latter. It is important to understand that someone who was neither a *ne'eman* nor a *ḥaber*, was not thereby regarded as a sinner, since the life of these special groups was one of supererogatory virtue, in the area pertaining to their vow, or 'undertaking'.
*tithes that which he eats*: this was not a biblical obligation, because, according to Scripture, it was the duty of the farmer to separate the tithes, and non-farmers could legitimately rely on the trustworthiness of farmers in this respect. However, since the farmers had come under suspicion of not separating some of the tithes, it had become a matter of supererogatory virtue to separate tithes even from cereals bought from dealers, though it was quite possible that these had already been tithed. The name given to such 'doubtful' cereals was *demai*. Societies were thus formed of people who had 'undertaken' to be 'trustworthy' in relation to tithes. Such people would always separate tithes from produce, unless they bought it from another member of a tithe-society, who could be trusted to have separated tithes, or to have bought it from a farmer whom he knew to be trustworthy. Since *demai* produce was not known to be untithed, and since there was no real obligation on anyone except the farmer to separate tithes, there were many leniencies in relation to *demai* produce: for example, it might be given to the poor, who were not required to suffer deprivation because of such scruples. (See M. Dem. 1:2 and 3:1 for other such leniencies.) The most important tithes (those due to the priests) were not made subject to the rules of *demai*, as the farmers were not suspected of neglecting them; also, the Levites' Tithe and the Poor

Man's Tithe were never included in the calculations, since they were regarded as only payable when full proof that the produce was untithed was available.

Consequently, even the *ne'eman* societies only concerned themselves with about half the tithes that were due. These considerations should be borne in mind, because there has been much exaggeration about the extent to which the tithe and purity societies divided the Jewish people. It should be noted that the rules of *demai*, so far from being biblical (*de-'oraita*) were not even regarded as being rabbinical (*de-rabbanan*), but rather as applying only to people who had given a voluntary 'undertaking' to observe them. It is clear from certain passages that the people who decided to give this 'undertaking' did not belong to any particular class; some of the learned Pharisaic class, for example, are known not to have been among them.

*and that which he sells and that which he buys*: this means that if he buys produce not to eat but to sell, he tithes it before he sells it: anyone buying from him knows that the produce has been certainly tithed. His customers, therefore, are likely to be other members of the society, who would not be obliged to separate further tithes, but would probably pay more than the market price.

*he does not accept an invitation to a meal with an 'am ha-'areṣ*: the term *'am ha-'areṣ* (literally 'people of the land', but employed to mean 'person of the land') means here simply someone who is not a member of a tithing or purity society (see, however, pp. 126 and 142 for other usages of the term). An *'am ha-'areṣ*, then, was not necessarily someone who deliberately ate produce which he knew to be untithed. He was much more likely to be someone who ate produce on the assumption that it had been tithed, relying on the fact that the biblical responsibility to tithe lay on the farmer, not on him. The prohibition against accepting an invitation to a meal with an *'am ha-'areṣ* does not, therefore, imply any strong disapproval of his way of life, or stigmatize him as a sinner. It simply means that the special vow or 'undertaking' of the society-member precludes him from partaking in meals that are not *guaranteed* to comply with the conditions of his vow. To give a modern analogy, someone who is on a special diet might refuse an invitation to dinner without in any way casting reproach on his intended host. It should be noted, furthermore, that such a refusal would *not* lead to the breaking off of friendly relations between the *ne'eman* and his *'am ha-'areṣ* friend, since there was no objection whatever to their sharing a meal at the house of the *ne'eman*, while the *'am ha-'areṣ* perfectly understood that his friend's vow precluded him from accepting invitations. Such arrangements are quite common even among modern Jews who have different standards of observance of food laws (*kašrut*).

*Rabbi Judah says: Even if he accepts an invitation to a meal with an ʿam ha-ʾareṣ, he is a neʾeman*: Rabbi Judah here means Rabbi Judah ben Ilʿai, a very prominent authority in the Mishnah, where he is always called simply 'Rabbi Judah' (not to be confused with Rabbi Judah the Prince, the redactor of the Mishnah, who is called 'Rabbi'). Rabbi Judah ben Ilʿai was a pupil of Rabbi Akiba, and flourished about AD 130 (see p. 45).

Rabbi Judah's point here is that a *neʾeman* may be trusted to know whether his friend, the *ʿam ha-ʾareṣ*, can be relied on to respect his friend's vow to the extent of putting before him at a meal only food bought from a *neʾeman* shopkeeper. Even one who normally does not keep to *neʾeman* rules can be trusted to do so on occasion, when hospitality demands such conduct. Rabbi Judah's attitude would be unintelligible on the view often put forward, that all friendship between society-members and the *ʿam ha-ʾareṣ* was impossible. On the other hand, there is no great gulf between Rabbi Judah and his opponents on this issue, since both would agree that a meal in the *neʾeman*'s house to which the *ʿam ha-ʾareṣ* was invited would be unobjectionable.

*They said to him:* an expression implying that there was a majority against him. The view of the majority was that the vow of a *neʾeman* obliged him not to rely on anyone except a fellow-*neʾeman* in tithing matters. If he relaxed this rule in relation to his own conduct, he could not be trusted to observe the rules in relation to fellow members.

*He that undertakes to be a ḥaber*: to observe special rules of purity, in addition to special rules of tithing. Here, too, an 'undertaking' or vow was necessary because the society was under a special rule that went beyond the requirements of normal Judaism. The essence of a *ḥaber*'s 'undertaking' was 'to eat ordinary food (*ḥullin*) in purity', i.e. to avoid imparting ritual impurity to ordinary food. Normally, there was no obligation to do this, for biblical law forbade only the imparting of impurity to holy food (see p. 53). The *ḥaber* underwent ablutions in the ritual pool similar to those that were obligatory for the priest before eating his priestly food (*terumah*). Those who were not *ḥaberim* were even less under a stigma than those who were not *neʾeman*, for, whereas the *neʾeman* was concerned about a possible breach of the law of tithing (even though such a breach was not really his responsibility), the *ḥaber* was not concerned even about a possible breach, but only engaged in an exercise of supererogatory piety.

*does not sell to an ʿam ha-ʾareṣ*: an *ʿam ha-ʾareṣ* means here anyone who is not a *ḥaber*, and may even include a *neʾeman*, since the latter is 'trustworthy' only in relation to tithes, not ritual impurity. The reason why a *ḥaber* does not sell produce to an *ʿam ha-ʾareṣ* is that the *ḥaber* has undertaken not to be instrumental in the conveying of impurity to ordinary food. Consequently, the *ḥaber* sells produce only to his fellow-*ḥaberim*, who will handle ordinary food in the same way that he does himself. This does *not* imply disapproval of the way of life of the *ʿam ha-ʾareṣ*, who is not bound by any 'undertaking', and is quite entitled to ignore purity questions when eating ordinary food. Note that it is only in connection with produce of the Land of Israel that the *ḥaber* gives his 'undertaking'. Since the whole of the Land of Israel was regarded as an extension of the Temple, and thus as holy territory, it was natural for some people, as an exercise in piety, to undertake voluntarily to treat its products as if they were subject to the same restrictions that governed the handling of holy food, such as the *terumah*. There was also a practical reason why a small minority of laymen should keep themselves in a constant state of ritual purity: in order to assist the priests in the collection of the *terumah* (see p. 96).

*either wet or dry, and does not buy from him wet*: only produce that had been moistened was susceptible to ritual impurity, in accordance with Lev. 11:37–8, 'When any of their dead bodies falls on seed intended for sowing, it remains clean; but if the seed has been soaked in water and any dead body falls on it, you shall treat it as unclean' (see M. Makš.) The *ḥaber* may buy grain from the *ʿam ha-ʾareṣ* as long as it has never been purposely moistened and thus cannot have acquired any impurity. It is noteworthy that the *ʿam ha-ʾareṣ* is trusted to say whether grain, which may be dry at present, has been moistened at any time in the past. For the degree of trust in which the *ʿam ha-ʾareṣ* was held, see also p. 96. The *ḥaber*, however, must not sell grain to an *ʿam ha-ʾareṣ* whether wet or dry, because this would be to hand it over to impurity.

*does not accept an invitation to a meal with him*: here there is no dissenting opinion. Whereas it was conceivable for an *ʿam ha-ʾareṣ* to be trusted in relation to tithes since it was a simple matter to provide tithed food for a guest, it was far too much to expect an *'am ha-'areṣ* to put his food, his house and himself into a state of purity in order to receive a guest.

*and does not invite him to a meal in his own garment*: social relations between the *ḥaber* and the *'am ha-'areṣ* are not ruled out completely, for the *ḥaber* may entertain his friend who is an *'am ha-'areṣ*, as long as the latter puts on a garment provided by the *ḥaber* as he enters the house; this is rather like the donning of white coats and masks in a modern hospital by visitors to a surgical theatre. The *'am ha-'areṣ*, however, is not required to cover his face or hands, because he would see that these were at the required standard of purity before visiting his *ḥaber* friend. While it was relatively easy to avoid contact of face and hands with a source of impurity, such as the dead body of a 'creeping thing', it was regarded as more difficult to preserve the purity of one's clothes; this indeed formed part of the apprenticeship of one entering a *ḥaburah*. For a further instance of the distinction made between persons and their clothes in ritual-purity matters, see p. 94.

*he does not raise small cattle*: i.e. sheep or goats. By an ordinance of the rabbis, probably dated about AD 60, it was forbidden to raise small cattle in any areas where they might damage crops, though it was permitted in semi-wilderness areas. Rabbi Judah probably means that the *ḥaber*, being dedicated to a life of supererogatory virtue, should not raise small cattle anywhere, since they might stray and damage crops. It is somewhat ironic that sheep-rearing, associated with the Patriarchs and with ideal figures such as David, should have acquired such disrepute in our era.

*he is not free with vows*: Rabbi Judah is probably referring to idle vows made merely for emphasis, which were not considered legally binding; but the rabbis also frowned on the making of vows generally, unless for a special religious purpose.

*or with merriment*: he must preserve a grave demeanour. Similarly, the Community Rule of the Qumran sect prescribes 'Whoever has guffawed foolishly shall do penance for thirty days'.

*he does not allow himself to become unclean through a corpse*: according to the Bible, this rule applies only to priests (Lev. 21:1). Rabbi Judah thus wants the *ḥaber* to behave like a priest. Exaggerated as Rabbi Judah's attitude is, it is quite clear from his remarks that the practice of the *ḥaburah* was never intended as a norm for all Israelites. It

would be impossible to discharge important religious duties if everybody refused to become unclean through a corpse. Note that this is the only form of impurity forbidden to a priest, and even this is waived if the priest is the only person available to bury the corpse.
*he frequents the House of Study*: the *ḥaber* was to combine the character of the ritual-purity devotee with that of the *talmid ḥakam*, or man of learning.
*These things do not come under this heading*: Rabbi Judah is overruled by his colleagues, who do not want to extend the concept of the *ḥaburah* to make it into a kind of contemplative order, but to restrict it to its original purpose, which was to act as a special group devoted to ritual purity.

*The passage is very instructive about the nature of the *ḥaburah* and the *ne'eman* fellowship. Neither of these groups was like the Qumran sect, which regarded itself as an oasis of righteousness in a desert of wickedness. On the other hand, they were not quite like the Christian monastic orders, leading a life isolated from the community. The essence of these Jewish groups was that they dedicated themselves to the perfection of one particular aspect of Judaism, while by no means abandoning the rest. The imperfect analogy with Christian monastic orders is, however, helpful. Just as a Trappist monk does not regard the ordinary church member as sinful because he talks, so a *ḥaber* did not repudiate as sinful the practice of the *'am ha-'areṣ*, who followed biblical law in not bothering about ritual purity except on special occasions, and in leaving tithing to the farmers.
**Note that 'ritual purity' is quite a different thing from the 'dietary laws', though these two topics are often confused. The 'dietary laws' consist of prohibitions against the eating of certain animals, birds, fish and insects. These prohibitions are biblical (see Lev. 11), and are obligatory on all Jews (but not on non-Jews). Consequently, no societies of *ḥaberim* were formed to observe these laws, since they were obligatory, not supererogatory. Included also in the dietary laws is the prohibition against eating the flesh even of permitted animals unless they have been slaughtered by the method called *šeḥiṭah*; this law is not found explicitly in the Bible, but was regarded as an *halakah le-Mošeh mi-Sinai* (see p. 4). If permitted meat was not available, Jews would sometimes resort to vegetarianism, as did Daniel and his companions (Dan. 1:8–16), not as a matter of 'ritual purity' but of *kašrut* ('permitted food'). The matter is somewhat complicated by the fact that the language of 'defilement' is occasionally used in relation to forbidden foods, which are sometimes called 'unclean', but this word has a different connotation in this context from its connotation in a 'ritual-purity' context. Also, there are some repercussions between the two systems of 'dietary law' and 'ritual purity'; for example, someone who touches the carcase of a forbidden animal becomes ritually unclean (Lev. 11:26). He is not *forbidden* to touch such a carcase, but is required to undergo ablution before entering holy areas, or eating or touching holy food, if he has become ritually

unclean in this or any other way. Thus to eat 'forbidden food' was a very serious matter, while to incur 'ritual impurity' was not serious at all, but was an inevitable part of everyday living, for which the easily available remedy was the ritual bath (*miqweh*).

## Two Kinds

*Mishnah Kil'ayim 9:1*

Nothing is forbidden as Two Kinds except wool and linen; and nothing becomes unclean through leprosy except wool and linen. The priests put on, to serve in the Temple, only wool and linen. The wool of camels and the wool of sheep that have been combed together – if the majority is from the camels, it is permitted; and if the majority is from the sheep, it is forbidden. If half and half, it is forbidden. So too flax and hemp that were combed together.

¶ The Torah forbids the wearing of a garment made of a mixture of wool and linen (Deut. 22:11), a mixture designated as *ša'aṭnez*, a word of doubtful origin, possibly Egyptian. See also Lev. 19:19, where *ša'aṭnez* is defined only as an instance of *kil'ayim* (literally, 'two kinds', i.e. forbidden mixtures), the other instances being sowing a field or vineyard with Two Kinds and causing Two Kinds of animal to mate together. The tractate *Kil'ayim* is concerned with all these prohibitions, and our present passage deals with *ša'aṭnez*, and incidentally gives an interesting clue to the meaning of this particular prohibition.

*nothing becomes unclean through leprosy except wool and linen*: it is characteristic of the Mishnah and Tosephta to digress from the subject at hand when some mnemonic purpose is served. Here the subject of leprosy-contamination in clothing is quite irrelevant to the subject of Two Kinds in clothing, but it is a useful memory-aid to say that the same two substances, wool and linen, are involved in both contexts, even though, in the case of leprosy, no mixture is involved: *either* wool or linen (but no other textile) is susceptible to leprosy-contamination (see Lev. 13:47). Leprosy in such a context does not mean Hansen's Disease, but something like mildew.

*the priests put on, to serve in the Temple, only wool and linen*: here again, no intrinsic connection is intended, but only the mnemonic advantage of grouping all contexts in which wool and linen feature together. Nevertheless, the Mishnah has achieved here, unwittingly, a significant connection. For it is no accident (though at first sight a surprising fact) that the very mixture which is forbidden under the law of *ša'aṭnez*, wool and linen, is actually enjoined for the garments of the priests (Exod. 39:29 shows that the girdle or sash of the ordinary priests was made of woven linen decorated with coloured wool, and the ephod and breast-piece of the High Priest were similarly worked, Exod. 39:2ff). This indicates that the reason for the prohibition of *ša'aṭnez* to the ordinary Israelite was not that such a mixture was considered evil, but that, on the contrary, it was reserved for holy purposes. Yet, in recognition of the Jewish doctrine of the priesthood of the laity (Exod. 19:6), the ordinary Israelite was allowed to wear *ša'aṭnez* in one garment, the *ṭallit*, or praying-shawl, the fringes of which could consist of both linen and wool, at least according to the House of Hillel (M. 'Ed. 4:10). The rationale of *ša'aṭnez*, however, does not appear to have been known to the later rabbis, who regarded it as an inexplicable law, not to be questioned by the human intellect; but it was still known to Josephus, who states explicitly 'Let not anyone of you wear a garment made of wool and linen, for that is appointed to be for the priests alone' (*Ant.* iv.8.11 (208)).

*if the majority is from the camels, it is permitted*: to be used in a garment together with linen. The term 'wool', as used in the biblical prohibition against joint use of wool and linen, applies only to the wool of sheep. A mixture in which camel-wool predominates counts as camel-wool, and may therefore be woven with linen.

*So too flax and hemp that were combed together*: linen is made from flax, but if hemp predominates in the mixture, it counts as hemp and may be woven or combined with wool in a garment. The word used for 'hemp' is *qanbos*, derived from the Greek *kannabis*, from which the English word 'canvas' is also derived.

## Hillel's *prosbol*

### *Mishnah Šebiit 10:3–6*

A loan for which a *prosbol* has been written is not cancelled by the Seventh Year. This is one of the things that Hillel the Elder ordained. When he saw that the people were refraining from loans to each other and were transgressing against what is written in the Torah (Deut. 15:9), 'Beware that there be not a base thought in thy heart', Hillel ordained the *prosbol*.

This is the content of the *prosbol*: 'I declare to you, so-and-so and so-and-so, the judges in such-and-such a place, that I shall collect any debt owing to me at any time that I wish'. And the judges sign below, or the witnesses . . .

A *prosbol* may be written only on immovable property. If the borrower does not have any, the lender may give him title to a part, however small, of his own land.

¶ The Pharisees were a reforming movement, using exegesis to adapt the Written Law to changing circumstances. In the present instance, the Pharisaic leader, Hillel (see p. 41), institutes a far-reaching agrarian reform – so far-reaching that it becomes a problem as to how he justified it by the usual Pharisaic methods of exegesis.

*prosbol*: the name of this document is derived from Greek, probably *probole*, meaning a 'declaration', but possibly from *pros boulei*, meaning 'to the council', since the affirmation had to be made before judges. No similar document, however, has been found in Graeco–Roman use, since the background of the document is the biblical law of the seventh-year cancellation of debts (*šemiṭṭah*).
*transgressing against what is written in the Torah*: the Torah's idealistic legislation, by which people were admonished to lend to poor people (without exacting interest, forbidden by Exod. 22:25) even though the *šemiṭṭah* would cancel the debt, was leading to the drying up of lending. The people who suffered most by this were poor tenant-farmers, who needed loans to buy seed and tools, and were not able to give valuables as pledges (such mortgaged loans were not subject to seventh-year cancellation). Hillel, therefore, in effect abolished the biblical law to the advantage of both lenders and borrowers (lenders could gain profit even from interest-free loans by lending to their tenant-farmers, who would then farm the land and pay rent). The biblical law had been suitable for a primitive agrarian economy of smallholders, in which loans were a form of charity, rather than a business transaction. (Later Judaism retained the idea that lending money to a poor man was a superior form of charity to giving it to him, since his self-respect was left undamaged.) Hillel's bold reform, by which a biblical law was abrogated, gave rise to much puzzlement in rabbinic literature later than the Mishnah. The Sifre offers a biblical justification for Hillel's enactment (i.e. that it can be deduced from a biblical verse, Deut. 15:3, that the seventh-year cancellation of debts does not apply to debts

handed over to a court for collection: the Sifre also amends the text of the *prosbol* slightly to accord with this interpretation). The Talmud (b. Giṭ. 36a–b) adopts the different line that the biblical law did not have full legal force in the times of the Second Temple, when Hillel lived, since the Jubilee was not in operation. Hillel was therefore able to abolish it by virtue of the power invested in rabbinical courts. Another possible explanation of Hillel's enactment is that it could be biblically justified on the ground that the biblical law was intended to apply only to the debts of the utterly destitute (*'ebyon*). This may explain why a *prosbol* could be drawn up only for a borrower who owned land; though, by a legal fiction which satisfied the letter of the biblical law, he could be given title to a small portion of the lender's land. Whatever the justification, Hillel's measure was a much-needed reform that helped the economic life of the country and showed the willingness of the Pharisees to adopt a flexible approach to biblical law.
*on immovable property*: a term which usually means 'on the security of immovable property' (*qarqaʿ*), but here the security aspect may be less important than the removal of the borrower from the status of the landless (*'ebyon*), for whom no *prosbol* would be effective. Note that for the *'ebyon*, or for anyone for whom no *prosbol* was drawn up, the seventh-year cancellation of debts was still in operation, even after Hillel's enactment. Note also that it was considered a meritorious action, though not obligatory, to pay one's debts even when subject to seventh-year cancellation (M. Šeb. 10:9).

## Hygiene

*Mishnah Terumot 8:4*

If wine that is *terumah* has become uncovered, it should be poured out; and it goes without saying that this is so of common wine. Three liquids are forbidden because of uncovering: water, wine and milk. And all other liquids are permitted. How long should they wait before being forbidden? As long as it takes for a reptile to come out from a nearby place and drink.

¶ The rabbis regarded matters of hygiene, where there might be danger to life or health, as having priority over all ritual matters. Although it was normally forbidden to destroy *terumah* (the holy food of the priests), this had to be done if there was any suspicion that it might become poisonous.

*it should be poured out*: because some poisonous reptile may have drunk from it and deposited poison in it.
*it goes without saying that this is so of common wine*: which need not be treated with such great respect as *terumah*.
*all other liquids are permitted*: because reptiles do not drink them. The Palestinian Talmud, however, adds other substances that should be kept covered: honey, brine, pickles, and crushed garlic. If left uncovered, these too should be destroyed.
There is evidence from the Palestinian Talmud (y. Taʿan. 23a) that the *Ḥasidim* did not approve of this and other hygienic ordinances of the rabbis, preferring to rely on Providence in matters of health. For the episode in the Gospels in which Jesus disapproved of hand-washing, see p. 122, where this episode is explained as concerned with hygiene, not ritual purity. It is quite probable that Jesus belonged to the Ḥasidic Pharisees. The incorrect notion that the *Ḥasidim* were lax in the observance of ritual purity arises from the failure of some scholars to distinguish between instances of hygiene and of ritual purity.

## The First-fruits

*Mishnah Bikkurim 3:1–4*

How do they separate the First-fruits? A man goes down in the middle of his field and sees a fig that has ripened, or a bunch of grapes that has ripened, or a pomegranate that has ripened; he binds them with reed-grass, and says 'Behold these are First-fruits!' And Rabbi Simeon says: Nevertheless, he calls them First-fruits again after they are plucked from the ground.

How do they take up the First-fruits? The men of all the smaller towns that belonged to the *maʿamad* gather together in the *maʿamad*-town, and they spend the night in the town square, and they do not enter the houses, and in the early morning the appointed one says 'Arise and let us go up to Zion, to the house of the Lord our God'.

Those that are near bring figs and grapes; and those who are far bring dried figs and raisins. And the ox goes before them, with its horns overlaid with gold and an olive-crown on its head. The flute plays before them until they come near to Jerusalem. When they came near to Jerusalem, they sent (messengers) before them and adorned their First-fruits. The rulers and the chiefs and the treasurers go out to meet them. According to the honour of those who entered were those who went out. And all the craftsmen of Jerusalem stand before them and greet them 'Our brothers, men of such-and-such a place, you are welcome!'

The flute plays before them until they reach the Temple Mount. When they have reached the Temple Mount, even King Agrippa takes his basket on his shoulder and enters until he reaches the Court. When he reached the Court, the Levites spoke in song, 'I will exalt Thee, O Lord, for Thou has set me up and not made mine enemies to triumph over me' (Ps. 30).

¶ In this passage, ostensibly halakic, there is evident a strong feeling of nostalgia. The procession of the carriers of First-fruits from their native centre to Jerusalem is described in idyllic style. We are reminded of Keats's 'Ode on a Grecian Urn':

> To what green altar, O mysterious priest,
> Leadst thou that heifer lowing at the skies,
> And all her silken flanks with garlands drest?
> What little town by river or sea shore,
> Or mountain-built with peaceful citadel,
> Is emptied of this folk, this pious morn?

The alternation of past and present tenses is an unconscious device for the conveying of nostalgia. King Agrippa was long dead at the time of the redaction of the Mishnah and the Temple was in ruins, but he is portrayed as if still alive, carrying his basket into the Temple Court. Yet this is far from being a lament for the passing of a golden age. It is a portrayal of how things ought to be, and, one day, will be again (see Part I, p. 33).

*the First-fruits*: these are prescribed in Deut. 26:1–11, together with the declaration to be made on bringing them to the Temple. First-fruits were brought only from the Seven Kinds (the main products of the Land of Israel): wheat, barley, grapes, figs, pomegranates, olives and dates.

*'Behold these are First-fruits!'*: it is this 'designation' that constitutes the act of separating the First-fruits.

*Rabbi Simeon*: this is Rabbi Simeon ben Yoḥai, who is always called simply Rabbi Simeon in the Mishnah. He was a pupil of Rabbi Akiba, and flourished in the generation of *c.* 130–60. Although a keen halakist, he was also a mystic, and acquired a strange posthumous *persona* as the hero and pseudepigraphic author of the medieval classic of Qabbalah, *The Zohar* (a mystical commentary on the Torah, composed in the thirteenth century, probably by Moses de Leon).

*he calls them First-fruits again*: Rabbi Simeon's reason is not fully known, but he seems to have been influenced by the procedure in relation to tithes, which were separated after harvesting. (The explanation given in the Palestinian Talmud is forced.) Rabbi Simeon's meaning is that the designation made while the crop is still standing is merely the declaration of an intention to set aside these particular fruits as First-fruits, and the designation must be repeated in the same words after the fruit is plucked before it becomes valid. The *halakah*, however, is not in accordance with Rabbi Simeon, since the majority of rabbis considered that the designation of unplucked First-fruits was a valid act of dedication.

*The men of all the smaller towns that belonged to the ma'amad*: an explanation of the term *ma'amad* is to be found in M. Ta'an. 4:2–4. For every one of the twenty-four 'courses' of the priesthood (hereditary divisions, each taking a turn of duty of one week), there was a *ma'amad*, or 'standing' of laymen, who associated themselves with the activities of that course. (For the priestly courses, see I Chron. 24:1–9, also Luke 1:5–8.) Some members of the *ma'amad* travelled to Jerusalem for the week of their associated priestly course and took part in prayer, together with priests and Levites, while priests of the course officiated in shifts in the Temple. Other members of the *ma'amad*, remaining at home, took part in special prayers and observances during the week of office of the course. The origin of the synagogue has been traced to this institution. The Land of Israel was thus divided into twenty-four districts, each supplying a *ma'amad* of laymen, who also, as here, engaged in activities not directly connected with the associated priestly course.

*the ma'amad-town*: this was the home-town of the current president of the *ma'amad*.

*they spend the night in the town square, and they do not enter the houses*: this was to avoid any ritual impurity, such as that caused by the presence of a corpse in a house (in the open air, a corpse could cause ritual impurity only by direct contact, or by walking over its resting-place in the cemetery). It was necessary, even for laymen who were not members of a *ḥaburah* ('table-fellowship'), to be in a state of ritual purity when entering the Temple grounds, and laymen were trusted to be in such a state when necessary.

*And the ox goes before them*: this ox will be sacrificed as a 'peace-offering' at the time of the offering of First-fruits.

*The rulers and the chiefs and the treasurers*: the word for 'rulers' (*paḥot*, a word of Assyrian origin found in Scripture) seems to refer to secular grandees. The other two words refer to leading administrators among the priests.

*According to the honour of those who entered were those who went out*: i.e. to greet them. The Palestinian Talmud, reluctant to admit that one *ma'amad* might be treated with more honour than another ('Is there such a thing as great and small in Israel?'), explains that this refers only to numbers. The more numerous the *ma'amad*, the more numerous would be the body coming out to greet it. It seems likely, however, that the reference is to the element of grandees, the eminence of which would vary according to the status of the provincial notables in the *ma'amad*.

*even King Agrippa*: mentioned also in M. Soṭ. 7:8 (see p. 106). He may have been Herod Agrippa I, who was much loved by the Pharisees, or possibly Herod Agrippa II, who lived in the last days of the Temple.

*takes his basket on his shoulder*: in accordance with the biblical prescription, '. . . and you shall put them in a basket . . . The priest shall take the basket from your hand . . .' (Deut. 26:2–4). The picture of King Agrippa, humbling himself to obey the biblical precept, adds to the idyllic and even messianic atmosphere of our passage.

## The Passover liturgy

*Mishnah Pesaḥim 10:4–5*

They have mixed for him the second cup: and here the son interrogates the father; and if there is no knowledge in the son, the father teaches him. 'How is this night different from all other nights, that on all other nights we may eat leavened or unleavened bread, on this night only unleavened bread? That on all other nights, we eat various herbs, on this night, bitter herbs? That on all other nights, we may eat meat that is roasted, stewed or boiled, on this night only roasted? That on all other nights, we dip once, on this night, twice?' And according to the knowledge of the son, his father teaches him. He begins with disgrace, and ends with praise, and he expounds from, 'A wandering Aramean was my father . . .' (Deut. 26:5), until he finishes the whole passage.

Rabban Gamaliel used to say: Anyone who has not said these three words on Passover has not discharged his duty, and these are they: *pesaḥ*, *maṣah* and *maror*. *Pesaḥ* ('Passover') – because the All-present passed over the houses of our ancestors in Egypt. *Maṣah* ('unleavened bread') – because our ancestors were redeemed in Egypt. *Maror* ('bitter herbs') – because the Egyptians made the lives of our ancestors bitter in Egypt. In every generation, a person is obliged to regard himself as if he personally has gone forth from Egypt, as it is said, 'And you shall tell your son on that day, saying, For the sake of this, the Lord acted for me when I went forth from Egypt' (Exod. 13:8). Therefore we are obliged to thank, to praise, to extol, to laud, to raise up high, to beautify, to bless, to declare supreme and to glorify him who did for our ancestors and for us all these miracles: he brought us out from slavery to freedom, from sorrow to rejoicing, and from mourning to festival, and from deep darkness to great light and from servitude to redemption, and let us say before him, Halleluiah.

¶ The *Seder* service is celebrated in the home on the night of the Passover. In times when the Temple was standing, the Passover meal was held in Jerusalem, if possible, and the central purpose of the meal was to eat the flesh of the paschal lamb which had been sacrificed that day, in accordance with the injunction of Exod. 12:43–9. In post-Temple times, however, the paschal lamb could not be eaten, except symbolically, so the centre of the service shifted to the 'telling' (*haggadah*) of the story of the Exodus. This 'telling' was itself a biblical precept (Exod. 13:8). Thus nowadays, the liturgy for Passover night is called the *Haggadah*, though the service itself as performed in the home is still called the *Seder* ('order'), which is short for *seder ha-pesaḥ*, 'the order of the paschal offering'. (The term *Haggadah* meaning the liturgy of Passover night in the home should not be confused with the general term *haggadah* or *'aggadah*, meaning the non-legal aspect of the Oral Torah.) The Mishnah, in accordance with its general policy (see Part I, p. 33), does not describe the post-Temple ritual, but recreates the practice of Temple times. In Jerusalem, in Temple times, each person enrolled in a 'company' (*ḥaburah*) for the Passover service. These 'companies' often took their meal in the open air, but it was not permitted to wander from 'company' to 'company' (Exod. 12:46 was understood in this sense). The *Haggadah* liturgy, as practised by Jews today, has acquired many additions from medieval times, but, as our present passage shows, its basic structure is the same as in ancient times: the four cups of wine, the interrogation by the son followed by the 'telling', the eating of unleavened bread and bitter herbs, the meal, and the singing of the *Hallel*.

*They have mixed for him the second cup*: we would say 'poured the cup', but wine was always mixed with water as it was served (see p. 56). The 'second cup' means the second of the four that were obligatory during the service.
*the son interrogates the father*: this interrogation echoes the biblical texts Exod. 12:26; 13:14 and Deut. 6:20.
*and if there is no knowledge in the son*: this echoes a further text, Exod. 13:8, in which the 'telling' takes place without a previous interrogation. All four texts were later interpreted as referring to four different types of son (the wise one, the wicked one, the simple one, and the son who does not know how to ask), as found in the developed *Haggadah*. The germ of this elaboration is the present clause. 'No knowledge' or 'no intellect' means lack of capacity to ask questions.
*the father teaches him*: this does not mean that the father teaches the son a formula of interrogation. The clause is a parenthesis, and the interrogation follows from the previous clause '. . . and here the son interrogates the father'. The specimen questions which now follow, however, later became a fixed part of the liturgy, with some modifications.
*on this night only roasted*: this question applied only in Temple times, when the paschal lamb was eaten. This had to be roasted (Exod. 12:8–9). This question is thus omitted in post-Temple practice, since it was not only not obligatory, but even regarded as wrong, to eat roast meat on Passover night, when this might be construed as performing sacrifice in some place other than the Temple in Jerusalem.

*on all other nights, we dip once, on this night, twice*: the Talmud finds this puzzling, and therefore emends to '. . . on all other nights we need not dip even once, but on this night we must dip twice'. The two dippings referred to are: the dipping of the *karpas* ('parsley' or 'celery') into salt water, immediately after the *Qidduš*; the dipping of the *maror* ('bitter herbs') into the *ḥaroset* (a mixture of fruit and spices with wine, used to sweeten the *maror*, and supposed to represent by its colour and texture the mortar used by the Israelites to build up their enforced brickwork in Egypt). The second dipping has symbolic relevance to the story of the Exodus, but the first dipping has no clear relevance. A strained halakic reason was found for the eating of parsley or celery (the blessing over it renders unnecessary a blessing over the bitter herbs, and thus provides an escape from the unsolved problem of whether one ought to make a blessing over something so unpleasant as bitter herbs), while the salt water into which the parsley was dipped was regarded as symbolic of the tears shed by the Israelites in Egypt. Recent scholarly research, however, into Graeco–Roman menus at the ceremonial meal, or *symposium*, has shown that the eating of parsley or celery at the commencement of the meal was quite standard (corresponding to the modern eating of *crudités*). The reading of the Mishnah, therefore, '. . . on all other nights we dip once', should be retained, as referring to the usual eating of *crudités*, which were dipped into salt water merely as a relish, while the son's question refers only to the unusual part, which was the eating of bitter herbs, dipped into a substance representing mortar.

*He begins with disgrace, and ends with praise*: this means that the low condition of the Israelites before their redemption is to be stressed, so that the ensuing praise for God's grace can be all the more heartfelt. In our present *Haggadah*, two elements of 'disgrace' are emphasized: that 'our ancestors were slaves to Pharaoh in Egypt', and that the Israelites were descended from idolaters, the forebears of Abraham. Thus Jews are not to regard themselves as enjoying God's favour because of their noble or racially superior descent; they are the descendants of idolaters and slaves.

*he expounds from, 'A wandering Aramean was my father'*: the exposition of this passage (which is, in fact, the declaration to be made when bringing the First-fruits) as found in the extant *Haggadah* translates the first phrase as 'An Aramean (Laban) tried to destroy my father (Jacob)', an interpretation found elsewhere in rabbinic literature. It may be, however, that the original *Haggadah* practice was to regard this phrase as part of the 'beginning with disgrace', being a reference to the humble Aramean origins of the Israelites.

*Rabban Gamaliel used to say*: this passage has been incorporated into the *Haggadah*, with considerable expansion of the explanations given for the three features mentioned. See Exod. 12:8; Num. 9:11 for the three features. For the link between redemption and unleavened bread, see Exod. 12:39 – deliverance was so swift that the bread did not have time to rise.

*as if he personally has gone forth from Egypt*: the inner purpose of the *Seder* service is here stated: to renew the basic religious experience of Judaism, the redemption from Egypt.

*Therefore we are obliged to thank*: here begins the proem to the *Hallel* (see p. 36). Psalms 113 and 114 are said before the meal, and Psalms 115 to 118 after the meal.

*from slavery to freedom*: that the basic concept of the Torah is freedom is asserted in many rabbinic passages.

*from deep darkness to great light*: echoing Isa. 9:2.

## Charity and the Temple

*Mishnah Šeqalim 5:6*

There were two chambers in the Temple. One was the Chamber of Secrets, and the other the Chamber of Vessels. The Chamber of Secrets – sin-fearers used to put (gifts) into it in secret, and poor people, of good family, were supplied from it in secret. The Chamber of Vessels – anyone who made a gift of a vessel would throw it into there, and once every thirty days the treasurers opened it, and any vessel that they found there that was needed for the upkeep of the Temple they left there, and the rest were sold for their value and the money went to the Chamber for the upkeep of the Temple.

¶ This passage gives rise to some puzzling questions. Why was the charity dispensed by the Chamber of Secrets given only to 'poor people of good family', whereas all other forms of charity were dispensed without regard for the antecedents of the recipients, or indeed for their own deserts? How does the Chamber of Secrets relate to other forms of poor-relief mentioned in the Mishnah, the *quppah* and the *tamḥuy*? (See p. 64 and M. Pe'ah 8:7; M. Pes. 10:1.)

The answer seems to be that this was the only form of charity in which there was *complete* secrecy, since the recipients could come to the Chamber and take what they needed without being seen. Other forms of charity were less secret: the poor taking the *pe'ah* (see p. 62), for example, were publicly identified as poor by resorting to the fields for that purpose, and even those who took from the poor-box (*quppah*) had to make themselves known to the three people who acted as distributors. Such identification would be particularly hard on 'people of good family' (by which public respectability and honour is meant, rather than virtue, though the categories are not quite distinct). It was a principle of charity that unusual susceptibilities should be respected (see p. 135), so the function of the Chamber of Secrets was to cater for those who would be too embarrassed, because of their respectable antecedents, to apply to the usual sources of charity, and might therefore be in danger of starvation. By the nature of the secrecy involved, there was no check on who was using the Chamber of Secrets; it was simply assumed that it would be used by those for whom it was intended, while the majority of the poor would be content with the usual channels of charity. There was thus no intention, in the Chamber of Secrets, to apply a 'virtue-test', or to exclude the 'undeserving poor' from charity. On the contrary, the secrecy made it impossible to apply any test to the recipients, and the provision 'of good family' is merely an indication of the category for whom this form of charity was intended. Indeed, the appellation 'sin-fearers' given to those who supplied the funds for this charity shows that they were regarded as specially virtuous in that they exercised no personal choice over the recipients of their generosity, made no discriminations, and asked for no gratitude or public acknowledgement. (See b. B.B. 10b and b. Ket. 67a).

*Note that wherever in the rabbinic writings mention is made of interrogation of applicants for charity or 'examination', this refers not to enquiries about their general moral character, but specifically about whether they are genuinely poor. Such 'examination' was permitted (though not enjoined) except when an applicant asked not for money or for clothes but for food; in such a case, the food must be given without enquiry, as it was assumed that no one would ask for food unless genuinely in want.

## Those honoured and dishonoured

*Mishnah Yoma 3:10–11 (see also Mishnah Nazir 3:6)*

Ben Qaṭin made twelve spigots for the laver, which (previously) had only two; and he also made a device for the laver so that its water should not become unfit by remaining overnight. King Monobaz made all the handles of the vessels for the Day of Atonement of gold. His mother Helena put a golden lamp over the door of the Sanctuary. She also made a golden tablet on which was written the paragraph of the Suspected Adulteress. As for Nicanor, miracles occurred to his gates, and they caused his name to be remembered for praise.

And these (they caused to be remembered) for dishonour. Those of the house of Garmu – they were not willing to teach how to make the Shewbread; those of the house of Abtinas – they were not willing to teach how to make the incense; Hygras ben Levi – he knew a special art of song, but was not willing to teach it; Ben Qamṣar – he was not willing to teach the craft of writing. Of the first it is written, 'The memory of the just is for a blessing'; but of these it is written, 'But the name of the wicked shall rot' (Prov. 10:7).

¶ The account of the Day of Atonement service is here interrupted to allot honour to those who had donated special rich gifts to beautify the Temple; and this leads to the mention of those remembered, on the contrary, with reproach, because their selfishness had caused the loss of skills that had contributed to the beauty of the Temple service. The passage is interesting too because of its mention of the royal house of Adiabene, which had been converted to Judaism in the first century AD, and had been notable for its devotion to Judaism.

*Ben Qaṭin*: a High Priest.
*the laver*: this was in the Temple Court between the porch and the altar (see M. Mid. 3:6 and also Exod. 30:18). The priests washed their hands and feet by using its water, and the innovation enabled twelve priests to wash simultaneously.
*so that its water should not become unfit by remaining overnight*: water that had remained in a vessel overnight was regarded as no longer living water, which was required for the Temple ablutions. The device (of cog-wheels) enabled the heavy brass laver to be lowered into the well, and thus its water retained its status as living water.
*King Monobaz*: the royal house of Adiabene (formerly the homeland of the Assyrians from which they embarked on the acquisition of the Assyrian Empire) was converted to Judaism about AD 30. Queen Helena, an enthusiastic convert to Judaism, visited Jerusalem

in AD 43 with her son Izates. Queen Helena sent shiploads of wheat and figs to Palestine in AD 48 to relieve a famine. Her son Izates was succeeded as King in AD 55 by his brother, Monobaz II, to whom the Mishnah is here referring. He was a firm adherent to Judaism, and his pious sayings are quoted in the Talmud.

*the paragraph of the Suspected Adulteress*: see Num. 5:11–31. The ordeal of the Suspected Adulteress was thus still performed at this date (about AD 50–60). Shortly afterwards, however, it was abolished by Rabban Joḥanan ben Zakkai (see M. Soṭ. 9:9).

*Nicanor*: the story of the miracle of Nicanor's gate is told in the Tosephta (Kippurim 2:4). When Nicanor was bringing his gift of two doors for a gate for the Temple Court by sea from Alexandria, a great storm arose, and one of the doors had to be thrown into the sea to lighten the ship's load. When the ship's crew wished to throw the other door into the sea too, Nicanor would not let them, saying 'If you throw it, throw me too'. The ship managed to reach port in Jaffa, and there the jettisoned door rose to the surface from beneath the ship. An even more miraculous account described how the jettisoned door was swallowed by a sea-monster, who disgorged it on the shore near Jaffa. The similarities between this story and the biblical story of Jonah are plain, though their heroes are very dissimilar. Nicanor (not to be confused with the Syrian general who fought against Judas Maccabaeus) was an Alexandrian Jew, and his gift of a gate to the Temple was made about AD 50. The 'Cave of Nicanor' on Mount Scopus contains a sarcophagus with the inscription 'The remains of the children of Nicanor of Alexandria who made the doors'. The Gate of Nicanor was situated at the east of the Temple Court (see M. Šeq. 6:3). The Talmudic account of the miracle of Nicanor (b. Yoma 38a) adds a further detail inspired by the story of Jonah: when Nicanor offered to be thrown into the sea, the storm was immediately stilled. The historical basis of the story is probably that the gate of Nicanor survived a very dangerous storm when transported from Alexandria to Palestine.

*the Shewbread*: the twelve Shewbread loaves which were placed on the golden table in the sanctuary from Sabbath to Sabbath (Exod. 25:30, Lev. 24:5–9). Great skill was needed to bake them with the required thinness, and in such a way that they remained fresh for the required time.

*the incense*: according to the Talmud, the special secret was a herbal ingredient which made the column of smoke ascend straight.

*a special art of song*: it seems that this was some secret of voice-

production by which he could increase the power of his singing voice.
*the craft of writing*: according to the Talmud, this was the art of writing with four pens simultaneously. Could this have been some early form of printing? It is puzzling what this has to do with the Temple service.

## Atonement and repentance

*Mishnah Yoma 8:9*
He who says 'I will sin, and repent: I will sin, and repent'; he will not be given the chance to repent. 'I will sin, and the Day of Atonement will atone'; the Day of Atonement does not atone. Transgressions between man and God; the Day of Atonement atones. Transgressions between a man and his neighbour; the Day of Atonement does not atone, until he appeases his neighbour. This Rabbi Eleazar ben Azariah derived from the verse, 'From all your sins before the Lord you will be purified' (Lev. 16:30): transgressions between man and God; the Day of Atonement atones. Transgressions between man and his neighbour; the Day of Atonement does not atone, until he appeases his neighbour. Said Rabbi Akiba: Happy are you, O Israel! Before whom are you purified, and who is your purifier? Your Father that is in Heaven. As it is said, 'And I will sprinkle clean water upon you and you shall be clean' (Ezek. 36:25). And it says, 'O Lord the pool of Israel' (Jer. 17:13). Just as the pool purifies those who are unclean, so the Holy One, blessed be he, purifies Israel.

¶ This is the final mishnah of the tractate *Yoma*, which is concerned with the ritual and observances of the Day of Atonement. Though the Mishnah is primarily a handbook of practice, it does occasionally give a glimpse of the concepts that lie behind the practice, and this is especially liable to occur at the end of a tractate. Here the function of the Day of Atonement as a purifier from sin is set in relation to the general principles of repentance. It is made clear that repentance and reparation are the primary methods of atonement, and that there is no magical efficacy in the rites of the Day of Atonement itself.

*'I will sin, and repent: I will sin, and repent'*: the repetition suggests the thought 'I will continue in this sin indefinitely, repenting from time to time in order to start sinning again with a clean slate'. Repentance is being used as a method for continuing to sin with a clear conscience.

*he will not be given the chance to repent*: this may mean that he will die before the time of his intended repentance. This explanation, however, is not entirely satisfactory, since it assumes that such repentance, if allowed, would be effective. A better explanation is that his own attitude cuts him off from the opportunity of genuine repentance, since the kind of repentance he practises is insincere, and therefore ineffective. True repentance must comprise the genuine resolve to give up the repented sin. The Hebrew word for 'repentance', *tešubah*, or 'return', shows that this is the essence of the biblical and rabbinic concept of repentance, rather than mere remorse, or sense of guilt.

*'I will sin, and the Day of Atonement will atone'; the Day of Atonement does not atone*: this asserts that the solemnity and sacrificial rites of the Day of Atonement, and even the personal rites of prayer and fasting, have no efficacy without repentance. Anyone who relies on the Day of Atonement alone to wipe away his sins, is without atonement – indeed, he is destroying the effectiveness of the Day of Atonement by ascribing to it some magical power, instead of regarding it as a means to repentance and as a mark that repentance has taken place. In general, the sacrificial system of sin-offerings, according to rabbinic thought (following that of the Prophets), has no efficacy except when accompanied by genuine repentance, though it does act as a seal to repentance and effects the final atonement.

*Transgressions between man and his neighbour; the Day of Atonement does not atone*: this statement goes further than the previous one. It says that even genuine repentance does not atone for a sin, even together with the rites of the Day of Atonement, if something has been left undone to repair the wrong. This means that offences against God are easier to wipe away than offences against man. For in the case of offences against God (e.g. violations of Sabbath law or laws of forbidden foods) simple repentance is sufficient; but in the case of offences against man, where someone has suffered loss of property or physical injury or insult, the wrong has to be put right by restoring the goods or money concerned, by compensating the injury, or by seeking pardon for the insult; and until this has been done, no full repentance has been performed, and consequently the Day of Atonement has no effect. In the New Testament, the Pharisees are represented as objecting to the pronouncement of forgiveness by Jesus (Matt. 9:2–4; Mark. 2:7) on the grounds that only God could forgive; but, in fact, in Pharisaic thought, even God could not forgive unless reparation had been made to fellow men injured by one's sins. In cases where such reparation was impossible (e.g. where a repentant tax-collector did not know the names of his victims), it was recommended to give an appropriate sum in public works (Tos. B.M. 8:26). (See p. 142, and Luke 19:8.)

*before the Lord*: this is taken with the preceding phrase (instead of with the subsequent phrase) in order to yield the required meaning, that only sins against God ('before the Lord') are referred to, not sins against man.

*Before whom are you purified*: Rabbi Akiba, on the other hand, takes the phrase 'before the Lord' in its more natural sense (meaning that the purification takes place in the presence of the Lord, in the Temple service). His saying is not thematically connected with the preceding part of the mishnah, but is brought in as an alternative interpretation of the verse from Leviticus, and as an appropriate sentiment for the conclusion of tractate *Yoma*, expressing thanks to God for providing the Day of Atonement as a means of purifying Israel from its sins. He supplements the verse from Leviticus, which says that Israel is purified *before* God, by other verses which involve God more intimately in the process of purification: firstly one which depicts God as actively purifying Israel, and secondly one which even depicts God as himself the medium in which Israel is purified. Rabbi Akiba thus finally stresses the aspect of atonement that the preceding part of the mishnah seeks to qualify and limit: the action of God in extending forgiveness, rather than the action of man in adopting new paths and remedying the effects of past conduct.

*the pool of Israel*: the Hebrew word *miqweh* is usually translated 'hope' here, but exactly the same word also means 'pool' and in particular it is used for the ritual pool in which people and vessels are immersed in order to cleanse them from ritual impurities. Rabbi Akiba is using this as a metaphor for the spiritual impurity caused by sin (ritual impurity itself is not sinful, any more than physical dirtiness, which is also used at times as a metaphor for spiritual impurity). Rabbi Akiba's translation 'the pool of Israel' instead of 'the hope of Israel' may be regarded as merely a pun, of a kind often used in rabbinical *deraša*. On the other hand, on the level of language study there is something to be said for this translation of the phrase *miqweh Yisrael* wherever it occurs in the Bible, in the sense 'the reservoir of Israel' *or* 'the resource of Israel', rather than 'the hope of Israel'. (This seems to be the sense of *miqweh geburah* ('reservoir of strength') in QS 4:21.) See the full verse in Jeremiah from which Akiba took the phrase, where God, in the parallel limb of the verse, is called 'the fountain of living water'. The usual word for 'hope' in Hebrew is *tiqwah*, and there is no difficulty in supposing that the word *miqweh* is always derived from the homonymous but different root *qawah*, meaning 'to collect'. Rabbi Akiba's introduction of the special meaning 'ritual pool' is, of course, a pun on any reckoning.

## The Rain-maker

*Mishnah Ta'anit 3:8*

For every misfortune that may come upon the community they proclaim a fast by sounding the *šopar*, except for over-abundance of rain. It once happened that they said to Ḥoni the Circle-maker 'Pray that rain may fall'. He said to them 'Go out and carry in the Passover ovens so that they will not melt (in the rain)'. He prayed, but the rain did not fall. What did he do? He drew a circle and stood inside it and said before him 'Lord of the Universe, your children have set their faces upon me, since I am like a member of your household. I swear by your great name that I will not stir from here until you have mercy on your children'. Rain began to fall in drops. Said he 'I did not ask for rain like this, but for enough to fill cisterns, ditches and caverns'. The rain began to fall furiously. Said he 'I did not ask for rain like this, but for rain of goodwill, blessing and graciousness'. The rain then fell in correct measure (but went on) until Israel went out from Jerusalem to the Temple Mount from before the rain. They came and said to him 'Just as you prayed for it to fall, so pray for it to go away'. He said to them 'Go out and see whether the Stone of Claims has been washed away'. Simeon ben Shetaḥ sent to him 'If you were not Ḥoni, I would decree excommunication against you. But what shall I do to you? For you behave with a high hand before the Omnipresent, and he does your will, like a child who demands imperiously of his father, and his father does his will; and it is about you that Scripture says, "May your father and mother be glad, and may she who bore you rejoice" (Prov. 23:25)'.

¶ This is the unusual occurrence of an extended, well-structured story in the Mishnah, which usually avoids such stories in order to preserve its character as a law code. Nevertheless, even this story is introduced for the sake of the legal point which it illustrates, though the story has features of great interest going far beyond that. The introductory sentence gives the legal point at issue: a fast should be instituted for communal misfortunes, but not for excessive rain (since it would be ungrateful to complain of an over-abundance of good). The story is then given to illustrate what is meant by 'excessive rain'. It does *not* mean destructive rain, which beats down the crops or causes floods: such rain one may seek to stop by prayer, as Ḥoni did when he prayed against the rain that came down 'furiously'. It means moderate rain which goes on so long that it becomes inconvenient; Ḥoni refuses to pray for the cessation of rain such as this. But the story was not told originally to illustrate this legal point. The protest of Simeon ben Shetaḥ (irrelevant to the legal point) gives the original theme of the story, namely, the tension between the charismatics of the Pharisaic movement (the *Ḥasidim*) and the more rationalist rabbis (see p. 43). It should be noted that there is no crude antagonism between these two religious tendencies, which formed part of the same movement. Our present story (as well as other similar stories to be found in the Talmudic literature) holds a delicate poise between Simeon's disapproval of Ḥoni's 'high-handed' methods of prayer and his admiration of Ḥoni's charismatic power and nearness to God. Moreover, the very fact that the Mishnah cites Ḥoni's actions in illustration of a point of law shows that no irreconcilable gap is envisaged between the legal approach and the charismatic approach.

*that may come upon the community*: the literal meaning is 'that may not come upon the community' – a euphemistic or prophylactic expression.

*šopar*: the ram's horn blown on solemn occasions to sound a note of warning, especially on the New Year and the Day of Atonement (see Lev. 25:9).

*Passover ovens*: these were kept in the open air of the courtyards for cooking the Passover lambs, and were made of clay, so could be expected to melt in prolonged rain. Ḥoni shows his somewhat boastful confidence in a favourable answer.
*drew a circle*: this suggests magical practice, but this is not alleged here against Ḥoni. The circle merely indicates his firm resolve not to budge until he receives a favourable answer.
*like a member of your household*: Ḥoni stresses his intimacy with God.
*until Israel went out from Jerusalem to the Temple Mount*: the covered porticos of the Temple Mount afforded better shelter. The meaning is not that the lower regions were flooded, for this would have come into the category of harmful rains, previously prayed against by Ḥoni. The rain is now over-prolonged but not harmful.
*'Go out and see whether the Stone of Claims has been washed away'*: the reading *'eben ha-ṭoʿim* ('the stone of wanderers', i.e. of those wandering about looking for their lost property) should be emended to *'eben ha-ṭoʿan* ('the Stone of Claims') in accordance with b. B.M. 28b. It was a stone where lost property could be claimed, and was a well-known landmark in Jerusalem. For laws of lost property see M.B.M. 1–3, based on Deut. 22:1–4. The Palestinian Talmud explains, probably correctly, that this was Ḥoni's emphatic way of refusing to pray. There is also an echo of Ḥoni's previous promise to bring rain that would melt clay ovens, as if to say 'I warned you that the rain might have some inconvenient consequences, but after all, it is only heavy enough to wash away clay, not stone, so you'll have to put up with it'.

## Ritual purity

*Mishnah Ḥagigah 2:7*

The clothes of an *ʿam ha-'areṣ* count as having *midras*-uncleanness for *perušim*; the clothes of *perušim* count as having *midras*-uncleanness for those who eat *terumah*; the clothes of those who eat *terumah* count as having *midras*-uncleanness for (those who eat) holy things; the clothes of (those who eat) holy things count as having *midras*-uncleanness for (those who handle) the sin-offering water. Joseph ben Joezer was the most saintly person in the priesthood, but his apron had *midras*-uncleanness for (those who eat) holy things. Joḥanan ben Gudgada used to eat according to the cleanness of holy things all his days; but his apron had *midras*-uncleanness for (those who handle) sin-offering water.

¶ This passage contains a conspectus of the Mishnaic system of ritual purity. It particularly shows that ritual impurity or uncleanness was *not* regarded as, in itself, sinful, but merely as a state disqualifying a person from certain ritual acts relating to sacred foods and areas. A person might be quite clean enough for partaking in such acts at one level of sacredness, but not at a higher level of sacredness. Even a person who was most particular about the observance of ritual purity was not necessarily in a fit state to partake in certain acts involving a very high degree of sacredness in the objects concerned; and, on the other hand, a person who did not observe ritual purity at all was guilty of no sin unless he performed religious acts for which some degree of ritual cleanness was required. The mishnah is at pains to stress that ritual purity is not a matter of virtue. This point is particularly important in relation to the status of the *ʿam ha-ʾareṣ*. The mishnah also shows that the system of ritual purity lent itself to the voluntary acceptance of a supererogatory level of observance as a kind of religious vow rather than the biblical vow of the Nazirite. Such a voluntary undertaking can be seen at two different levels in this passage, but was subject to great variation.

*ʿam ha-ʾareṣ*: the meaning of the expression *ʿam ha-ʾareṣ* is a complex topic, since it bears several different meanings and was used sometimes in a pejorative, sometimes in a non-pejorative, way (see p. 126). Here it is used in its basic non-pejorative sense of 'layman', and is applied in the context of the ladder of ritual purity. On this ladder, the *ʿam ha-ʾareṣ* occupied the lowest rung, since he was not a priest, nor was he a member of the fraternities, known as *ḥaberim* or *perušim*, which undertook to practise a special standard of ritual purity higher than that required of the layman, but not so high as that required of the priest (see p. 70).
*perušim*: this word should not be translated 'Pharisees' in this context. It can also mean 'sectarians' or 'those who deviate from the norm' or 'those who are abstinent'. Only when the word *perušim* is opposed to *ṣedukim* ('Sadducees') does it mean unambiguously 'Pharisees'; in other cases its meaning must be judged from the context. When opposed to *ʿam ha-ʾareṣ*, as here, it is equivalent to *ḥaberim*, and means those who undertook a voluntary programme of ritual purity. The *ḥaberim* were not co-extensive with the Pharisees, who, as a religious party (otherwise known as *ḥakamim*,

'Sages' or *soperim*, 'Scribes') claimed great authority over the whole field of Jewish law and thought, and had much wider aims than the *ḥaberim*. It seems probable that the *ḥaberim*, apart from practising a regime of abstinence as a spiritual exercise, served a useful social purpose by acting as tax-collectors for the priests, since the tithes had to be handled in a state of above-normal ritual purity. But it was far from being the case that such a state was advocated as obligatory for everyone: on the contrary, there were also fraternities (*ḥaburot*) who dedicated themselves, from at least equally pious motives, to a life of ritual *impurity*, by concerning themselves with the laying out and burial of the dead (contact with a corpse made a person ritually unclean). Even these people, however, had to be ritually clean for certain occasions, e.g. when visiting Jerusalem for the Pilgrim Festivals, and cleanness could easily be achieved by the prescribed ablution, i.e. a simple immersion in a river or specially constructed pool (*miqweh*, see p. 53). The layman, or *ʿam ha-ʾareṣ*, was also careful to achieve ritual cleanness on such special occasions, and by rabbinic law, it was assumed without further enquiry that the *ʿam ha-ʾareṣ* was conscientious in acquiring ritual purity at such times (see M. Ḥag. 3:6). Maimonides, the greatest medieval philosopher and codifier of Judaism, writes 'The uncleanness of common people (*ʿam ha-ʾareṣ*) is deemed to be clean during a feast, for all Israelites count as Associates (*ḥaberim*) during the feasts; and all their vessels, and their foodstuffs, and their liquids count as clean during a feast, since they all make themselves clean to go to Jerusalem for the feast' (*Mishneh Torah*, *Tohorah*, *Miškab u-Mošab* 11:9). Also, the *ʿam ha-ʾareṣ* was assumed to be ritually clean during the season of wine-presses and olive-presses, when particular care was needed to preserve the purity of the Priest-tithe (M. Ḥag. 3:4). There was, therefore, a considerable degree of trust in the *ʿam ha-ʾareṣ* in matters of ritual purity even though he was assumed to be in a state of ritual uncleanness usually, as he had a right to be. The idea that the ritual-purity laws made mutual trust, friendship and social intercourse impossible between the different sections of the community is thus incorrect (see also p. 69).

*midras-uncleanness*: this is a serious degree of uncleanness, since it means the degree of uncleanness imparted by a person with a 'running issue' (*zab*) or by a menstruating woman (*niddah*). *Midras* means 'pressure', and is a general word covering the 'sitting', 'lying' or 'riding' mentioned in Lev. 15. A garment on which a *zab* has lain, sat or ridden has '*midras*-uncleanness'. What the mishnah is saying, then, is that despite the fact that each rung on the ritual-purity ladder has its own standard of purity, this counts only on its own level, but in relation to the rung above, each rung counts as having no cleanness at all. For example, a priest who is on duty in the Temple handling *qodašim* must treat as totally unclean a priest not on duty (i.e. avoid touching him), even though the latter, objectively, may be in the state of cleanness required for eating the priestly food, *terumah*. This extra precaution was instituted by the rabbis to prevent all possibility of contact between holy foodstuffs and impurity.

*terumah*: translated by AV as 'heave-offering', but 'offering' is better; it refers in the Mishnah to the tithe given to the priests, as opposed to the tithe (*ma'aser*) given to the Levites (Deut. 18:3–4). Also included under the term *terumah* were the priests' dues payable from the Levites' Tithe (*terumat ma'aser*). The amount of the *terumah* was not precisely fixed, but varied from a sixtieth to a fortieth of the crop. It was biblically forbidden for a non-priest to eat the *terumah* (unless a member of a priestly household), and also, it was biblically forbidden to allow the *terumah* to become ritually unclean, or for the priest to eat it, if it had by chance become unclean. Thus the priests had to eat their *terumah*, their staple food, in a condition of ritual cleanness, an obligation not imposed on an ordinary Israelite eating his ordinary food, which he was permitted to eat when he or the food or both were ritually unclean. *Some* Israelites, however (the *ḥaberim*), made a voluntary undertaking to eat ordinary food (*ḥullin*) 'in cleanness', and these are the people called in the present mishnah *perušim*. Note that the *perušim* did not have to keep up the same standard of ritual purity as the priests, since *ḥullin* was not so susceptible to uncleanness as *terumah*. That is why the present mishnah states that, in relation to the priests, the *perušim* were regarded as unclean. (Thus it is not correct to say, as some scholars have said, that the *ḥaberim* tried to keep up the same standard of purity as the priests. Moreover, the cleanness of the *ḥaberim* was a far less serious matter than that of the priests, who risked sacrilege, while a *ḥaber* risked only a failure to observe his 'undertaking'.)

*holy things*: Hebrew, *qodeš*, in this instance, but often the plural *qodašim* is used. This refers to the sacrifices offered in the Temple, which were regarded as more susceptible to ritual uncleanness than the *terumah*: thus a 'third-degree of uncleanness' would not render *terumah* unclean, but would render a sacrifice unclean. Uncleanness was regarded as diminishing as it became further removed from the primary source of uncleanness, say a corpse. Thus something that actually touched a corpse was unclean to such a high degree that it was called a 'father of uncleanness'; something that touched a 'father' became unclean 'in the first-degree'; something that touched a 'first-degree' source became unclean 'in the second degree'; something that touched a 'second-degree' source became unclean 'in the third-degree', and so on. Ordinary food (*ḥullin*) was not susceptible of 'third-degree' uncleanness but *terumah* was. *Terumah* was not susceptible of 'fourth-degree' uncleanness, but sacrifices (*qodašim*) were. Thus *perušim* (who had 'undertaken' to eat *ḥullin* without rendering it unclean) had to avoid being in a 'first-degree' of uncleanness while eating their meals; priests had to avoid being in a 'second-degree' of uncleanness while eating *terumah*, and had to take care not to allow anything with a 'third-degree' of uncleanness to come in contact with sacrifices. Thus the normal state of ordinary people (*ʿam ha-'areṣ*), since they did not have to worry about whether they were conveying uncleanness to their food, was 'first-degree' uncleanness, except during harvesting of grapes and olives, and during festival pilgrimage to Jerusalem. The normal state of the *perušim* was 'second-degree' uncleanness, since such a degree could not affect the *ḥullin* which they ate (as non-priests, they were not allowed to eat *terumah*, so did not have to worry about attaining a state of cleanness sufficient to eat *terumah*). In practice, this meant that while both priests and *perušim* had a ritual bath every morning, the *perušim* could then proceed to their meal immediately, while priests (see M. Ber. 1:1) had to wait until the evening before eating *terumah* (since between the morning bath and the evening, a person was called a *tebul yom* ('he who bathed that day') and was unclean in the 'second-degree'). A priest could, of course, eat ordinary food if he wished, and would then not have to observe any more rules of ritual purity than the *ʿam ha-'areṣ*, except when fulfilling his stint of Temple service.

*sin-offering water*: this was the water which contained the ashes of the Red Cow (see Num. 19). It was used for the purification of those who had incurred uncleanness from contact with a corpse. The sin-offering water was so-called because of the use of the word *ḥaṭ'at* in Num. 19:9, a word usually translated 'sin-offering'. In this context, however, a better translation is probably 'purification'. By biblical law this water is one of the 'holy things', and therefore no more susceptible to uncleanness than the sacrifices, but the rabbis enacted many extra precautions to prevent it from incurring uncleanness (see M. Ḥag. 2:5–6), since so many purifications depended upon it. The placing of those who handled the sin-offering water in a separate category was one of these extra precautions.

*Joseph ben Joezer*: he appears in M. ’Ab. 1:4 as a member of the ‘pairs’ who received the tradition, his partner being Jose ben Joḥanan, in the fourth generation before Hillel (*c.* 150 BC). He is there called ‘a man of Zereda’ (see also M. ʿEd. 8:4, where some traditions are given in his name). In *’Abot* and *ʿEduyot*, his name is given not as ‘Joseph’, but as ‘Jose’, which is a derived form of ‘Joseph’, current in post-biblical times. The name of Jesus’ brother is given as ‘Joses’ (Greek form of ‘Jose’) in Matt. 13:55; Mark 6:3. Such derived forms of biblical names were common; Jesus’ own name, for example, was in Hebrew *Yešu*, derived from the biblical *Yehošuʿa* (‘Joshua’) – which had been modified even in biblical times to *Yešuʿa* (see Ezra 2:2).

*was the most saintly person in the priesthood*: the word here for ‘saintly’ is *ḥasid*, which means ‘pious to the point of going beyond the letter of the law’. The point emphasized here is that one’s state of ritual cleanness is not related to one’s state of virtue.

*Joḥanan ben Gudgada*: traditions are given in his name in M. Giṭ. 5:5; and M. Yeb. 14:2, though in M. ʿEd. 7:9 the same traditions are cited in the name of Neḥunya ben Gudgada. Evidently, he was a priest, but instead of eating his *terumah* in the degree of cleanness suitable to it (i.e. avoiding being in a ‘second-degree’ of uncleanness), he voluntarily treated it as if it were ‘holy things’, which required one degree of cleanness higher (i.e. he took care that his food did not come into contact even with a ‘third-degree’ of uncleanness). This means that he practised, on a higher rung of the ritual-purity ladder, the same kind of supererogatory observance that the *perušim* practised on the level of the non-priest. This shows that many variations of the supererogatory type of observance were practised; in fact, we come across other variations elsewhere, such as a non-priest treating *ḥullin* as if it were *terumah* (thus observing a standard *two* degrees higher than that required of him by the law); see b. Ḥul. 34b. The important thing to note is that all these practices were purely personal undertakings which had no implications for general observance. They gave an outlet for exercises of unusual piety, but in no way pointed to a condemnation of those who did what the law required and no more. Thus the theory expounded by J. Neusner in *From Politics to Piety: the Emergence of*

*Pharisaic Judaism* (New York, Ktav, 1979), pp. 82–90, that the 'table-fellowships' were a sect which hoped to convert all Jews to their way of life, is incorrect.

## The rights of wives

*Mishnah Ketubot 5:1*

Even though they said that a virgin is entitled to 200 *dinars* and a widow to one *minah*, if he wished to add even a hundred *minahs*, he may add them. If she became a widow or was divorced, whether while betrothed or after marriage, she may claim the whole.

¶ It was laid down in rabbinical law that no marriage was valid unless the husband gave a document, called the *ketubah*, to the wife, in which he undertook to pay her a statutory sum in the event of divorce. In the event of the husband's death, this sum was also payable by his heirs. According to rabbinic tradition, the *ketubah* was first instituted by Simeon ben Shetaḥ (about 100 BC) in order to safeguard wives against arbitrary divorce. The sum stipulated in the *ketubah* was not payable if the wife were divorced because of adultery or other disgraceful conduct on her part. It should be noted, too, that any property brought into the marriage by the wife belonged to her, and had to be returned to her in the event of divorce (even if she was divorced because of misconduct). The husband, however, was entitled to any profits accruing from his wife's property during the marriage. Thus the view often pronounced that 'in rabbinic law, a wife has no rights', was very far from the truth. She had the right to own property (a right granted to wives by English law only in 1870). She also had the right to divorce if the marriage had become intolerable to her (see p. 101). The husband had to treat her with respect: for example, he had no right to beat her (a right abrogated in English law only in 1891). In rabbinic law, a wife could claim damages against a violent husband just as she could against any other person who offered her violence. Further, she had various rights of maintenance: a husband was even obliged to provide his wife with cosmetics. These rights arose from the status of Jewish marriage as a contract into which husband and wife freely entered, each remaining a separate legal personage. Jewish marriage was not a sacrament, by which individuality was lost in an indissoluble mystic union and legal rights abolished – a concept which, in practice, could work to the detriment of the wife.

*200 dinars*: a sum regarded as sufficient to pay for food and clothing for a person for a year. A *dinar* is equivalent to a *zuz*.
*one minah*: this is equivalent to 100 *dinars*. The divorce of a woman who was virgin at marriage is regarded as a greater hardship to her than that of a woman who was a widow at marriage.
*while betrothed*: the betrothal (*'erusin*) constituted the beginning of the marriage, but the bride continued to live in her father's home for a period of about a year until the completion of the marriage (*nissu'in*).

## The wife's right to divorce

*Mishnah Ketubot 7:10*
These are compelled to divorce their wives: he who is afflicted with boils, or who has a polypus, or who is a scraper, or who is a coppersmith or a tanner, whether this was the case before they married or only after they married. And in all these cases, Rabbi Meir said: Even if he made it a condition, she may say 'I thought I could bear it, but, as it is, I cannot bear it'. But the Sages say: She must bear it despite herself, except in the case of one who is afflicted with boils, because she will sap his strength. It once happened in Sidon that a tanner died and had a brother who was also a tanner. The Sages said: She may say 'I could bear your brother, but I cannot bear you'.

¶ Rabbinic law allows a wife to be released from an unbearable marriage, even if her husband is unwilling to divorce her. In such a divorce, she retains the usual rights of a divorced woman: i.e. her property must be returned to her, and the amount stipulated in her *ketubah* (see p. 100) must be paid to her.

*These are compelled*: nevertheless, the husband has to express willingness, since, in theory, a divorce requires the decision of the husband (Deut. 24:1). Thus, the procedure in the case of a husband whom the court compels to divorce his wife is: They compel him until he says 'It is my will' (M. 'Arak. 5:6). In practice, in the case of a recalcitrant husband, this means that he is flogged until he expresses willingness to give the divorce (see Maimonides, *Mishneh*

*Torah, Našim, Gerušin*, 2:20). In most cases, however, the direction of the court is sufficient to secure the husband's consent. Thus the frequent error that in rabbinic law a husband cannot be compelled to give a divorce is based on the form, not on the reality, of rabbinic law. The rabbis, in their usual way, liberalized the biblical law without formally revoking it. A wife who wished to be released from an unbearable marriage had only to apply to the court.
*is afflicted with boils*: has a chronic skin disease or leprosy.
*a polypus*: a growth in the nose or mouth causing an intolerable smell.
*a scraper*: the Gemara explains that this means one who collects the excrements of dogs.
*a coppersmith or a tanner*: both are regarded as professions which cause their practitioners to acquire a bad smell.
*Even if he made it a condition*: if the wife explicitly accepted, as a condition of marriage, the husband's handicap.
*But the Sages say: She must bear it*: this applies only to the case in which an explicit condition was accepted by the wife. This does not mean that the wife is bound to the marriage for life, but only that if she insists on a divorce in these circumstances, she is not entitled to the amount stipulated in her *ketubah*, though she is still entitled to the return of her property.
*because she will sap his strength*: the Sages consider that it is medically inadvisable for such a person to be married anyway, and are therefore willing to accept Rabbi Meir's view in this case.
*a tanner died*: without having children, so that by the levirate law (Deut. 25:5) the widow is automatically married to his brother unless the brother elects to divorce her in a special ceremony (Deut. 25:7–10) known as *ḥaliṣah* (literally, 'loosening', from the loosening of the shoe, Deut. 25:9). Here, too, though in theory such a divorce depends on the will of the man, in rabbinic law he can be compelled to give the divorce if the woman regards the marriage as unbearable, and in such circumstances her rights are safeguarded. In the present case, it might be argued that since she did not request a divorce from her previous husband on the ground that he was a tanner, she was not entitled to this plea in the case of the brother: but the Sages did not accept this argument.

*The above are by no means the only valid grounds for a wife's claim to divorce. For example, a wife may demand a divorce if a husband insists on moving to significantly different surroundings, such as from a town to a city, or vice versa (M. Ket. 13:10).

## Vows and parents

*Mishnah Nedarim 9:1*

Rabbi Eliezer says: They open for a man with the honour of his father and his mother. But the Sages forbid (this). Said Rabbi Ṣadoq: Rather than opening for him with the honour of his father and mother, let them open for him with the honour of God! If so, there are no vows. And the Sages agree with Rabbi Eliezer that in a matter that is between him and his father and mother, they may open for him with the honour of his father and mother.

¶ This passage deals with the question of the annulment of vows. The rabbis believed (though they admitted that there is no explicit warrant for this in Scripture) that a vow could be annulled if it could be established by a competent authority that the vow was made under some kind of misapprehension. Thus a person who had made a rash vow from which he wished to be released would go to a court of three rabbis who would seek by enquiry to find an 'opening' by which the vow could be annulled. The present passage says that a vow can be annulled on the ground that it affects the interests of a parent, though not merely on the ground that the making of *any* rash vow brings dishonour on the parent of the person involved. The unanimous ruling that if the interests of a parent are affected by a vow, it can be annulled, seems to contradict the account of the Pharisaic attitude to vows and parents given in the New Testament (Mark 7:9–13; Matt. 15:3–6).

*They open*: the expression is typical of the use of the third person plural of the present tense throughout the Mishnah to express the impersonal 'one': 'one may open . . .', or 'one opens . . .', or 'a way may be opened'. The locution expresses not only what may, or must, be done, but also what is customarily done. It is to be contrasted with the style of the Bible with its direct commands, 'thou shalt . . .' or 'thou shalt not . . .'. The Mishnah is a manual of practice, and purposely does not adopt a biblical style of direct command, since the Mishnah does not claim Divine inspiration (see p. 8). Contrast here the style of the Qumran documents, which claim far greater authority.
*with the honour of his father and his mother*: Rabbi Eliezer thinks that a blanket method of annulling a vow can be adopted in the form:

Would you have made this vow if you had borne in mind the honour due by the Fifth Commandment to your parents? In other words: Would you have been ashamed to make such a vow in the presence of your parents? If the answer is 'Yes', the vow can be annulled as having been made in a mood of moral blindness.

*with the honour of God*: Rabbi Ṣadoq thinks such a blanket method is inadmissible, and as a *reductio ad absurdum*, argues that one might as well resort to an even more undifferentiated and unparticularized method of 'opening' by asking: Would you have made this vow if you had reflected that it might involve lack of respect to God?

*a matter that is between him and his father and mother*: i.e. if the vow specifically affected the area of his relationship with his father and/or his mother. Thus a blanket method of 'opening' is rejected; enquiries must be addressed to the specific content of the vow.

## The abandoned corpse

*Mishnah Nazir 7:1*

A High Priest and a Nazirite may not become unclean because of their relatives; but they must become unclean because of an abandoned corpse. If a High Priest and a Nazirite were walking on a road and found an abandoned corpse, Rabbi Eliezer says: Let the High Priest become unclean rather than the Nazirite. But the Sages say: Let the Nazirite become unclean rather than the High Priest. Said Rabbi Eliezer to the Sages: Let the priest become unclean, since he does not have to bring a sacrifice on account of his uncleanness, rather than the Nazirite who does have to bring a sacrifice. Said the Sages to Rabbi Eliezer: Let the Nazirite become unclean, since his holiness is only temporary, rather than the priest whose holiness is permanent.

¶ Priests and Nazirites are the only kind of Israelites, (apart from soldiers in a holy war), commanded in the Bible to avoid ritual impurity even when not in contact with holy places or foods and even these two classes are forbidden only in relation to corpse-uncleanness, not to other kinds of uncleanness. For the High Priest, see Lev. 21:11 (an ordinary priest may incur uncleanness from the corpse of a relative, see Lev. 21:2, but not a High Priest); for the Nazirite, see Num. 6:6; he is like a High Priest in this respect. But the duty of burying an abandoned corpse overrides the holiness of both High Priest and Nazirite. The name given to an abandoned corpse is *met miṣwah*, literally 'a corpse of commandment'. The problem of this passage, however, is one of precedence: which of the two, High Priest or Nazirite, should, by preference, sacrifice his state of ritual cleanness, if they are together faced with the task of burying an abandoned corpse? A conundrum of this kind is often used by the Mishnah to bring out the legal characteristics of a situation or category. Note that this passage refutes the explanation sometimes given of the New Testament parable about the Good Samaritan: that the priest and Levite in the story were anxious not to become contaminated by a corpse by the wayside. Even a High Priest had to regard a wayside corpse as demanding his care, and Levites were not forbidden to incur corpse-uncleanness even in ordinary circumstances. This is quite apart from the fact that the duty of saving life overrode all ritual laws including those of ritual purity. Thus the parable portrays not a priest and Levite putting Jewish law before humane considerations, but a priest and Levite in defiance of Jewish law showing less concern than a Samaritan for saving human life: the moral being that goodness does not depend on rank (a familiar Jewish moral).

*unclean*: corpse-uncleanness could be contracted either by touching a corpse or by being under the same roof with one. It was a seven-day uncleanness and required sprinkling with the ashes of the Red Cow (see Num. 19:11–13).
*Nazirite*: one who vows to be a *Nazir* ('separated one') must not drink wine, cut his hair or become unclean through corpse-uncleanness, even for a close relative (Num. 6:1ff). The vow seems to have been quite frequently practised in mishnaic times, and was usually for thirty days. The best-known biblical Nazirite was Samson, who was a lifelong Nazirite.
*bring a sacrifice*: see Num. 6:10–11. Moreover, the Nazirite then has to begin the term of his vow again. Thus it is much more trouble for the Nazirite than for the High Priest to sacrifice his state of cleanness.
*holiness is permanent*: the Sages take the view that the matter should be decided by the superior holiness of the High Priest, rather than by the amount of trouble involved. The Talmud, however, takes the view that the dispute is about which has the greater sanctity, the High Priesthood or the Nazirite status. Even a lifelong Nazirite is not a Nazirite from birth.

## The Torah-Portion of the King

*Mishnah Soṭah 7:8*

How is the Portion of the King? After the conclusion of the first festival day of the Festival of Tabernacles, in the eighth year, after the conclusion of the Seventh Year, they make for him a platform of wood in the Temple Court, and he sits on it: as it is said, 'At the end of seven years, at the set time, etc.' (Deut. 31:10). The Beadle of the Synagogue takes the scroll of the law and gives it to the Head of the Synagogue, and the Head of the Synagogue gives it to the Vice-High Priest, and the Vice-High Priest gives it the High Priest, and the High Priest gives it to the King; and the King receives it standing and reads it sitting. King Agrippa received it standing and read it standing, and the Sages praised him. And when he reached, 'You may not put over you a foreign man' (Deut. 17:15), his eyes streamed with tears. They said to him: Do not fear, Agrippa. You are our brother, you are our brother, you are our brother.

¶ By a conflation of Deut. 17:18–20 with Deut. 31:10–13, it was held that a public reading from the Torah should be performed by the King once every seven years at the Feast of Tabernacles. The present passage gives the details of how this was done. A vivid historical sidelight on the personality of King Agrippa I is included (but see p. 81 and p. 109).

*How is the Portion of the King?*: the use of the present tense throughout the passage, despite the fact that this rite had not been performed for many years at the time of the redaction of the Mishnah, shows how the rabbis kept alive the picture of a functioning Jewish state. This aim of the Mishnah can hardly be called 'nostalgia', since it regards such ceremonies as that of the Portion of the King as being merely in abeyance (see Part I, p. 34). The Messiah, who, in Jewish eyes, would be a fully functioning Jewish King in the political sense, would restore this practice, and meanwhile, its details were carefully preserved in the Oral Law. There is thus a distinct political aspect to the Mishnah; its hope of the restoration of the Jewish monarchy in an independent state is hardly that of a people reconciled to Roman rule. The present passage, if made known to the Roman authorities, might well have been regarded as subversive.

*After the conclusion of the first festival day*: the first and eighth day of Tabernacles were full festival days in which work was forbidden, though not so stringently as on a Sabbath. The intervening days were called *ḥol ha-moʿed* ('the non-holy part of the Festival'), which were part of the Festival, but on which work of most kinds was permitted. The Jewish day ended at nightfall when the stars came out, so 'the conclusion of the first festival day' would be in the evening.

*in the Temple Court*: most Tannaitic authorities hold that this means the Court of Women, but some hold that it means the Court of Israel, which was a smaller area within the Court of Priests. In the Court of Women, the ceremony would have been watched by women in the balconies surrounding the Court. If it was in the Court of Israel, women would have had to be admitted, as the Torah specifically includes women (and children) in this rite (Deut. 31:12).

*'At the end of seven years'*: this biblical passage does not actually mention the King, but merely says that a reading of the Torah must take place every seventh year at Tabernacles in the presence of 'all Israel'. Deut. 17:19, on the other hand, prescribes that the King should have a copy of the Torah of his own and that he should 'read from it all the days of his life', for his private instruction. At what stage the two passages were taken together to mean that the King should perform the reading every seven years is difficult to decide. According to Josephus (*Ant.* iv.8.12 (209)), the reading was performed by the High Priest, but this could refer to periods in which there was no King, or perhaps this is an instance of Josephus' tendency to glorify the High Priesthood. The graphic reference to Agrippa seems historically authentic, but some scholars think that the King referred to here was not Agrippa I (AD 40–44) but Agrippa II, who reigned just before the destruction of the Temple in AD 70. We thus have no evidence of the reading of the law by the King before the first century AD. The reading by King Josiah (2 Kings 23:2) is depicted as a unique occasion; but it is possible that this was the pattern on which the regular rite was modelled and if so, it may be that the rite dates from the reinstitution of the monarchy by the Hasmoneans (104 BC). It is possible, however, that, as some scholars have argued, it was Josiah himself, not the Hasmoneans, who instituted the reading by the King as a regular yearly rite. Most

modern scholars hold that Josiah's reading was the Book of Deuteronomy alone, and it is interesting that the reading by the King at Tabernacles was entirely from the Book of Deuteronomy. The reason given for this in the rabbinic sources, however, is that the King is enjoined to 'write him a copy of this law' (Deut. 17:18), and the expression 'copy of the law' (*mišneh torah*) was a common rabbinic designation for the Book of Deuteronomy because of its repetition of laws and narrative found in the earlier books of the Pentateuch.

*the Beadle of the Synagogue*: Hebrew, *ḥazan ha-keneset*. He was the superintendent at prayer-meetings, giving the signals for response, assigning seats and performing other supervisory duties. This should not be confused with the later Hebrew usage by which *ḥazan* meant 'cantor', or 'singer and intoner of the service'. This particular Synagogue was not a building but a community of lay worshippers in the Temple. Its services of prayer were conducted by Israelites, not priests (see M. Taʿan. 4:2), delegates from twenty-four regions who participated in a rota system, so that there would always be lay participation in the Temple service (see Glossary, *maʿamad*, and p. 80).

*the Head of the Synagogue*: he was an elected honorary official, neither a priest nor a rabbi, but a respected householder, who headed the administration of the Synagogue. This system of voluntary lay administration has survived in the Synagogue to the present day. In later Judaism, his title was *Parnas*. In the New Testament the office is called that of the 'President of the Synagogue' (*archon tes synagoges*, e.g. Luke 8:41, applied to Jairus).

*Vice-High Priest*: Hebrew, *segan ha-kohanim*, usually, but here simply *sagan*. He took the place of the High Priest on occasion, accompanied him when he officiated and supervised the daily offering. The word is found in biblical Hebrew in the sense of 'ruler' and is rendered by Septuagint as *strategos* (e.g. Jeremiah 51:23). In Josephus the word *strategos* is used for a Temple official probably identical with the functionary mentioned here. In the New Testament too, *strategos* probably means the Vice-High Priest (see Acts 4:1, 5:24, 26). In Luke 22:4, 52, however, the plural *strategoi* probably refers to police officers. In the years leading up to the Destruction, the Vice-High Priest was usually a Pharisee, while the High Priesthood itself was in the hands of the Sadducees. The Vice-High Priest thus acted as a guard on the High Priest, preventing him from applying Sadducean views to the Temple service. One Vice High-

Priest, Eleazar ben Ḥananiah, took a prominent part in the Jewish War against Rome, further evidence that the Pharisees were by no means non-political, even in the years following the advent of Hillel.

*the High Priest gives it to the King*: this series of ceremonious handings-over gave due honour to the dignity of the King.

*reads it sitting*: this is held by the Talmud to show that the ceremony took place in the Court of Women, since sitting was forbidden in the Court of Priests (even in that part of it called the Court of Israelites) even to a King (unless of the House of David).

*King Agrippa*: he was remembered with affection, despite his descent from the usurper Herod I. On the female side, he was descended from the Hasmoneans.

*read it standing*: showing supererogatory virtue, in his desire to show honour to the Torah. The Talmud discusses whether it is, in fact, permitted to a king to waive his own dignity in this way, but decides that it is, where a virtuous act is involved.

*'You may not put over you a foreign man'*: in its context, this injunction excludes from the monarchy only non-Jews. Someone like Agrippa, descended from a convert to Judaism, but also with many born Jews in his ancestry, would not be excluded – indeed King David himself was in the same case, being descended from the Moabite convert Ruth, while Rehoboam, the son of Solomon was the son of the Ammonitess Naamah (I Kings 14:21), and yet his right to the succession was never questioned. The *halakah* found in the Talmud (b. Yeb. 45b) is that a convert is excluded from kingship, but someone with one parent a born Jew and the other a convert is not excluded. It is therefore difficult to understand why Agrippa became distressed at reaching the verse requiring that the King should be 'thy brother', and why he had to be reassured by the Sages. It is even more difficult to understand why some rabbis in the Talmud take the view that the Sages were *wrong* to reassure Agrippa, and even that the destruction of the Temple was a punishment for this 'flattery' (b. Soṭ. 41b; Tos. Soṭ. 7:27; y. Soṭ. 7:7). Commentators have laboured to solve this problem without success. It seems probable that the real question about Agrippa's right to the throne was not his eligibility under the law of Deut. 17:15, but his descent from the usurper Herod I, who supplanted the Hasmonean dynasty by a violent coup. At any rate, it is clear that the Mishnah takes the view that the Sages were right to reassure Agrippa. The right of the Davidic dynasty to kingship was not a bar

to Agrippa's occupation of the throne. The Hasmoneans too were of non-Davidic descent. The promise to David of perpetual kingship was regarded as referring to the messianic age, and did not preclude intervening dynasties of non-Davidic descent.

## The rights of workers

*Mishnah Baba Meṣi'a 7:1*

If a man hired labourers and told them to work early or to work late, if the custom of the area is not to work early or not to work late, he is not permitted to compel them. If the custom of the area is to provide workmen with food, he must give it to them; and where the custom is to provide them with dessert, he must do so: everything is in accordance with the custom of the region. It once happened with Rabbi Joḥanan ben Mattia that he said to his son: Go, hire workers for us. He went, and agreed to give them food. When he returned to his father (and told him what he had done), his father said to him: My son, even if you were to make for them a meal like those of King Solomon in his prime you would not have fulfilled your duty with them, for they are the children of Abraham, Isaac and Jacob. But before they begin work, go forth and say to them 'It is on condition that I am obliged to give you only bread and beans'. Rabban Simeon ben Gamaliel says, however: It was not necessary to say this: everything is according to the custom of the region.

¶ This mishnah begins by stressing the rights of workers: that they must not be compelled to endure harder conditions of work than are customary in the neighbourhood. It ends by stressing the rights of employers: that they are not bound to supply *better* conditions than are customary in the neighbourhood. The illustrative story about Rabbi Joḥanan ben Mattia and his son, however, provides a glimpse of the underlying principle governing relations between employers and workers: that every Israelite must be regarded as a prince. The use of such stories in the Mishnah frequently raises it above the humdrum level of a legal textbook (which, on the whole, it tries to be) and gives an insight into the moral concepts behind the Mishnah. Though, halakically, Rabbi Joḥanan's point (that an employer's obligation to his employees is unlimited unless qualified by specific agreement) is overruled as too hard on employers, his point remains valid on the moral level and has a place in the supererogatory code of conduct known as *middat ḥasidut* ('the saintly measure').

*work early or to work late*: i.e. before dawn or after sunset. The Talmud comments that this is so even if he is paying above-normal wages, since the workers can say that they understood this was to pay for an above-normal standard of work. It is open to the employer, of course, to *specify* that he wants extra hours worked, and if the employees agree to this beforehand, they are bound to work accordingly.
*a meal like those of King Solomon in his prime*: the reference is to I Kings 4:22–3, 'And Solomon's provision for one day was thirty measures of fine flour, and threescore measures of meal. Ten fat oxen, and twenty oxen out of the pastures, and an hundred sheep, besides harts and roebucks and fallow deer and fatted fowl'.
*for they are the children of Abraham, Isaac and Jacob*: compare M. Šab. 14:4: Kings' children may anoint their wounds (on the Sabbath) with rose-oil since it is their custom to do so on ordinary days. Rabbi Simeon says: All Israelites are Kings' children.
*everything is according to the custom of the region*: when no special conditions have been agreed, and when the custom is not contrary to some biblical or rabbinic law.

## Workers: the privilege of eating

*Mishnah Baba Meṣiʿa 7:2*
And these (workers) may eat by the authority of the Torah: he who works on produce that is attached to the ground at the time of its harvesting, and also he who works on what has been detached from the ground before its preparation is complete; and only on produce that grows from the earth. And these may not eat: he who works on what is attached to the ground at a time when it is not being harvested, and he who works on what is detached from the ground after its preparation is complete; or on something that does not grow from the earth.

¶ This mishnah gives legal substance to the law found in Deut. 23:24–5, 'When thou comest into thy neighbour's vineyard, then thou mayest eat grapes thy fill at thine own pleasure; but thou shalt not put any in thy vessel. When thou comest into the standing corn of thy neighbour, then thou mayest pluck the ears with thine hand; but thou shalt not move a sickle unto thy neighbour's standing corn'. The Mishnah takes for granted, as an established interpretation, that these verses apply not to passers-by, but to workers, working in the vineyard or field of a fellow Jew. (These verses thus cannot be used to solve the difficulty in the corn-plucking incident in the Gospels (Mark 2:23–6; Matt. 12:1–8), that Jesus' disciples, in plucking ears of corn, were offending not only against Sabbath laws but against the law of theft.) But the Mishnah seeks to define the kinds of produce to which the Deuteronomic law applies, and the kinds to which it does not apply. May a worker, for example, in a cheese factory, eat freely of the cheeses on the assembly-line, relying on his rights under the Deuteronomic law? Clearly, some distinctions are needed, to prevent a piece of kindly legislation from getting out of hand to the unjustified loss of the employer.

*by the authority of the Torah*: i.e. without previous arrangement with the employer, and without reference to local custom; this connection with the previous mishnah explains why this mishnah begins with 'and'. Even where the Torah gives no authorization, however, the worker may eat of the produce by previous agreement with the employer.

*at the time of its harvesting*: but not on unripe produce.

*before its preparation is complete*: while it is still undergoing the agricultural processes of primary production. When these are complete, the produce becomes liable for tithes (see M. Maʿas. 1:2–8, where the times are laid down for various kinds of produce). Once the time for tithing has arrived, the special privilege of the worker ceases. Thus workers in a bakery, for example, do not have the scriptural privilege. This privilege is thus interpreted to cover not merely produce plucked by the workman (as a literal reading of the biblical passage might suggest), but already plucked material on which he is working in an agricultural way (e.g. winnowing). Moreover, it is extended from the grapes and corn mentioned in the Bible to all other produce.

*something that does not grow from the earth*: thus workers on cheese or meat are excluded.

## Liability of a guardian

*Mishnah Baba Meṣiʿa 7:8*

Those whose work is only to guard (gathered) produce may eat of it if that is the local custom, but they have no scriptural right to do so. There are four kinds of guardian: he who guards without pay; he who borrows; he who guards for pay; and he who hires. He who guards without pay may take an oath in every case; he who borrows must pay in every case; he who guards for pay and he who hires may take an oath on an animal that was lamed or captured or dead, but they must pay if the animal was lost or stolen.

¶ The mishnah begins by discussing the case of a person whose work is to guard agricultural produce which is still undergoing agricultural processes. Does mere guarding constitute 'work' of the kind that entails the biblical privilege of eating the produce? The answer is 'No', since guarding does not properly constitute work on the produce; but local custom may nevertheless sanction the inclusion of guardians among other categories of agricultural workers. Even local custom, however, the Talmud adds, cannot allow a guardian to eat produce while it is still attached to the tree or ground. The mishnah now continues by analyzing the concept of 'guardian', which has been raised in incidental fashion as part of the laws of the eating-privilege of the agricultural labourer. This somewhat unmethodical sequence (one would expect the definition of 'guardian' to come in a separate section of the Mishnah) is rather typical of the Mishnah, which is only roughly divided into separate topics of law, and can often digress into different areas or even into anecdotes or reflections of a general character. The effect is that the system of the Mishnah appears as a seamless whole, in which all divisions are arbitrary and a given topic may be reached by an infinite variety of sequences.

*he who borrows:* he is also regarded as a kind of guardian, since he is responsible for returning the animal or object intact; the same applies to the hirer.

*He who guards without pay may take an oath in every case*: if the object or animal is lost or damaged, he does not have to pay its value to the owner, but must take an oath that the loss was not due to his negligence. Since he was guarding as a mere favour to the owner, his liability is the least of all the kinds of guardian. If, however, he

admits negligence, he must pay the value to the owner, since in agreeing to be guardian, he took on some responsibility.
*he who borrows must pay in every case*: the borrower, on the contrary, is the most liable of all guardians, since he brings no benefit to the owner by his guardianship, but only to himself. Even if the loss is due to unavoidable accident, he must pay the value. The Talmud adds, however, that if the animal dies in the normal course of work, the borrower does not have to pay its value, for this was the purpose for which the animal was borrowed and to which the owner agreed.
*lamed or captured or dead*: these expressions are taken from the biblical passage which lies behind the Mishnaic treatment, Exod. 22:9–13. They are taken to mean loss by unavoidable accident. The Mishnah often omits explicit reference to its biblical sources (unlike the Halakic Midrashim and the Talmud), but these are readily discernible in the vocabulary employed.

*Even the distinctions made here between different types of guardian are mostly derived from biblical sources. For the unpaid guardian, see Exod. 22:7–8. For the borrower, see Exod. 22:14. For the paid guardian, see Exod. 22:10–11 (though that this refers to the paid rather than the unpaid guardian is a result of rabbinic exegesis and harmonization). The fourth type of guardian, the hirer, is not mentioned in the Torah (though an attempt was made to find him in Exod. 22:15), and this category is a rabbinic, or at least post-biblical classification. There is dispute about his status (see b. B.M. 93a) but the present passage takes his obligations to be the same as those of a paid guardian.

## Liability: what constitutes an accident?

*Mishnah Baba Meṣiʿa 7:9*

One wolf is not an accident: two wolves are an accident. Rabbi Judah says: At a time of a plague of wolves, even one wolf is an accident. Two dogs are not an accident. Yadua the Babylonian says, on behalf of Rabbi Meir: From one direction, it is not an accident: from two directions, it is an accident. A brigand constitutes an accident. A lion or a bear or a leopard or a panther or a snake constitute an accident. When? At the time when they come of their own accord: but if he took them (the flock) to a place of numerous wild animals or brigands, it is not an accident.

¶ This rather picturesque mishnah is written in characteristically laconic style (fifty-nine words in Hebrew). The question addressed is under what circumstances a shepherd (classified as a paid guardian, and therefore responsible for loss or theft, but not for damage by unavoidable accident; see previous mishnah) may plead that an unavoidable accident has occurred. Thus though he may be absolved by taking an oath that he was not responsible, this claim may be made only within certain guidelines.

*One wolf is not an accident*: if a sheep is attacked by only one wolf, the shepherd should have been able to drive the wolf away, and therefore cannot plead 'unavoidable accident'.
*two wolves*: are considered beyond the capacity of a single man to drive away from the sheep.
*a plague of wolves*: the Hebrew word here for 'plague' is *mišlaḥat* meaning literally a 'letting-loose' or 'visitation', with the implication that this is an act of God. The word has a biblical ring ('the letting-loose of evil angels', see Ps. 78:49).
*even one wolf is an accident*: because wolves, with the backing of a nearby pack, become unusually daring so that even one wolf cannot be driven away by a single man.
*brigand*: Hebrew, *listes*, from the Greek *lestes*. The Talmud comments that even if the shepherd is armed, he cannot be expected to drive away an armed bandit, since the latter is reckless of his own life: 'He comes to kill or be killed'.
*Yadua the Babylonian*: mentioned only here. Since he does not have the title 'Rabbi', he must have remained in the status of a scholar without ordination (*semikah*). There was constant interchange between the Jewish communities of Babylonia and Palestine, Babylonians coming to study in Palestine, and, at a later stage, vice versa.
*Rabbi Meir*: one of the most famous rabbis of the Tannaitic period. He was the pupil of Rabbi Akiba, and the husband of the celebrated Beruriah, the only female authority of the Talmud.

## The value of a human life

*Mishnah Sanhedrin 4:5*

How does one cast awe on the witnesses in capital cases? They used to bring them in and cast awe on them as follows: Perhaps you will speak by guesswork, or by hearsay, or from previous evidence, or on the authority of someone you consider trustworthy; or perhaps you are unaware that we intend to examine you with searching enquiry. Know that capital cases are not like non-capital cases. In non-capital cases, a witness may atone by payment for having given wrong evidence; but in capital cases, a witness is responsible not only for the blood of the accused, but for the blood of his (unborn) descendants until the end of the world. For so we have found with Cain, who killed his brother, that it is written, 'The bloods of thy brother cry' (Gen. 4:10). It does not say, 'The blood of thy brother', but 'The bloods of thy brother', meaning his blood and the blood of his descendants. For that reason, man was created as a single individual (from whom all mankind descended), to teach you that Scripture regards one who destroys a single soul as if he has destroyed a whole world; and also Scripture regards one who saves the life of a single soul as if he has saved the life of a whole world. And also (man was created as a single individual) for the sake of peace among mankind, so that no man may say to his neighbour 'My father (*'abba*) was greater than your father'. And also that heretics should not say 'There are many powers in heaven'. And also to proclaim the greatness of the Holy One, blessed be he, for though a human being may stamp many coins with one seal, they are all identical, while the King of all Kings, the Holy One, blessed be he, has stamped every human being with the seal of Adam, yet not one of them is like his fellow. Therefore everyone is obliged to say 'For my sake the world was created'. And perhaps you (the witnesses) may say 'Why should we bother with this troublesome matter?' But has it not been said (Lev. 5:1), 'He being a witness, whether he has seen or known, if he does not utter it, then he shall bear his iniquity'? And perhaps you may say 'Why should we be responsible for the blood of this man?' But has it not been said (Prov. 11:10), 'When the wicked perish there is rejoicing'?

¶ The Mishnah confines itself, on the whole, to the task of being a law book, but here a practical context (the wording of admonishment to witnesses in capital cases) gives rise to a sublime statement of the essence of Judaism.

*cast awe on the witnesses*: the witnesses were to be solemnly admonished about the awesome seriousness of their task.

*previous evidence*: i.e. evidence heard by the present witness in some other court of law. Only eyewitness evidence was admitted.
*The bloods of thy brother*: Hebrew, *damim*. This is a plural form, but the use of such a plural is actually not uncommon grammatically. The present exegesis comes under the heading of *deraša* ('secondary, elaborative exegesis'), not *pešat* ('literal, straightforward exegesis'). A secondary exegesis merely reinforces the legal point, but does not form its main basis, which is here the common-sense perception that to deprive a man of life involves depriving his potential descendants of the chance to live.
*a single soul . . . a whole world*: every human being, like Adam and Eve, could have been the progenitor of a whole human race. Another interpretation is that just as Adam and Eve once comprised the entire human race, so even now no single human being is diminished by the co-presence of millions of fellow humans; his death is a disaster as great as that of Adam would have been before he begat descendants. Another interpretation, consonant with Jewish mysticism, is that each human being is a microcosm of the universe. The above three interpretations are not mutually exclusive.
*one who saves the life of a single soul*: the reading given in the Babylonian Talmud is 'a single soul from Israel', but the reading in the Parma text (see Part I, p. 31) of the Mishnah is 'a single soul', which is undoubtedly the correct reading in view of the universalistic context dealing not with Israel but with Adam, the father of all mankind. This is the reading given by Maimonides (*Mišneh Torah, Šopeṭim, Sanhedrin* 12:3), and was evidently found in the text of the Mishnah before him.
*has stamped every human being with the seal of Adam, yet not one of them is like his fellow*: Robert Gordis comments in 'A basis for morals', p. 35, 'The implications are clear: man's innate dignity is the source of his right to be different, which is the essence of freedom. The equality of men, as seen in their common origin, is the source of all men's right to justice'.

## Hanging

*Mishnah Sanhedrin 6:4*

A man is hanged with his face to the people and a woman with her face towards the gallows. This is the opinion of Rabbi Eliezer. But the Sages say: A man is hanged but a woman is not hanged. Said Rabbi Eliezer to the Sages: Did not Simeon ben Shetaḥ hang women in Ashkelon? They answered: He hanged eighty women, and two should not be condemned in one day.

¶ The 'hanging' referred to in this passage is not a form of execution, but the hanging up of the corpse of an executed person, in accordance with Deut. 21:22. The next verse directs that the corpse must not be left hanging overnight, 'For a hanged man is a reproach to the Lord' (Paul's interpretation (Gal. 3:13) that this refers to a curse upon the executed person is not in accordance with any rabbinic interpretation, since the execution of a criminal was regarded as atoning for his sin). Rabbi Eliezer thinks that this post-execution hanging should be performed whether the executed person is a man or woman. The Sages say that it applies only to a man, probably because the exposure of a woman was regarded as more indecent that that of a man. Rabbi Eliezer quotes a precedent: the famous authority Simeon ben Shetaḥ once hanged eighty women on one day, after their execution (for a crime unspecified in the Mishnah, but other sources say that it was witchcraft). The Sages, however, reply that this precedent is too irregular to be accepted, since normally the law does not allow more than one person to be condemned on one day; there must have been special circumstances which make this case unsuitable as a precedent.

*Simeon ben Shetaḥ*: Pharisaic leader during the reigns of King Alexander Jannai (102–76 BC) and Queen Salome Alexandra (76–67 BC). According to rabbinic tradition, he became the chief adviser of Queen Salome Alexandra, and her reign was regarded as a golden age. In the chain of tradition (M.'Ab.) he is bracketed with Judah ben Tabbai as 'receiving the law' from Nittai the Arbelite, and as having transmitted it to Shemaiah and Abtalion, the predecessors of Hillel and Shammai.

*Rabbi Eliezer*: Eliezer ben Hyrcanus, sometimes called 'Eliezer the Great', flourished about AD 90–110. He was the teacher of Rabbi Akiba. Though highly respected by the other rabbis, he eventually became estranged from them because of his obstinacy in clinging to his opinions in the face of adverse majority decisions.

*The strange case of Simeon Ben Shetaḥ and the witches, which seemed to contradict halakic norms, has puzzled many commentators. Some modern scholars have argued that the case shows that Mishnaic laws relating to executions were not in force in pre-Mishnaic times. Some have even seen the 'hangings' as crucifixions. The probable explanation, however, is that the story was originally not a legal case at all, but a folk-legend about a contest between Simeon ben Shetaḥ and a coven of witches. A version of this folk-legend can be found in the Palestinian Talmud (y. Ḥag. 2:2). Here Simeon outwits the band of eighty witches through his knowledge that a witch loses her power if she is not in contact with the earth. He tricks the witches into dancing with eighty young men, whom he has instructed to lift the witches from the ground at a pre-arranged signal. Then the young men 'went and hanged them'. This was not a legal execution, but a defeat of malign witches who could be killed only by a death that kept them above the earth from which they derived their demonic power; it was no more a legal precedent than Perseus's beheading of the Gorgons. This story, however, was transformed by the law-minded rabbis of later times into a possible legal precedent; so that they had to suppose that there must have been special circumstances to account for the apparent halakic irregularities.

## Majority decision

*Mishnah ʿEduyyot 5:6–7*

Aqabia ben Mahalale'el testified to four things. They said to him: Aqabia, recant about the four things that you have said, and we shall make you Father of the High Court of Israel. He said to them: It is better that I should be called a madman all my days than that I should become even for one hour a wicked person before God, that people may not say 'For the sake of office, he recanted'. So they excommunicated him, and he died while excommunicated, and the Court stoned his coffin. Said Rabbi Judah: God forbid that Aqabia was excommunicated! For the Temple Court was not shut in the face of any man of Israel so wise and God-fearing as Aqabia ben Mahalale'el. But whom did they excommunicate? Eliezer ben Ḥanok, who criticized the ritual cleansing of hands; and when he died, the Court sent and put a stone on his coffin. This teaches that anyone who dies while excommunicated has his coffin stoned.

At the time of his (Aqabia's) death, he said to his son: My son, retract the four things that I have been asserting. Said he: And why did you not then retract them yourself? He replied: I heard them from a majority and they heard them from a majority; I relied on what I heard, and they relied on what they heard. But you have heard from an individual, and also from a majority. It is better to leave the words of the individual and take hold of the words of the majority. Said he: Father, recommend me to your comrades. He replied: I do not recommend you. Said he: Have you perhaps found some fault in me? He replied: No, but let your deeds bring you near, or your deeds remove you afar.

¶ The majority vote of the High Court (*Bet Din*) was held to be binding on all Israel. Dissident rabbis, however, sometimes refused to accept a majority decision, being quite sure that their own view was correct, or that a tradition in their possession was authoritative. The ethics of majority decisions are thrashed out in many stories, in which the individual conscience of a recalcitrant rabbi of high stature comes into conflict with the equally urgent moral need to bow before a constitutionally valid majority decision. See for example the Talmudic story of the great Rabbi Eliezer (b. B.M. 59b), who, like Aqabia in the present passage, was excommunicated by his colleagues despite their reverence for him.

*Aqabia ben Mahalale'el*: his moral sayings are quoted in M.'Ab. 3:1. His dates are uncertain, but he probably lived before the destruction of the Temple.

*testified*: the tractate from which this passage is taken is called *'Eduyyot*, 'testimonies', because many of the opinions cited in it are introduced by the verb 'testified', as here. Some scholars have thought that the tractate *'Eduyyot* was the nucleus from which the rest of the Mishnah was developed (or, at least, contains that nucleus) and this is why it contains such miscellaneous 'testimonies', comprising a first effort towards the collection and arrangement of the traditional oral material after the destruction of the Temple. Later, the material was amplified and put into thematic order, so that the 'testimonies' found in *'Eduyyot* are mostly found repeated elsewhere in the Mishnah. If Aqabia lived *before* the Destruction, his testimony cannot have been given at the synod in Jabneh of about AD 90 (known as 'that same day') at the time of the election of Eleazar ben Azariah to the position of President, though according to tradition (b. Ber. 28a) that was the time of the drawing up of the tractate *'Eduyyot*. But it was held that on 'that same day' older testimonies were also recalled. A modern view is that *'Eduyyot* was composed at a relatively late stage of the compilation of the Mishnah.

*Father of the High Court*: this position (*'Ab Bet Din*) was second to that of the *Nasi* (literally, 'Prince') who was President of the High Court. The title could therefore be translated as 'Vice-President'. (See M. Ḥag. 2:2, where the 'pairs' are regarded as succeeding generations of *Nasi* and *'Ab Bet Din*; some scholars regard this as anachronistic.) The terms 'Great Sanhedrin' and 'Great *Bet Din*' are equivalent. There were smaller bodies which also had the name 'sanhedrin' or '*bet din*', but our present passage refers to the Great Sanhedrin, as is shown by the designation '*Bet Din* of Israel'. This body consisted of seventy-one members, including the President, though at some periods (when there were joint presidents) it contained seventy-two members. Since the time of the later Hasmoneans (first century BC), the Great Sanhedrin had only religious functions, including the decision of disputed matters of *halakah*. Its political functions were taken away from it and given to another body, also called a sanhedrin, over which at times the King presided, and at other times the High Priest. It was such a political sanhedrin, as much evidence suggests, that condemned Jesus.

*excommunicated*: this ban, called *nidduy*, consisted of social isolation, usually lasting for thirty days. The banned person had to stay at home, and could not be included in a prayer-quorum (*minyan*). The punishment was given for offences amounting to contempt of court and for offensive or obstructive behaviour. If the ban was ineffective, a severer ban, called *ḥerem*, might be imposed, in which normal relations were forbidden in study and business, as well as in prayer and social intercourse. There was nothing equivalent to the 'bell, book and candle' procedure of medieval Christian excommunications, in which supernatural sanctions were imposed.

*the Court stoned his coffin*: i.e. a single stone was laid on his coffin; see later in this passage in reference to Eliezer ben Ḥanok. This was done simply to mark the fact that he had died under the displeasure of the Court, but did not imply any punishment in the afterlife; on the contrary, it may have been meant to be a symbolic punishment atoning for the offence, just as an executed person was held to have atoned for his sin by undergoing execution.

*Rabbi Judah*: this is Rabbi Judah ben Il'ai, one of the leading figures of the Mishnah (see p. 45). He took an important part in reconstituting the Sanhedrin after the disaster of the defeat of Bar Kokhba in AD 135 and the subsequent Hadrianic persecution. He was a teacher of Rabbi Judah the Prince, the redactor of the Mishnah, and his sayings show him often at variance with Rabbi Akiba and Rabbi

Meir, whose traditions and opinions are also important sources for the Mishnah. Here we find Rabbi Judah disagreeing strongly with the anonymous account given of the excommunication of Aqabia. It is not clear, however, whether he disagrees also with the account given of Aqabia's refusal to accept the majority opinion of the 'four things'; perhaps Rabbi Judah is only saying that this disagreement did not lead to excommunication, in view of Aqabia's acknowledged wisdom and piety. He seems to be alleging, also, that the case of Aqabia has been confused with the case of another dissident rabbi, Eliezer ben Ḥanok.

*the Temple Court was not shut*: according to the Talmud (b. Pes. 64b), the meaning of this phrase is simply, 'No man in Israel was so wise and God-fearing as Aqabia ben Mahalale'el'. The expression 'The Temple Court was not shut in the face of any man so wise . . .', according to this interpretation, is simply a graphic way of saying, 'No man in Israel . . .', since the whole of Israel was present in the Temple Court at the time of its ceremonial closing at Passover (see M. Pes. 5:5). At this time, the whole people was *inside* the Temple Court engaged in offering the Passover sacrifice, in accordance with the biblical injunction, 'And the whole assembly of the congregation of Israel shall slaughter it' (Exod. 12:6). (Actually, the Temple Court could not contain so many, so they were admitted in three shifts). Nevertheless, a more natural way of understanding the Mishnah's expression is that it is equivalent to saying 'No man so wise and God-fearing as Aqabia was shut *out* of the Temple Court by being excommunicated' (an excommunicated person being barred from the Temple Court, though not from the Temple Mount, see M. Mid. 2:2).

*Eliezer ben Ḥanok*: in some readings, Eleazar. This is the only mention of his name.

*who criticized the ritual cleansing of hands*: this criticism is interesting, especially in view of the criticism ascribed to Jesus in Mark 7:1–23; Matt. 15:1–9, when asked by 'Pharisees and lawyers' why his disciples 'break the tradition of the elders' by not washing their hands before meals. It is doubtful, however, whether the ritual washing of hands was required for laymen by Pharisaic law in the time of Jesus; its institution is ascribed by the Talmud (b. Šab. 15a) to the time of the Eighteen Decrees (about AD 65). The *hygienic* washing of hands, however, was part of all ancient etiquette, and this can be found in Jewish sources at a date much earlier than the ritual washing prescribed in the Mishnah tractate *Yadayim*. It is this hygienic etiquette that Jesus' disciples, in all probability, did not observe, since Jesus, as a Hasidic Pharisee, may have held that hygienic precautions showed a lack of faith in Providence (the *Ḥasidim* are known to have held such views). (See p. 78.) Jesus' justification of his disciples supports this interpretation, since it is couched in terms of hygiene (Mark 7:14–19). (Providence has arranged that the self-purging of the body carries away all harmful substances.) The similarity between Jesus and Eliezer ben Ḥanok on this issue is thus only apparent. The ritual washing of hands to which Eliezer ben Ḥanok objected was a late refinement of the ritual-purity system by which a person's hands were held to be unclean even if his whole body was ritually clean. A special washing was thus prescribed for the hands only. There was no pretence that there was any scriptural authority for this washing. It was held that ritual hand-washing had been instituted *for priests only* and for *qodašim* only by King Solomon, that this had been extended by Hillel and Shammai for *terumah*, and that the Eighteen Decrees had extended it to laymen. The offence of Eliezer ben Ḥanok was thus not the flouting of an ancient tradition, but the rejection of a *recent* rabbinical ordinance which he regarded as unjustified and tiresome. That is why the disciplinary procedure of excommunication was thought appropriate. There were other respected rabbis who were not at all pleased about the Eighteen Decrees. The Tosephta remarks (Tos. Šab. 1:17) 'That day was as hard for Israel as the day that they made the Golden Calf' (see Exod. 32:4): i.e. the day when, by a Shammaiite majority, the Eighteen Decrees were passed. See also b. Šab. 17a and y. Šab. 1:4.

*I heard them from a majority*: it seems that the point at issue between Aqabia and the other rabbis was a historical rather than a strictly legal one: what had been the majority view in past sessions of the *Bet Din* on the 'four things'? Aqabia was convinced that he was in possession of the facts about these previous decisions; the other rabbis, however, thought that the views advocated by Aqabia had been minority views only. If the conflict between Aqabia and his colleagues had been more substantive than this (i.e. if they were reconsidering the 'four things' *ab initio*), Aqabia would have had to give way even on his own principles, for a *Bet Din* had the right to reverse a decision made by a previous *Bet Din* on a matter of law basing itself on the precedent of a previous minority opinion (M. 'Ed. 1:5). (To cancel an 'enactment', or *taqqanah*, of a previous court, as opposed to reversing an interpretation of law, required, however, a court 'greater in wisdom and in numbers': see Maimonides, *Mišneh Torah, Šopetim, Mamrim* 2:1–2.) Aqabia, in other words, was in the paradoxical situation of opposing the majority of his colleagues because of his respect for the principle of majority decision. This is thus one of the perplexities that arise from that principle: what happens when a minority or individual disagrees with a majority about whether a past decision was passed by a majority or not? Aqabia thought it his duty to stick to his view, but advised his son, who had followed him out of loyalty, to bow to the majority in the matter.

*and they heard them from a majority*: i.e. they (the opponents of Aqabia) based their view on their claim (mistaken, in Aqabia's view) that it was based on a past majority decision.

*let your deeds bring you near*: this little moral tale is appended to the main story, and has no bearing on the issue of majority decisions. It shows, however, that despite his excommunication (the historicity of which only Rabbi Judah ben Il'ai disputes), he was still regarded as a moral authority, since his moral sayings are transmitted, here and in *'Abot*; and his son takes it for granted that his father's standing remains so high that the rabbis would accept a recommendation given by him.

The 'four things' were:

1. a type of leprosy, which Aqabia declared unclean, the Sages clean;
2. a type of menstrual blood, which Aqabia declared unclean, the Sages clean;
3. the making use of the dropped-out hair of a blemished first-born animal, which Aqabia permitted, the Sages forbade;
4. the application of the law of the Suspected Adulteress (Num. 5:11–31): did it apply to a proselyte woman or to a freed bondwoman? Aqabia said it did not, the Sages said it did.

## Learning and morality

*Mishnah 'Abot 2:5–6*

Hillel says: Do not separate from the community; and do not trust yourself until the day of your death; and do not judge your neighbour until you come to his place; and do not say 'A thing that it is impossible to understand!' – for, in the end, it will be understood;

and do not say 'When I have leisure, I will study' – perhaps you will not have leisure.

He used to say: A boor cannot be a fearer of sin; an ignorant man cannot be a saint; a bashful man cannot learn; and an impatient man cannot teach; nor can anyone who engages in much business become wise; and in a place where there are no men, strive to be a man.

¶ These sayings of Hillel are based on the premise that the process of a person's life should be a continual development through learning. Such progress is possible only when the personality is kept open to development: it should not be made fixed and static through complacency; nor should it be deprived of movement through too much self-distrust. This passage thus illustrates what is the main theme of the tractate *'Abot*: the ethical character of the process of learning, i.e. that virtue is not to be found in mere simplicity or innocence, but through striving by intellectual effort towards a higher standard. The final sentence of the tractate is thus 'According to the effort is the reward'. The tractate *'Abot*, with its concept of study as an ethical process, thus presents a view of morality that contrasts with that of the New Testament, where virtue tends to be equated with innocence, and salvation is defined as the recovery of primal innocence (e.g. Matt. 18:3). The tractate *'Abot* is concerned, on the contrary, with the morality of learning and the learning of morality.

The first set of Hillel's sayings has a common theme: the importance of humility, in learning and character-development.

*Do not separate from the community*: do not prize your own worth so much that you despise the community and withdraw from it, failing to realise how much you owe to it. This warning against élitism is in keeping with the character of the Pharisees depicted by Josephus, as the party of the common people. The name 'Pharisees', though derived from the same verb *paraš*, 'to separate', used here, cannot signify an intention on the part of the Pharisees to separate themselves from the people. It was not, in any case, the name that they preferred for themselves, and was probably at first an opprobrious name given to them by their opponents the Sadducees, meaning 'sectarians'.
*do not trust yourself until the day of your death*: or, 'do not believe in yourself'. This means that one should never think that one has

overcome one's 'evil inclination', for it is active in a human being as long as he has breath.

*do not judge your neighbour until you come to his place*: do not assume that you would have done any better than your erring neighbour, if you had been faced with his temptation.

*do not say 'A thing that it is impossible to understand'*: do not think that just because you do not understand something, nobody will ever be able to explain it. This injunction has been variously translated (e.g. 'Do not say something that cannot be understood at once in the hope that it will be understood eventually'), and the above is only one possible interpretation, but it fits the Hebrew satisfactorily, and has the merit that it continues the theme of humility, whereas the other interpretations do not.

*perhaps you will not have leisure*: don't put off study until a suitable moment; how do you know how many suitable moments God will allow you?

The next group of Hillel's sayings has a tendency opposed to that of the first group: they warn against excessive self-distrust as a hindrance to development both in study and morality. Taken together, the two groups point to an awareness of human limitations combined with a respect for human dignity and capabilities: this combination of attitudes is characteristic of mishnaic and Talmudic Judaism.

*A boor*: one without cultivation or self-respect. He is defined in M. Miq. 9:6 as one who does not care about stains on his garments. Here the foundation of morality is located in a sense of one's own dignity.

*an ignorant man*: Hebrew, *'am ha-'areṣ* (literally, 'a person of the land'). This expression can have different meanings in different contexts (see pp. 69–71), but here it means one who lacks expert knowledge of the law, or a 'layman' relative to the learned man, or *talmid ḥakam* (literally, 'scholar and sage') (not, here, relative to the *ḥaber*, or member of a 'table-fellowship'). Note that it is not said that the *'am ha-'areṣ* cannot be a 'fearer of sin', i.e. a decent, honourable person. This is said only of the 'boor', and the *'am ha-'areṣ* is carefully distinguished from the boor. It is said only that the *'am ha-'areṣ* cannot be a saint, i.e. cannot rise to the highest reach of morality, which goes beyond the letter of the law. Only he who has intimate knowledge of the law can transcend it. Thus saintliness is not a matter of grace alone, but can be attained (though, of course, not inevitably) by a process of training and effort.

*a bashful man cannot learn*: over-humility is a hindrance to learning, since a pupil must have sufficient self-confidence to question his teacher and put forward objections and difficulties.

*an impatient man cannot teach*: only one who has due respect for his pupils, treating their questions seriously, can be a good teacher. This is the corollary of the last saying, for a bad teacher wants his pupils to be docile, passive and 'bashful'.

*nor can anyone who engages in much business become wise*: this apparently humdrum saying, translated thus, says simply that worldly affairs leave little time for study; it thus repeats the idea of the previous saying: And do not say 'When I have leisure, I will study' (see also Ecclus. 38:24ff and M. 'Ab. 4:10). A better translation, possibly, is that suggested by M. Jastrow in his *Dictionary of the Targumim, the Talmud Babli and Yerushalmi and the Midrashic Literature*, p. 462, 'Not everyone who has a large trade becomes experienced'. This is a warning (metaphorically expressed in terms of trade) to scholars 'Do not be over-ambitious: by trying to know too much too soon, you run the danger of superficiality': i.e. take time to learn each department of knowledge thoroughly, even though this means that your progress towards full knowledge will be gradual and slow, and you will have to confess ignorance of many things while still learning.

*in a place where there are no men, strive to be a man*: this sums up the individualism of rabbinic Judaism, which despite its stress on communal endeavour, bases itself ultimately on the worth and self-respect of the individual. This saying, winding up the series, balances the opening saying 'Do not separate from the community'. Do not be a lone individual, despising the community: but do not be afraid, if there is no community to support you, to act as a lone individual to uphold true values.

## The young and the old

*Mishnah 'Abot 4:20*

Elisha ben Abuyah says: He who learns as a child, to what may he be likened? To ink written on new paper. And he who learns while old, to what may he be likened? To ink written on used paper. Rabbi Yose bar Judah of Kefar ha-Babli said: He that learns from the young, to what may he be likened? To one that eats unripe grapes and drinks wine from his winepress. And he that learns from the old, to what may he be likened? To one that eats ripe grapes and drinks old wine. Rabbi says: Do not look at the jar but at what is in it. There may be a new jar that is full of old wine and an old one in which there is not even new wine.

¶ The unifying motif of this passage is the antithesis of youth to age. What are the advantages of being young, or being old, in the acquisition of knowledge, whether as giver or receiver?

*Elisha ben Abuyah*: he was the rabbi (*c.* AD 100–150) who defected from Judaism and was known usually not by his name, but by the epithet *Aḥer* ('another') (see p. 44). His pupil Rabbi Meir kept contact with him, in the hope of inducing him to repent. His halakic opinions are nowhere quoted in the Mishnah, yet here, surprisingly, his opinion on education is cited. In the later compilation, *'Abot deRabbi Nathan*, the whole of chapter twenty-four is devoted to his sayings. The rabbis regarded his case with pain rather than with hatred, and a legend arose that he repented with his dying breath (see y. Ḥag. 2:1). The residual respect in which he was held accounts for this citation of his views; yet it is noteworthy that the view actually chosen contains a measure of dramatic irony. For Elisha ben Abuyah was the prime example of someone whose early training did *not* make a permanent impression on him. Though the 'ink' in his case was written on 'new paper' (i.e. in infancy), it did not last. In striking contrast, Elisha's great contemporary, Rabbi Akiba, received no early training, and did not begin his study of the law until he was forty years old; yet his faith and learning remained until his death as a martyr in great old age. Thus the choice of this particular saying out of all the corpus of sayings that must have been available in Elisha's name is significant. The implication is 'Yes, early training is indeed important; but it is by no means all-important, for look who is the author of this saying – Elisha ben Abuyah! And think who his greatest colleague was – Akiba!' The sayings cited in the name of Elisha in *'Abot deRabbi Nathan* all carry a similar charge of dramatic irony, for they are all concerned with the question, 'What kind of Torah-learning lasts?'

*used paper*: from which previous writing has been erased: the paper thus does not absorb the ink so deeply, and the writing is less legible and more easily removed by wear.

*Rabbi Yose bar Judah of Kefar ha-Babli*: a well-known teacher, son of the great Judah ben Il'ai, and contemporary and friend of Judah the Prince, with whom, as here, he is often in friendly dispute.
*Rabbi*: Judah ha-Nasi (*Nasi* means 'Prince', the title of the head of the Sanhedrin), leader of the generation of *Tanna'im* which flourished from about AD 165–200, and redactor of the Mishnah. Because of his eminence he was known simply as 'Rabbi', i.e. 'teacher *par excellence*'.
*a new jar that is full of old wine*: a young man who has mature wisdom. Rabbi disagrees with Yose's too sweeping statement extolling the old above the young.

*It is interesting to compare this passage with the Gospel parable warning against putting 'new wine into old wineskins' (Mark 2:22; Matt. 9:17; Luke 5:37–9). The intention of the Gospel parable as edited is clearly that the 'new wine' of Jesus' new doctrine cannot be contained in the outdated forms ('old wineskin') of Judaism. The difficulty, however, is that 'old wine' was (and is) universally regarded as superior to 'new wine', as our passage shows. Moreover (a point usually missed), 'old wineskins' were also regarded as superior to 'new wineskins' since leather becomes less liable to burst as it matures (see Job 32:19 in AV, unnecessarily emended in NEB). Survivals of the original meaning (regarding new as bad and old as good) can be detected in the relevant Gospel passages themselves: thus, in the parallel parable about the patch on the cloak, Matt. 9:16 and Mark 2:21 use the derogatory word *agnaphou* ('unseasoned') for 'new' (as against Luke 5:36, *kainou*); while Luke 5:39 says plainly that old wine is better than new wine, which contradicts the ostensible meaning of the parable. Thus, the original meaning of Jesus' saying must have been 'Do not introduce new, untried doctrines into religion, as this endangers the fabric' – a sentiment quite out of accord with the prevailing Gospel picture of Jesus as a rebel against Judaism.

## The holiness of the land

*Mishnah Kelim 1:6*

There are ten degrees of holiness (lit. holinesses). The Land of Israel is holier than all other lands. And what is its holiness? That they bring from it the '*Omer*, and the First-fruits and the Two Loaves, which they may not bring from any other land.

*Mishnah Menaḥot 8:1*

All the offerings of the community or of the individual may be offered either from the Land or from outside the Land, from the new or from the old, except the *'omer* and the Two Loaves, which come only from the new and from the Land.

¶ These two passages are juxtaposed here in order to illustrate the attitude of Mishnaic Judaism to the holiness of the Land of Israel. The halakic approach precludes a mystical concept of this holiness, and ensures that the Land of Israel is not demarcated as an area of holiness surrounded by a world of unholiness. On the contrary, by the same criterion by which Israel is defined as holy, the other lands of the world are assigned their own degree of holiness too. The Temple, by accepting the produce of the whole world as fit for its offerings, acts as a centre of holiness for the world, not just for the Land.

*what is its holiness?*: i.e. how is its holiness expressed in practical terms?

*'Omer*: this was a sheaf of barley, which was offered, in accordance with Lev. 23:10 as 'the first of your harvest'. See M. Men. 10:3 for a description of the rite, and for the controversy between Pharisees and Sadducees about the date when it should be performed, the Pharisees holding that it should always be on the sixteenth of Nisan, while the Sadducees held that it should be on the first Sunday after the fifteenth of Nisan. Only after the bringing of the *'Omer* was the new corn permitted to be eaten (Lev. 23:14). It is because the *'Omer* is called 'the first of *your* harvest' (Lev. 23:10) that it was held that it could not be brought from an outside land.

*First-fruits*: similarly, Scripture says, 'Thou shalt take the first of all the fruit of earth which thou shalt bring from *thy* land . . .' (Deut. 26:2).

*the Two Loaves*: these are brought on Pentecost (Lev. 23:17) and are also called 'First-fruits' (*ibid.*). The Mishnaic view is that the Two Loaves mark the period from which the use of new corn is permitted in the Temple service, as opposed to the use of new corn outside the Temple, permitted from the time of the offering of the *'Omer*. The same verse says that the Two Loaves must be brought 'from *your* dwelling-places', which was held to exclude produce of outside lands.

*All the offerings*: in the context, this means 'all the meal-offerings', but in M. Par. 2:1, the same dictum is given a wider reference, applying to animal-offerings too, including even the Red Cow, from whose ashes the 'water of purification' was made (see p. 98). See, however, M. Tem. 3:5, for two exceptions in animal-offerings. It should be noted that the offerings from outside lands permitted here include offerings brought by Gentiles, permitted by the Torah (Lev. 22:25) and widely practised in rabbinical times (see M. Šeq. 1:5; 7:6).

*except the ʿOmer and the Two Loaves*: the First-fruits are omitted here, probably because the distinction between 'new' and 'old' does not apply to them, since they are new by definition.

It may be thought a difficulty that, by a rabbinical decree dated about AD 70, all gentile lands were regarded as ritually unclean (b. Šab. 15a). How then was it possible for the produce of gentile lands to be offered in the Temple? This is actually no difficulty. Ritual uncleanness and unholiness are very different things. The holiest things can become unclean (see p. 139) without losing their holiness. So the rabbinical decree did not cancel the eligibility of produce from outside lands as offerings in the Temple. Moreover, such produce would not necessarily share in the uncleanness of the lands themselves. Corn would not become unclean unless it was purposely moistened to make it susceptible to ritual impurity (see M. Makš.). Animals can never become unclean while alive (M. 'Oh. 8:1). So the rabbinical decree neither argues lack of holiness in outside lands, nor interferes with the supply of offerings from them. The reason for the rabbinical decree was that it was thought that Gentiles did not take great care to mark the sites of graves; consequently, anyone travelling in gentile lands was assumed to have acquired ritual uncleanness by passing over a gravesite. There was no prohibition against travelling to gentile lands; but on returning to the Land, the traveller was required to take a ritual bath before coming into contact with holy areas or foodstuffs.

## Tax-gatherers and uncleanness

*Mishnah Tohorot 7:6*

If tax-gatherers entered a house, the house becomes unclean. If there is a Gentile with them, they are trusted to say 'We did not enter', but not trusted to say 'We entered, but we did not touch'. If thieves entered a house, it becomes unclean only where the feet of the thieves have been.

¶ This passage has often been misunderstood, and wrongly applied to the explanation of Gospel passages involving tax-collectors. The passage does *not* mean that tax-collectors were regarded as exuding a special kind of uncleanness; they were, in fact, regarded as no more unclean than ordinary persons. Consequently, the objection recorded in several Gospel passages to Jesus' association with tax-collectors cannot have been on grounds of ritual purity, as is often asserted. The objection was that the tax-collectors (Jews who collaborated with the Roman tax-farmers in collecting exorbitant taxes often by violent means) were regarded as gangsters and also as traitors. Jesus associated with them not because he pitied them as innocent outcasts, but because he wished to bring them to repentance for their life of crime (see p. 143). Jesus' attitude towards the tax-collectors was thus no different from that of the Pharisees as regards condemnation of their sinful activities (see Matt. 5:46; 18:17), but, in the enthusiasm of his messianic mission, he had greater hopes of bringing them to repentance (though the Pharisees by no means ruled out the possibility of repentance by tax-collectors, see p. 143).

The passage gives some interesting evidence of social relations under the Roman Occupation between those who became tools of the infamous tax-farming system and their fellow Jews, by whom they were detested, yet were still regarded as Jews.

*If tax-gatherers entered a house, the house becomes unclean*: this means that all the contents of the house are assumed to be unclean. The reason is that tax-gatherers are assumed to have handled everything in the house in order to assess the wealth of the owners. An ordinary person, not a tax-gatherer, could be trusted not to rummage around the house, and therefore did not affect the contents of the house as a whole. The 'house' referred to here is the house of a *ḥaber*, who had undertaken to keep his house in a state of ritual cleanness; this is not required of ordinary persons, to whom, therefore, the entry of tax-gatherers would not matter from a ritual-purity point of view.

*If there is a Gentile with them*: the tax-gatherers were Jews, and though regarded as sinners because of their extortionary activities, they were still trusted to some extent as having some respect for the pious observances of their fellow Jews. Thus, if there was some doubt whether they had entered the *ḥaber*'s house or not, and they themselves testified that they had not, they were believed, even if they were in company with their Roman supervisor. In the absence of the supervisor, they were even believed if they testified that they had entered the house but had not touched its contents. But this latter testimony was not believed if they were in company with the supervisor, since it was not regarded as credible that the supervisor would not have insisted on the handling of the contents of the house.

*If thieves entered a house*: thieves, unlike tax-collectors, would not handle objects for the purpose of assessment, and therefore only the part of the house visibly disturbed by them became unclean.

## THE TOSEPHTA

See Part I, pp. 35 to 36, for a general characterization of the Tosephta.

The Tosephta is divided into the same six Orders as the Mishnah. It has not been studied, through the centuries, with quite the attention given to the Mishnah, with the result that its text has not been so well preserved, and presents many problems. The outstanding scholarly work, during the present century, of Saul Lieberman (*Tosefta Ki-Fshuṭah*, 9 vols., New York, 1955–73) has solved many of these problems, and has put the study of the Tosephta on a new footing.

### The Forgotten Sheaf

*Tosephta Pe'ah 3:8*

It once happened with a certain *Ḥasid* that he forgot a sheaf of corn which was in the middle of his field. He said to his son: Go and sacrifice for me a bull for a burnt offering and another bull for a peace-offering. Said his son: Father, why do you see fit to rejoice over this duty more than over all the duties mentioned in the Torah? Said his father: All the other duties of the Torah were given to us by God to be performed intentionally, but this one comes to us by inattention, so that if we perform it purposely before God, the fulfilment of this commandment does not come to our hand.

¶ This passage expresses what later became known as 'the joy of the commandment' (*simḥat ha-miṣwah*), i.e. the idea that the opportunity to perform a good deed prescribed in the Torah should be regarded as a piece of good fortune, rather than as a meritorious act for which one should claim credit. The *Ḥasid* ('saint') in this story has striven to fulfil all the biblical commandments, but one has so far eluded him – the commandment to leave a forgotten sheaf for the poor, 'When you reap the harvest in your field and forget a swathe, do not go back to pick it up; it shall be left for the alien, the orphan and the widow' (Deut. 24:19). Not being a forgetful person, the *Ḥasid* has not, until now, been able to fulfil this precept; and 'forgetting on purpose' would not count! Consequently, to celebrate his good fortune in having, for once, suffered a loss of memory, he makes a rich thanksgiving offering in the Temple.

*Ḥasid*: the category of *Ḥasid* included such charismatic figures as Ḥanina ben Dosa and Ḥoni the Circle-maker (see pp. 43 and 92). The *Ḥasidim* were members of the Pharisaic movement who aimed at a standard of conduct higher than the mere fulfilment of the laws of the Torah. Their mode of behaviour was known as *middat ḥasidut* ('the measure of the saints'), and many stories were told about their often unexpected reactions and deeds. Some *Ḥasidim* were criticized by the more middle-of-the-road Pharisees as pursuing saintliness at the cost of common sense, as when they neglected hygienic precautions out of faith in God (see p. 78). The expression *ḥasid šoteh* ('foolish saint') was coined to describe the extremist; but the *Ḥasidim* on the whole were venerated by their fellow Pharisees.
*a bull for a burnt-offering and another bull for a peace-offering*: for burnt-offerings as thanksgiving offerings, see Jer. 17:26, and for peace-offerings in thanksgiving, see Lev. 7:11–12. The burnt-offering (*'olah*) was entirely burnt, while the peace-offering (*šelamim*) was eaten, in part, by the offerer. The burnt-offering expressed the entire devotion of the offerer to God, while the peace-offering expressed fellowship with God in a shared meal. The *Ḥasid* wished to express both approaches to thanksgiving.
*this commandment does not come to our hand*: the *Ḥasid* does not mean that there is no merit in leaving behind a sheaf purposely for the poor; but such an act would be a normal act of charity, which would be a fulfilment of the biblical commandment to feed the poor (Lev. 25:35ff), not of the specific commandment concerning 'the Forgotten Sheaf'.

## Charity

*Tosephta Pe'ah 4:9–10*

The *tamḥuy* is every day, the *quppah* is from Sabbath-eve to Sabbath-eve. The *tamḥuy* is for everyone, the *quppah* is for the poor of that city. If he stayed there thirty days, he becomes like the people of the city for the *quppah*, but for clothes (he must stay) six months. And for the city-taxes, twelve months.

If a poor man put a *peruṭah* into the *quppah*, or a portion of food into the *tamḥuy*, they accept them from him; but if he did not put them in, they do not oblige him to do so. If they gave him new garments, and he returned to them old garments, they accept it from him. If he did not give, they do not oblige him to give. If he was accustomed to fine wool clothes, they give him fine wool clothes; if he was accustomed to money, they give him money; to dough, they give him dough; to bread, they give him bread; to be fed into his mouth, they feed him into his mouth; as it is said, '. . . sufficient for his need, whatever may be lacking to him' (Deut. 15:8): i.e. even a slave, even a horse. 'To him': this means a wife, as it is said, 'I will make *for him* a help meet for him' (Gen. 2:18). It happened with Hillel the Elder that he bought for a poor man of good family a horse with which he worked and a slave to serve him. Again, it happened with the men of Galilee that they used to bring for a certain old man of Sepphoris a pound of meat every day.

¶ The *tamḥuy* and the *quppah* are mentioned in the Mishnah as forms of poor-relief, but their operation is taken for granted and not explained (see p. 64). The Tosephta, as so often, fills out our understanding of the matter, and also formulates an important principle of charity.

*tamḥuy . . . quppah*: for an explanation of these terms, see p. 65.
*for the city-taxes, twelve months*: this applies not to the poor, but to ordinary citizens. This kind of loose connection is typical of rabbinic codificatory style, which sometimes aims at memorability at the expense of strict categorization.
*a peruṭah*: the smallest copper coin.
*they accept them from him*: the obligation to give charity is incumbent on the poor too, but this cannot be made an excuse for any compulsory deductions from poor-relief given to them.
*If he was accustomed to fine wool clothes*: charity must be adapted to the psychological needs of the recipient. Someone whose previous life has accustomed him to rough fare may be given rough fare in charity; but someone accustomed to delicate living would pine away if given rough fare. Jewish humour often dwells on the sublime arrogance of the Jewish beggar, who expects only the best – an attitude arising out of the *halakah*.

*'I will make for him'*: the Hebrew *lo* can mean either 'to him' or 'for him'. The exegesis is an instance of the hermeneutic method, *gezerah šawah* ('similar expression'), which deduces some similarity in meaning between two far-removed passages in the Bible because they both contain the same quirk of expression. In this instance, both passages, one in Genesis and one in Deuteronomy, contain the word *lo*, which is a common enough word, but in these two cases the word seems to have a similar redundancy, so that the verse in Deuteronomy is regarded as deliberately recalling the verse in Genesis. The upshot is that charity must go even so far as to find a wife for a man who needs one.

*Hillel the Elder*: the famous Hillel, legendary patriarch of the Pharisees, founder of the House of Hillel. He was called Hillel the Elder because of his patriarchal status. His great contemporary and rival, Shammai, was also given the title, 'the Elder'.

*for a poor man of good family*: this expression means a family with a high standard of living. For the special provision for wealthy people fallen on hard times see also p. 85.

## The perils of mysticism

*Tosephta Ḥagigah 2:3–4*

Four entered the Garden, Ben Azzai, and Ben Zoma, Aḥer and Rabbi Akiba. One looked and died; one looked and was smitten; one looked and cut the shoots; and one went up in peace and came down in peace. Ben Azzai looked and died; to him the scriptural verse applies, 'Precious in the eyes of the Lord is the death of his saints' (Ps. 116:15). Ben Zoma looked and was smitten; to him the scriptural verse applies, 'Have you found honey? Eat what is sufficient for you' (Prov. 25:16). Elisha looked and cut the shoots; to him the scriptural verse applies, 'Suffer not thy mouth to cause thy flesh to sin' (Eccles. 5:6). Rabbi Akiba went up in peace and came down in peace. To him the scriptural verse applies, 'Draw me, we will run after thee: the King hath brought me into his chambers' (S. of S. 1:4).

¶ This famous passage (of which another version is found in b. Ḥag. 14b) testifies to the practice of mysticism in rabbinic circles, though it issues a severe warning about the danger of such practice, even to those apparently well-prepared.

*the Garden*: Hebrew, *pardes*, a word derived from Persian, which also gave rise to Greek *paradeisos* and English 'paradise'. It is used to mean the sphere of mystical experience, or possibly the region in heaven to which the mystic is transported in his trance.

*Ben Azzai*: his full name was Simeon ben Azzai, but because he was never ordained as a rabbi (preferring a life of study and mystical contemplation), he is known as Ben Azzai, a form of familiar address.

*Ben Zoma*: the same applies to Ben Zoma, whose name in full was Simeon ben Zoma. They were both younger contemporaries of Rabbi Akiba. For further details of Ben Zoma's ill-fated venture into mysticism, see p. 226.

*Aḥer*: this appellation, meaning literally 'another', was given to Elisha ben Abuyah, who was at first a highly-respected colleague and rival of Rabbi Akiba, but who later became a renegade from Judaism and even joined hands with the persecutors of the rabbis. Some of his sayings were nevertheless preserved (see p. 127). His defection is traced here to the psychological effects of the incautious pursuit of mysticism, though elsewhere in the rabbinic writings, other causes are cited.

*Ben Azzai looked and died*: just before this, in the version of the story preserved in the Babylonian Talmud, comes a warning from Rabbi Akiba to his companions: when you reach the stones of pure marble, do not say 'Water, water', for it is said, 'He who speaks lies shall not be established before my eyes' (Ps. 101:7). Parallels to this warning can be found in rabbinic mystical writings (see p. 229) and also in gnostic prescriptions for negotiating the dangers of the ascent to heaven. The story in the Babylonian Talmud, however, does not continue with a failure by Rabbi Akiba's companions to heed his warning, so we must conclude that two different stories had been collated. In the main story, the mistake made by those who failed was not using the wrong words, but 'looking'. The Hebrew word here for 'looked', *heṣiṣ*, can mean 'peeped', or 'looked prematurely'. It signifies that the offender was overcome by curiosity, and looked at God's glory before full preparation had been made, thus showing an immaturity of mystical approach that proved dangerous. The aim of Jewish mysticism is always a visual experience, such as those of Isaiah and Ezekiel.

*'Precious in the eyes of the Lord is the death of his saints'*: this quotation is hard to reconcile with the general drift of the story warning against mysticism, except for a tiny minority. The quotation suggests, on

the contrary, that Ben Azzai died a blessed death through mystical union with God. The quotations, however, are probably a later addition to the story.

*'Have you found honey? Eat what is sufficient for you'*: the biblical passage continues, 'lest thou be filled therewith and vomit it'. Ben Zoma had bitten off more than he could chew of the 'honey' of mysticism, and became 'smitten' (i.e. deranged).

*Elisha looked and cut the shoots*: here Aḥer is given his real name, though some sources have 'Aḥer' at this point too. 'Cut the shoots' is an expression not often used except in relation to Elisha ben Abuyah, and there have been various opinions about its exact meaning. Some think it means that he attempted to corrupt the young people by dissuading them from studying the Torah (a story exists to this effect in y. Ḥag. 77b; S. of S. R. 1:4). More probable is that 'cut the shoots' means simply 'broke contact with the springs of religious faith'. Support for this interpretation comes from a passage in Homiletic Midrash: Make not the fence (around the laws) more important than the essentials, lest it fall down and cut the shoots (Gen. R. 19:3). Unlikely, therefore, is the interpretation that 'cut the shoots' refers to some illegitimate mystical operation in the Garden.

*'Suffer not thy mouth to cause thy flesh to sin'*: this text was probably considered appropriate because of the continuation, '. . . neither say thou before the angel that it was an error, wherefore should God be angry at thy voice . . .?' This mysterious verse suggests a context of mystical ascent to the realm of the angels; though it seems to fit better a story of 'saying the wrong thing' than one of illegitimate 'looking'.

*'Draw me, we will run after thee: the King hath brought me into his chambers'*: the Song of Songs was the focus of much mystical meditation, being interpreted as symbolic of the love between God and Israel. Rabbi Akiba, in particular, was a great devotee of the Song of Songs, defending it against those who wished to exclude it from the canon (M. Yad. 3:5).

* A rather puzzling question about the expression 'Four entered the Garden . . .' is the following: does this mean that they entered simultaneously in a joint mystical expedition, or that they entered separately? The latter is much more likely, in view of evidence from rabbinic and later sources that mystical experience took the form of solitary trance. Moreover, Ben Zoma's tragic mystical mishap is elsewhere described as a solitary trance (see p. 226). The only detail telling against this is the speech of Rabbi Akiba recorded in the Babylonian Talmud (see above), which, at first sight, is the

speech of a leader to a band of companions ascending together. This speech, however, should probably be understood as a warning issued by Rabbi Akiba to his colleagues before they separately attempted the ascent.

## Immersing the moon

*Tosephta Ḥagigah 3:35*

If the Table becomes ritually unclean, they immerse it in its time, and even on the Sabbath. It once happened that they immersed the Menorah on a Festival day, and the Sadducees were saying: Come and see the Pharisees, who immerse the orb of the moon.

¶ This is one of the Tannaitic passages in which the *perušim* are shown in conflict with the *ṣeduqim* (i.e. Pharisees versus Sadducees), and in these texts only does the word *perušim* mean unambiguously 'Pharisees', as opposed to the other possible meanings of the word ('ascetics', 'secessionists', 'heretics', 'table-fellowships'). The lack of a capital letter in Hebrew is responsible for much confusion; in English there would be no difficulty in distinguishing between, say, Republican and republican, Puritan and puritan, Liberal and liberal.

In the above passage, the Pharisees are mocked by the Sadducees for carrying out a ritual purification of the sacred Temple candelabra, the Menorah. The usual interpretation of the passage is that the Sadducees are mocking the Pharisees for their undue scrupulosity in ritual-purity matters. This interpretation, however, is almost certainly incorrect, since recent research has shown that the Sadducees were *more* scrupulous in ritual-purity matters than the Pharisees. Another interpretation must therefore be sought.

*the Table*: this is the golden Table in the outer sanctum of the Temple, on which the Shewbread was displayed (see Exod. 25:23–30; Num. 4:7; 1 Kings 7:48; 2 Chron. 4:19). The twelve loaves were changed every Sabbath.
*becomes ritually unclean*: even the holiest things could become ritually unclean, without losing their holiness. In the case of holy food, no method of purification was available, so it had to be burnt. In the case of vessels, however, purification was effected by immersion in the ritual pool (*miqweh*).
*they immerse it*: the use of the third person plural, corresponding to our impersonal 'one' or the passive, is characteristic of the Mishnah and Tosephta, which do not give apodeictic commands in the style

of the Bible, but rather give a descriptive account of how things were done. In this way (unlike the Apocrypha, Pseudepigrapha and the Qumran literature), they make evident by their unassuming style that they make no claim to be holy writ.

*in its time*: this means at the time of the changing of the loaves, which was on the Sabbath.

*even on the Sabbath*: i.e. even though this necessarily had to be done on the Sabbath, since the loaves could not be disturbed until then. It was forbidden by a rabbinical decree to immerse objects for purification on the Sabbath (M. Ter. 2:3), but such rabbinical decrees did not apply in the Temple.

*who immerse the orb of the moon*: in the version of this story given in the Palestinian Talmud, the Sadducees are quoted as saying (y. Ḥag. 3:8): See the Pharisees are immersing the sphere of the sun! (i.e. the crystalline sphere in which the sun was fixed, and the motion of which produced the motion of the sun). This makes the action of the Pharisees seem even more ridiculous in the eyes of the Sadducees, since they are representing the Pharisees as immersing not just a heavenly body, but a whole celestial sphere.

*The explanation of the above dispute between Pharisees and Sadducees would appear to be as follows. The Sadducees held that the holiest objects in the Temple could not be purified by immersion, since the Torah had enjoined that they should remain permanently in the Temple and never be removed (see, for the Table, Exod. 25:30, 'And you shall put the table of Shewbread before me *continually*', and for the Menorah, Exod. 27:20–1, 'to light a lamp *continually*'.) The only possible course for the Sadducees was to take care that the Table and the Menorah never became unclean, for if they did, no remedy was possible. They thus regarded the Menorah as immovable, like the sun or moon in their celestial spheres – indeed there is ample evidence that the Menorah symbolised the heavenly bodies (see Josephus, *War*. v.5.5. (217)). The Sadducees thus vilified the Pharisees for removing the Menorah for purification, not on the ground that this was a case of undue scrupulosity, but because it was a case of irreverence towards the Menorah, which was being treated just like any ordinary vessel. That this is the correct explanation can be verified by reference to the Tannaitic source (*baraita*) quoted in the commentary on M. Ḥag. 3:8 in the Babylonian Talmud; which shows that even among the Pharisees there was a group which thought that the Table and the Menorah should never be moved from their place for purification: instead one should just warn the priests: Take heed not to touch the Table or the Menorah. This stricter group, however, was overruled and the Pharisaic *halakah* became that both Table and Menorah could be removed and immersed. There was also an intermediate group among the Pharisees which held that the Menorah could be immersed, but not the Table: this group is represented by M. Ḥag. 3:8 itself. Our present passage in the Tosephta gives the finally accepted ruling, and is slightly later than the ruling of the Mishnah. The passage is very instructive about the type of conflict that took place between the Pharisees and the Sadducees. The latter stood for a more rigid and obscurantist attitude, while the Pharisees took a more rationalist and flexible approach, though there were stricter Pharisees who were closer to the Sadducees. In ritual-purity matters and in much else, the Sadducees were close to the Qumran sect; evidence is accumulating that the two sects were connected, the Qumran sect being a dissident branch of the Sadducees.

## Mourning for the Temple

*Tosephta Soṭah 15:11–13 (also b. B.B. 60b)*

When the Temple was destroyed, ascetics (*perušim*) increased in Israel, and they abstained from eating meat and drinking wine. Rabbi Joshua engaged them in discussion. He said to them: My sons, why do you abstain from eating meat? They replied: Shall we eat meat, which was offered every day continually on the altar, and now is abolished? He said to them: Why do you abstain from drinking wine? They replied: Shall we drink wine, which was offered as a libation on the altar, and is now abolished? He said to them: Should we also abstain from eating figs and grapes, since they used to bring them as First-fruits at Pentecost? Should we abstain from bread, since they used to bring the Two Loaves and the Shewbread? Should we abstain from drinking water, since they used to offer a water-libation on Tabernacles? They were silent. He said to them: Not to mourn at all is impossible, for the tragedy has happened (lit. the decree has been decreed), but to mourn too much is also impossible. But thus the Sages have said: When a man plasters his house, he should leave a small portion unplastered, as a remembrance of Jerusalem. A man should prepare everything that is necessary for a meal, and then leave one small thing undone, as a remembrance of Jerusalem. A woman should put on all her ornaments, and then leave aside one small thing, as a remembrance of Jerusalem. For it is said, 'If I forget thee, O Jerusalem, may my right hand forget its cunning. May my tongue cleave to my palate, if ever I think not of you, if ever I set not Jerusalem above my highest joy' (Ps. 137:5–6).

¶ This passage illustrates how the *halakah*, with its steady delineation of limits, came to the aid of the Jewish people in their despair after the destruction of the Temple by giving a behavioural outline to mourning that would allow due expression of grief without self-destructiveness.

*perušim*: this word (previously discussed on p. 139) is often translated indiscriminately as 'Pharisees', but it is obvious from the context that it does not mean 'Pharisees' here. Rabbi Joshua, who argues gently against the group in question, was a Pharisaic leader: also 'Pharisees increased in Israel' would not make sense. This passage is one of many in which *perušim* or *perušin* means 'ascetics', which is one of the non-pejorative meanings of the word.
*Rabbi Joshua*: this is the famous Joshua ben Ḥanania, who was ordained before the Destruction, and was a pupil of Rabban Joḥanan ben Zakkai. He is often portrayed in controversy, not only with fellow Pharisees, but with Alexandrian Jews, Sadducees, pagan philosophers, and even with the Emperor Hadrian (AD 117–138). He is always portrayed as an advocate of moderation and rationalism. On one occasion (b. B.M. 59b), he ruled God himself out of order, when He attempted to influence the decision of a conference of rabbis by a miracle – this story, the apex of Talmudic humanism, was declared blasphemous by the Christian prosecutors in the trial of the Talmud in 1240 at Paris (see Part I, p. 5).
*First-fruits at Pentecost*: see M. Bikk. 3:1. See p. 78.
*the Two Loaves*: these were brought at Pentecost (see Lev. 23:17), as first offering of the wheat harvest (see b. Men. 48b).
*water-libation on Tabernacles*: see M. Suk. 4:9. This rite was condemned by the Sadducees as having no basis in Scripture, but it was highly prized by the Pharisees, who observed it with great ceremony and rejoicing. See M. Suk. 5:1: He who has not seen the joy of the water-drawing has never seen joy in his life.

## Tax-gatherers and repentance

*Tosephta Baba Meṣ'ia 8:26*

Tax-collectors and publicans: their repentance is difficult. They should make restitution to those whom they know, and for the rest, he should make public utilities out of them.

¶ Those Jews who collaborated with the Roman tax-farmers by acting for them as tax-collectors were regarded as criminals, and specifically as robbers. This was because many of the taxes were regarded as unjust (e.g. the *fiscus Judaicus*, which was originally for the upkeep of the Temple, but, after the destruction of the Temple was collected by the Romans for the idolatrous purpose of the upkeep of the temple of Jupiter in Rome); and the methods of tax-collecting were often cruelly oppressive. Philo describes the tortures used by tax-collectors in Egypt (*De Specialibus Legibus* 3:159–63). Since the tax-farmers had bought the tax-concession, they were allowed to exact as much as they could extort from the people. Their violence and menaces forced many citizens into outlawry, both in Palestine and Egypt. Yet the tax-collectors were not regarded as beyond repentance. They were still Jews, and hope remained that they would return to a worthy way of life. The present passage throws much light on the incident involving Zacchaeus in Luke 19.

*publicans*: Hebrew, *mokesim*. These are the collectors of customs dues. The Talmud (b. B.Q. 113a) explains that these men were regarded as robbers only if they were non-government officials (i.e. if they were employees of tax-farmers) or were 'bound by no limit' (i.e. exacted as much as they could extort). If, however, they were government officials exacting a fixed amount, their work was regarded as legitimate, even when on behalf of the Roman authorities.

*their repentance is difficult*: the reason is that repentance was not regarded as complete without restitution. Even the Day of Atonement did not effect atonement for someone who had failed to make restitution for wrongs against his fellow man (see p. 90). The tax-collectors, who dealt with hundreds of people every day, could not possibly remember who they all were, and so make restitution to them all.

*for the rest*: i.e. the rest of the monies available for restitution.

*he should make public utilities out of them*: the principle behind this is quoted in the Talmud from an early formulation: If one robbed and he does not know whom he robbed, he must apply it to public purposes. What are such? Said Rabbi Hisda: Wells, ditches and grottoes (b. Beṣ. 29a).

*In the Gospel story of Zacchaeus, the repentant tax-collector says, 'Here and now, sir, I give half my possessions to charity: and if I have cheated anyone, I am ready to repay him four times over' (Luke 19:8). The double method of repayment is similar to that outlined in the Tosephta: payment to persons definitely known, and payment for general welfare to replace reparation to persons unknown. Zacchaeus, however, in supererogatory zeal, promises fourfold repayment to known victims. The remainder he promises to charity, not for public utilities. This may represent a mode advocated in times earlier than the Tosephta. The Tosephta and Talmud advocate a contribution to public utilities on the ground that this method may benefit actual victims of the extortion, since all use these utilities; the water-system is advocated as the best recipient of the reparation, since water is the most widely used form of public utility.

## The Noachian Laws

*Tosephta 'Abodah Zarah 8:4*

Seven commandments were given to the Sons of Noah:

to administer justice;
not to worship idols;
not to blaspheme;
not to engage in forbidden sexual relationships;
not to shed blood;
not to rob;
not to eat a limb taken from a live animal.

¶ This is the earliest listing of the Seven Laws of the Sons of Noah in the rabbinic writings. They are also listed in a different order in b. Sanh. 56a, and details of them are discussed in many different contexts. The term 'Sons of Noah' means Gentiles, and the Seven Laws constitute a *lex gentium*, or international code of law obligatory on all mankind. This means that the special provisions of the Jewish Torah, such as observance of Sabbath and festivals and the dietary laws, are not regarded as obligatory for anyone except Jews. To worship the One God, and to observe a code of elementary decency is sufficient to qualify as one of 'the righteous of the Gentiles' and thus to gain 'a portion in the World to Come' (b. Sanh. 105a). A Gentile may decide to become a full convert to Judaism, but this is not required to attain salvation or escape damnation, for he is perfectly acceptable to God as an adherent of the Noachian dispensation (Tos. Sanh. 13:2). There was some doubt and difference of opinion among the rabbis about when and how the Seven Laws were first promulgated. The majority opinion is that they were first given to Adam (except the seventh law, which did not apply to Adam since meat-eating was altogether forbidden before the Flood), and then repeated to Noah. In several Talmudic texts, the expression is used that the Sons of Noah 'accepted' the Seven Laws (rather than that they were commanded to obey them). This shows that a covenantal relationship was regarded as existing between God and the Gentiles, who freely entered into a covenant to worship him and obey his basic laws. In regard to the Jews too the language used about the giving of the Torah is sometimes that of command, and sometimes that of covenant, both aspects being regarded as essential to a commitment to God-given principles of behaviour. The Noachian Laws were frequently cited by John Selden (1584–1654) and Hugo Grotius (1583–1645) in their attempts to work out the principles of international law.

*to administer justice*: this means to set up courts and penal systems in order to ensure that the other laws are obeyed. The inclusion of this law shows that it is incorrect to interpret the Noachian Laws as merely intended to apply to the 'resident alien' (*ger tošab*) living within a Jewish society. Such a 'resident alien' is indeed included among the Noachians to whom the other laws apply, but the first of the Seven Laws envisages a world of sovereign gentile nations, each of which is responsible for the implementation of the Laws within its own territory, and this law is addressed to the governments of such nations.

*not to worship idols*: this and the next law imply that Noachians are required to adhere to monotheism. Forms of worship, however, are not laid down in this minimum code, and are left to the Noachians themselves to develop. Thus the Noachian concept implies a religious pluralism, in which many forms of monotheistic worship may coexist in the world.

*not to engage in forbidden sexual relationships*: the term used is 'the uncovering of nakednesses', the reference being to the laws against incest, adultery, homosexuality and bestiality in Lev. 18. Thus this one law actually comprises a great many laws. The Seven Laws, in fact, are merely the outline of a legal code which would be of considerable length if fully stated, and which is capable of the same kind of continuous development as the Torah.

*not to shed blood*: this is a prohibition against murder. The reason for this particular mode of expression lies in the wording of God's injunctions to Noah, regarded as the biblical source of the Seven Noachian Laws (Gen. 9:1–7, and particularly verse 6).

*not to rob*: this includes stealing and every form of dishonesty in matters of property, and thus represents a large department of legislation, rather than a single law.

*not to eat a limb taken from a live animal*: this is the rabbinical interpretation of Gen. 9:4, the literal meaning of which, however, seems to be a prohibition against the consumption of animal blood. In pre-rabbinic interpretation, indeed, this verse was interpreted in its literal sense as a prohibition against blood as food (see Jub. 7:28–31 and Acts 15:20, see below). In rabbinic law, blood was forbidden food to Jews (Lev. 7:26f), but not to Gentiles. Gen. 9:4 was thus translated as, 'Flesh that is alive you shall not eat', i.e. flesh taken from an animal while it is alive; and, since this verse was addressed to Noah, the patriarch of the Gentiles, as one of the Seven Noachian Laws, this left Gentiles free to eat blood itself. Eating the flesh of a live animal was forbidden, of course, to Jews too, who might only eat meat from an animal slaughtered by the method of *šeḥiṭah*, a method not required for Gentiles. The reason why the rabbis could not take Gen. 9:4 in a literal sense as forbidding blood-eating to Gentiles is that Deut. 14:21 explicitly permits Gentiles (in this context, resident aliens) to eat meat from an animal which has died of natural causes thus retaining its blood. It should be noted that though Lev. 17:15 prohibits the eating of blood to the 'stranger' as well as to the native Jew, the rabbis understood this verse to refer to the full convert to Judaism (*ger ṣedeq*) not to the resident alien (*ger tošab*).

*The short code of laws drawn up by James (Acts 15:19–20) to be observed by gentile converts to Christianity is best understood as a version of the Noachian Laws. There was nothing new in prescribing such rules for 'God-fearers' or Noachian monotheists, but such believers had not previously been incorporated into a messianic movement. James, an observant Jew, certainly had no intention of weakening the attachment of Jewish Christians to the observance of the Torah, or even of discouraging Gentiles from becoming full converts to Judaism if they so wished, thereby becoming Jewish Christians. James's rules were for those who wished to remain non-Jews, while sharing the belief of the Jerusalem Church in the kingship of Jesus and his imminent return. James's rules were, 'to abstain from things polluted by contact with idols, from fornication, from anything that has been strangled, and from blood'. This is only four laws instead of seven; but it may be remarked that the first law listed in the Tosephta ('to administer justice') was not applicable in this situation, being addressed to governments, not individuals. James's rule about 'idols' corresponds to laws two and three in the Tosephta, while James's law about 'fornication' corresponds to the Tosephta's fourth law. James's third law corresponds to the Tosephta's seventh law, for both evidently arise from Gen. 9:4, with James taking the older view of this verse's meaning as forbidding blood-eating to Gentiles (meat of animals that had been 'strangled' would retain the blood, as opposed to meat obtained through *šeḥiṭah*). James's fourth law, enjoining abstention 'from blood' is best understood as referring not to blood-eating (already covered by his third law) but to bloodshed, as in the Tosephta's fifth law. Thus the only essential law missing from James's list is 'not to rob', which may have dropped out of the text subject as it was to manuscript variations.

## THE TANNAITIC MIDRASHIM

See Part I, pp. 22 to 25, for a general characterization of the Tannaitic Midrashim.

It was recognized in nineteenth-century research that the Tannaitic Midrashim were of two types, those from the school of Rabbi Ishmael, and those from that of Rabbi Akiba, differing in style of exegesis and vocabulary, as well as in the names of authorities most prominently quoted. This distinction, however, has been qualified by more recent research, and it is now felt that, while valid for the (no longer extant) texts from which our present texts are derived, the distinction was blurred by redactors of the fourth century. Nevertheless, the classification holds good in the main, and the discovery by modern researchers of hitherto unknown works of the Tannaitic-Midrash type (though in fragmentary form) has made it possible to obtain a more complete picture of the genre.

The four Midrashim previously known were:

1. Mekilta (literally, 'collection'), a Midrash on Exodus, emanating from the school of Rabbi Ishmael;
2. Sifra ('book'), from the school of Rabbi Akiba, on Leviticus;
3. Sifre ('books') on Numbers, from the school of Rabbi Ishmael;
4. Sifre on Deuteronomy, from the school of Rabbi Akiba.

It now appears that there was originally a complete set of Midrashim on Exodus to Deuteronomy from each of the two schools, and three of the missing Midrashim have been reconstructed as follows:

1. A Midrash on Exodus, entitled *Mekilta of Rabbi Simeon ben Yoḥai*, from the school of Rabbi Akiba;
2. A Midrash on Numbers, entitled *Sifre Zuta*, from the school of Rabbi Akiba;
3. A Midrash on Deuteronomy, entitled *Mekilta on Deuteronomy*, or *Midrash Tanna'im*, from the school of Rabbi Ishmael.

This leaves only one Midrash still missing, that on Leviticus from the school of Rabbi Ishmael, but some fragments have been assigned plausibly to this work.

The Mekilta of Rabbi Ishmael, from which most of the following extracts have been taken, is divided into nine tractates: *Pisḥa* ('Passover'), covering Exod. 12:1 to 13:16; *Bešallaḥ* ('When he sent', first prominent word and title of the weekly lection beginning Exod. 13:17), covering Exod. 13:17 to 14:31; *Širata* ('Song'), covering Exod. 15:1–21; *Va-yassa'* ('And he caused to travel', first word of Exod. 15:22), covering Exod. 15:22 to 17:7; *'Amaleq*, covering Exod. 17:8 to 18:27; *Ba-ḥodeš* ('In the month', first word of Exod. 19:1), covering Exod. 19:1 to 20:26; *Neziqin* ('Damages'), covering Exod. 21:1; to 22:23; *Kaspa* ('Money'), covering Exod. 22:24 to 23:19; and *Šabbeta* ('Sabbath'), covering Exod. 31:12–17 and 35:1–3.

## *Mekilta*

### The Binding of Isaac

*Mekilta Pisḥa 7 on Exodus 12:13*
And I shall see the blood, and I shall pass over you.

I see the blood of the Binding of Isaac: as it is said, 'And Abraham called the name of that place Adonai-jireh' (Gen. 22:14). And elsewhere it says, 'And as he was about to destroy, the Lord saw and changed his mind' (I Chron. 21:15). What did he see? He saw the blood of the Binding of Isaac: as it is said, 'God will see for himself the lamb . . .' (Gen. 22:8).

¶ The Bible says that when God sees the blood of the paschal sacrifice on the doorposts of the houses of the Israelites, he will spare them from the plague of the first-born. The Midrash, while not denying the literal meaning of this text, adds another dimension: that God, in sparing the Israelites also 'sees', or has in mind, the blood shed by Isaac on the occasion of his Binding (*'Aqedah*). Thus we find in Judaism an idea having some apparent affinity to the atoning force of the Crucifixion in Christianity: the blood of Isaac saving the Israelites just as the blood of Jesus saves Christians. The difficulty is that, according to the biblical story, the Binding of Isaac was a bloodless occasion, since the intended sacrifice was called off. The meaning of our passage, then, is that God sees the blood that Isaac was *ready* to sacrifice, and counts it as an actual sacrifice. This, however, is not a complete explanation, as there is evidence, in Midrashic literature, of an extra-biblical version of the story of Isaac in which the Binding was not bloodless. Thus we find in Mek.

SbY. (ed. D. Hoffman, p. 4) that a quarter of a *log* of Isaac's blood was actually spilt on the altar. (This is sometimes misquoted in modern works as 'a quarter of Isaac's blood'; a *log* is equivalent to the contents of six eggs.) Further, some fragmentary Midrashim have been found which say that Isaac actually died, was reduced to ashes, and then brought back to life; and this throws some light on better-known Midrashic and Talmudic passages which refer cryptically to 'the ashes of Isaac'. On the other hand, Mid. Gen. R. 56:7 says firmly that not a drop of Isaac's blood was shed, which may be intended to quash the stories of a sacrifice, or partial sacrifice. The existence of such stories has been explained as being due to the influence of Christianity, or, alternatively, as deriving from a very ancient version pre-dating the redaction of the canon of the Torah (probably in the sixth century BC). It is clear, however, that even though a story did exist about the sacrifice, or partial sacrifice, of Isaac, this was of no central significance in Judaism, and therefore cannot really be compared to the Christian concept of the Crucifixion.

*Adonai-jireh*: this means 'the Lord will see', and the suggestion is that this name signifies that whenever the descendants of Isaac are in danger, the Lord will 'see', or remember, the blood shed, or willingly offered, by Isaac, and come to their rescue.
*the Lord saw*: this expression, found in the account of the staying of the plague provoked by David's census in I Chronicles, is cryptic, and gives room for the explanation that what God saw was 'the blood of Isaac'. The corresponding account in 2 Sam. 24 lacks this expression. A Talmudic comment (b. Ber. 62b) is that what God saw was 'the ashes of Isaac'.
*'God will see for himself the lamb'*: this is usually translated, 'God will provide . . .', but the literal meaning is 'see', which is taken here to be a prophecy (by Abraham) of the future efficacy of Isaac's sacrifice.

## On the Septuagint

*Mekilta Pisḥa 14 on Exodus 12:40*

Now the time that the children of Israel dwelt in Egypt and in the land of Canaan and in the land of Goshen was four hundred and thirty years.

(The text in Exodus actually reads: Now the time that the children of Israel dwelt in Egypt was four hundred and thirty years.)

This is one of the things which they wrote for Ptolemy, the King. Similarly, they wrote for him, 'God created in the beginning' (Gen. 1:1) (instead of, 'In the beginning God created'); 'I will make a man in an image and a likeness' (Gen. 1:26) (instead of, 'Let us make man in our image and our likeness'); 'A male with corresponding female parts created he him' (Gen. 5:2) (instead of, 'Male and female created he them'); 'And God finished on the sixth day . . . and rested on the seventh day' (Gen. 2:2) (instead of, 'And God finished on the seventh day . . . and rested on the seventh day'); 'Come, let me go down and confuse their speech' (Gen. 11:7) (instead of, 'Come, let us go down and confuse their speech); 'And Sarah laughed among her relatives' (Gen. 18:12) (instead of, 'And Sarah laughed within herself'); 'For in their anger they slew an ox and in their self-will they tore up a stall' (Gen. 49:6) (instead of, 'For in their anger they slew a man, and in their self-will they hamstrung an ox'); 'And Moses took his wife and his sons and mounted them upon a carrier of man' (Exod. 4:20) (instead of, '. . . and mounted them on an ass'); 'I have not taken one desirable thing from them' (Num. 16:15) (instead of, 'I have not taken one ass from them'); '. . . which the Lord your God has allotted to give light to all peoples' (Deut. 4:19) (instead of, '. . . has allotted to all peoples'); '. . . which I have forbidden the nations to worship' (Deut. 17:3) (instead of, '. . . which I have forbidden'); '. . . and the slender-footed' (Lev. 11:6) (instead of '. . . and the hare').

¶ We have here a rabbinic account of the composition of the Septuagint, explaining that the translators made certain alterations to the text in order to obviate misunderstandings or heretical misinterpretations. In a parallel account in b. Meg. 9a–b, a miraculous aspect is introduced: all seventy-two translators were isolated in separate cubicles, yet by Divine inspiration, they all introduced the same alterations. Other Jewish and Christian sources also emphasize the miraculous, though the earliest source, the Letter of Aristeas (see Bartlett, *Jews in the Hellenistic World*, vol. I, part I, pp. 11–34), merely says that the translators compared and harmonized their versions. The attitude of the rabbis to the Septuagint changed in the course of time from one of approbation (as here) to one of disapproval (as the Septuagint became the basis of Christian interpretation), and the Greek translation then preferred was that of Aquila (about AD 130). Only five of the twelve alterations cited here are to be found in extant texts of the Septuagint.

*and in the land of Canaan and in the land of Goshen*: this was added because the period of 430 years seemed far too long for the sojourn in Egypt, for Moses was only of the fourth generation since Jacob (Jacob, Levi, Kohath, Amram, Moses). Consequently, the period of 430 years was taken to date from the Covenant made with Abraham (Gen. 15), while the period of 400 years mentioned in Gen. 15:13 was held to date from the birth of Isaac (see p. 223). The actual period of sojourn in Egypt was held to have been 210 years, for which biblical support was found in Gen. 42:2 (the numerical value of the word *redu*, 'go down'). Extant texts of the Septuagint of Exod. 12:40 read, '. . . in the land of Egypt and the land of Canaan . . .'.

*'God created in the beginning'*: this change was designed to combat mystical interpretations of the term 'beginning', by which it was regarded as a Power contemporary with, or antecedent to, the Creator.

*'in an image and a likeness'*: the original 'our image and likeness' was cited by heretics to prove a plurality of divine Powers; later it was used to support the doctrine of the Trinity in Christianity.

*'a male with corresponding female parts'*: it was a rabbinic idea that the first Adam was a hermaphrodite, who was later separated by God into two separate beings, male and female. A similar idea is found in Plato's *Symposium*, and has been traced to a Babylonian origin. It is not clear, however, why, according to the rabbis, the Septuagint translators should have been concerned to import this idea into their text, since there was nothing heretical in taking the biblical account more literally.

*'finished on the sixth day'*: certain scoffers had accused God of working on the Sabbath. This alteration is found in extant texts of the Septuagint.

*'let me go down'*: again, the change from plural to singular combated pluralistic, dualistic or, later, Trinitarian doctrines.

*'among her relatives'*: the medieval commentator Rashi's interpreta-

tion is that this alternative was designed to meet the objection that when Abraham laughed (Gen. 17:17), he was not reproved, while Sarah was reproved for laughing (Gen. 18:13). A slight alteration of the Hebrew text makes it mean 'among her relatives' instead of 'within herself'; thus Sarah was reproved for public ridicule, while Abraham kept his doubts to himself. Perhaps this objection had been raised by sceptics or scoffers; yet it is remarkable that the rabbis here ascribe to the translators a bold emendation of the Hebrew text, rather than merely a discreet rendering.

*'slew an ox . . . tore up a stall'*: the alteration seems designed to reduce the crime of Simeon and Levi, and thus to alleviate the curse pronounced against them by their father Jacob; this verse may have been used by anti-Semites in Alexandria and elsewhere to argue that the Israelite tribes were accursed.

*'mounted them upon a carrier of man'*: scoffers may have jeered at Moses' humble mode of transport for his family. 'Carrier of man' is a vague term which might refer to camel-transport, which was regarded as more dignified. Extant texts of the Septuagint read, '. . . on beasts of burden' (instead of, '. . . on an ass').

*'one desirable thing'*: this alleged alteration requires only a slight change in the Hebrew, and gives a better sense, so it may be that this was in fact a variant reading. It is found in extant texts of the Septuagint.

*'to give light to all peoples'*: this, however, is to forestall the possible misunderstanding that God permits non-Israelites to worship the sun, moon and stars as deities.

*'forbidden the nations to worship'*: this is to forestall the misunderstanding that the heavenly bodies came into being without God's permission, and thus constitute independent cosmic Powers.

*'and the slender-footed'*: the Talmud explains that this alteration was made in order to avoid giving offence to King Ptolemy, whose wife was called 'Hare', and who might therefore feel insulted to know that the hare was designated an unclean animal. The Septuagint does actually (in verse 5, not verse 6) use the word *dasupoda* in place of the usual Greek word for 'hare', which is *lagos*, and Lagos was the name, not of Ptolemy's wife, but of his father. The word *dasupoda*, however, means not 'slender-footed', but 'hairy-footed'. A slight emendation in the text of the Mekilta, it has been suggested (*seʿirat* instead of *ṣeʿirat*), would make it read 'hairy-footed' instead of 'slender-footed'.

## Reconciliation with Egypt

*Mekilta Bešallah 1 on Exodus 13:17*
Now when Pharaoh let the people go . . .

'Letting go' (Hebrew, *šilluaḥ*); wherever this expression occurs, it means 'escorting'. For example, '. . . and Abraham went with them to let them go' (Gen. 18:16); and '. . . and Isaac let them go' (Gen. 26:31). The mouth that said: 'Moreover I will not let Israel go' (Exod. 5:2) is the same mouth that said, 'I will let you go' (Exod. 8:28). What reward did they (the Egyptians) receive for this? 'Thou shalt not loathe an Egyptian' (Deut. 23:7). The mouth that said, 'I know not the Lord' (Exod. 5:2) is the same mouth that said, 'Let me flee from before Israel, for the Lord fights for them against Egypt' (Exod. 14:25). What reward did they receive for this? 'In that day there shall be an altar to the Lord in the midst of the land of Egypt, and a pillar at its border to the Lord' (Isa. 19:19). The mouth that said, 'Who is the Lord that I should listen to his voice?' (Exod. 5:2) is the same mouth that said, 'The Lord is in the right, and I and my people are in the wrong' (Exod. 9:27). And what reward did they receive for this? They were given a place of burial, as it is said, 'Thou stretchedst out thy right hand, the earth swallowed them' (Exod. 15:12).

¶ This is a typical chain of biblical quotations showing resonances and ironies between apparently disconnected passages. The theme throughout is one of reconciliation between Israel and Egypt: Pharaoh is given credit for his expressions of contrition, even when he later cancelled them, and the end result, in messianic days, will be complete reconciliation with Egypt, which will unite with Israel in the worship of God.

*'escorting'*: Pharaoh did not merely expel the Israelites, but showed them respect and courtesy by accompanying, or escorting, them for some distance on their journey. The particular verbal form of the verb *šalaḥ* ('to send') used here undoubtedly does have this meaning of 'escorting' sometimes, though it is an exaggeration to say that it always has this meaning, and it is unlikely, from a literal point of

view, that the meaning is intended by the biblical text here. The Mekilta's interpretation is thus a *deraša* ('homiletic exegesis'), importing a meaning friendly to Pharaoh, and inculcating a mood of reconciliation with former enemies. The proof-texts, Gen. 18:16 and 26:31, are genuine instances of the meaning 'escorting'; further examples are Gen. 12:20 and 31:27. 'Escorting' (*lewayah*) was a highly regarded concept in the rabbinic culture. As an act of courtesy to a departing guest, it belonged to the sphere of polite behaviour (*derek 'ereṣ*), but when the guest was one distinguished in Torah-learning, it became an obligation of *halakah*. The duty was found in its most generalized form in the 'escorting' of a corpse to its last resting-place; all members of the local community had this obligation of *lewayah*.

*'Thou shalt not loathe an Egyptian'*: this text continues, '. . . because thou wast a stranger in his land'. Even though the Israelites were oppressed by the Egyptians, they were not exterminated, and for this owe a debt of gratitude. This reason, however, is omitted by the Mekilta, as it wishes to adduce a different reason; Pharaoh's courtesy in escorting the Israelites on their departure. The next verse says that the Egyptians, like Edomites, may 'enter the congregation of the Lord in their third generation'. This means that Egyptians may become converts and may marry other converts, but only in the third generation may marry full Jews. This restriction did not apply to converts of nations which had no record of enmity against Israel (such converts being allowed to marry a full Jew immediately on conversion). The Egyptians were thus penalized to some extent, but the penalty was to be a strictly limited one.

*'Let me flee from before Israel'*: since the speaker of this speech is 'Egypt', translators have rendered the speech in the plural, 'Let us flee from before Israel'. The Mekilta, however, understands 'Egypt' to be a royal title of Pharaoh (as in the Shakespearian 'I am dying, Egypt, dying', *Antony and Cleopatra*, Act 4 Scene 15), and the speech to be in the singular, which, grammatically, it is. Thus the blaspheming mouth of Pharaoh, in the hour of defeat, acknowledges the Lord, and, as a reward, his nation will worship the Lord in messianic days, and, as the passage from Isaiah goes on to say, will be delivered from its oppressors by a 'saviour'.

*They were given a place of burial*: the expression, '. . . the earth swallowed them', in the Song of the Sea, is taken to show God's compassion rather than his punishment, for the Egyptians were not left to drown unburied, but were given decent burial by being taken into the earth. This is a surprising interpretation, and cannot, of course, be regarded as the literal meaning of the text. Perhaps there is some resonance here with the beginning of our extract. Pharaoh has shown respect to the Israelites by 'escorting' them on their departure; in reward, the departure to death of the Egyptians is not without honour; they are given some of the respect due to the dead. As we have seen, an important observance of such respect is the *lewayah*, or 'escort', given to a corpse, and, by a submerged train of thought, this may have led to the topic of the Egyptians' burial, as if to say 'Pharaoh's *lewayah* for the Israelites was not answered by a *lewayah* for the Egyptians, but at least they had a decent burial'.

## The bones of Joseph

*Mekilta Bešallaḥ 1 on Exodus 13:19*
And Moses took the bones of Joseph with him.

To show the wisdom and saintliness of Moses: for all Israel were busying themselves with the spoil, but Moses busied himself with the duty of the bones of Joseph. It was about him that Scripture says, 'The wise of heart takes duties' (Prov. 10:8). But how did Moses know where Joseph was buried? They said: Seraḥ, the daughter of Asher, survived from that generation, and she showed Moses the burying-place of Joseph. She said to him 'The Egyptians made a coffin of metal for him, and sunk it into the midst of the Nile'. Moses came and stood by the Nile. He took a tablet of gold, and engraved on it the Explicit Name, and threw it into the river. He cried out and said 'Joseph son of Jacob! The oath which the Holy One, blessed be he, swore to Abraham our father has reached its time – that he would redeem his sons. If you rise, it is well; but if not, we are absolved from your oath'. Immediately, the coffin of Joseph floated up, and Moses took it.

¶ This is a good example of Midrashic legend, embellishing the biblical text. Miraculous additions are made to what, in the Bible, is straightforward, naturalistic narrative, and a moralistic touch is added to the character of Moses.

*'The wise of heart takes duties'*: the verb 'takes' is regarded as meaning 'takes upon himself' (rather than 'accepts' or 'takes to heart'), and the Hebrew word for 'duties' (*miṣwot*, literally, 'commandments') is given its rabbinical connotation of 'an act of special piety'.
*Seraḥ*: she became a focus of legends because she was the only woman to be mentioned among those who 'descended to Egypt' (see Gen. 46:17). Not only was she held to have survived the whole period of the Egyptian exile, but she was even held to have survived until the time of King David, being the 'wise woman' of Abel (2 Sam. 20:16–22). Moreover, she was held to have escaped death altogether and entered the Garden of Eden alive, together with Enoch, Methuselah, Elijah and others (Yalq. Š. II, 367).
*the Explicit Name*: Hebrew, *Šem ha-meforaš*. This was the Tetragrammaton, the letters of which were *yod*, *he*, *waw*, *he*, but which was normally pronounced as the quite different word, *'adonai*, meaning 'Lord' (the vowel-signs of *'adonai*, placed under the Tetragrammaton, produced in English transliteration, the name 'Jehovah', which is not a name of God in Jewish tradition). The correct vowels of the Tetragrammaton were no longer known in rabbinic times, and it was thought that a knowledge of them would confer miraculous powers on someone pronouncing the Name. The 'explicitness' of the Name in the present context, however (where the Name is written, not pronounced), cannot refer to the vocalization (since vowel-signs did not exist as a system in our period), but only to the explicit spelling of the consonants, as opposed to writing *'adonai*. The reluctance to pronounce or even write the name of God in its explicit form arose from reverence, and also possibly from a literal interpretation of Exod. 20:7.
*'your oath'*: see Gen. 50:25.

## Do not return to Egypt

*Mekilta Bešallaḥ 3 on Exodus 14:13*

For as you have seen the Egyptians today, you shall not continue to see them for ever.

In three places the Everpresent enjoined Israel not to return to Egypt: as it is said, 'For as you have seen the Egyptians today, you shall not continue to see them for ever'. And it says, 'You shall henceforth return no more that way' (Deut. 17:16). And it says, 'By the way of which I said to you: You shall see it no more again' (Deut. 28:68). In all three of them, they returned there, and in all three of them, they fell. The first was in the days of Sennacherib, as it is said, 'Woe to them that go down to Egypt for help' (Isa. 31:1). The second was in the days of Joḥanan, the son of Kareah, as it is said, 'Then it shall come to pass, that the sword, which you fear, shall overtake you there in the land of Egypt' (Jer. 42:16). The third was in the days of Trajan. In all three of them they returned, and in all three of them they fell.

Four parties arose among Israel at the sea. One said 'Let us fall into the sea'. One said 'Let us return to Egypt'. One said 'Let us make war against them'. And one said 'Let us cry out against them'. The party that said 'Let us fall into the sea', was told, 'Stand still and see the salvation of the Lord'. The one that said 'Let us return to Egypt', was told, 'For as you have seen the Egyptians today, you shall not continue to see them for ever'. The one that said 'Let us make war against them', was told, 'The Lord will fight for you'. The one that said 'Let us cry out against them', was told, 'And you shall hold your peace'.

¶ The three biblical injunctions not to return to Egypt are taken to refer prophetically to three occasions in Jewish history: 713 BC, 588 BC and AD 115. The lesson learnt by the rabbis from disastrous messianic movements is expressed here, in a context of biblical exegesis.

*'you shall not continue to see them'*: this is taken to be a command, rather than a prophecy.
*The third was in the days of Trajan*: there were great disturbances of the Jewish people in the years AD 115–17 of the reign of Trajan, involving the Jewish communities of Egypt, Cyrenaica, Libya, Cyprus, Mesopotamia and Babylonia, in the wake of Trajan's attempt to conquer the Parthian Empire. Our passage suggests that there was a significant movement of Jews to Egypt at this time, but there is no historical record of such a movement. The Jewish population of Egypt was estimated by Philo as about 1,000,000 around the year AD 40, so immigration of Jews to Egypt had been

taking place over a long period before the time of Trajan. Indeed, the Jewish population of Egypt declined rapidly during and after the reign of Trajan. The 'fall' referred to here is the persecution following the suppression of Jewish uprisings. Perhaps this persecution is here regarded as a punishment not for a return to Egypt in the actual period of Trajan, but for the gradual accumulation of Jewish population in Egypt up to this period.
*'Let us make war against them'*: the rabbis had seen the failure not only of the Jewish War (AD 66–70) and the above-mentioned Trajanic uprisings, but also of the Bar Kokhba revolt (AD 132–35). The period of the Mishnah saw a turning towards peaceful accommodation with Rome, reflected in this comment on the various parties at the Red Sea. In the future, though the messianic hope of Jewish independence from Rome was not given up, the deliverance was to be left to God, and meanwhile a practical political compromise was sought.

## The Oneness of God

*Mekilta Širata 4 on Exodus 15:3*
The Lord is a man of war, the Lord is his name.

Why is this said? Because he was revealed at the Sea like a warrior doing battle, as it is said, 'The Lord is a man of war'. He was revealed at Sinai like an old man full of mercy, as it is said, 'And they saw the God of Israel . . .' (Exod. 24:10). And when they were redeemed, what does it say? 'And the like of the very heaven for clearness' (*ibid.*). And it says, 'I beheld till thrones were placed, and one that was ancient of days did sit' (Dan. 7:9). And it says, 'A fiery stream issued . . .' (Dan. 7:10). This was so that no opening should be given to the nations of the world to say that there are two Powers; but, on the contrary, 'The Lord is a man of war, the Lord is his name'. He was in Egypt, he was at the Sea, he was in the past, he will be in the future, he is in this world, he will be in the coming world, as it is said, 'See now that I, even I, am he . . .' (Deut. 32:39). And it says, 'Who hath wrought and done it? He that called the generations from the beginning. I, the Lord, who am the first, and with the last I am he' (Isa. 41:4).

¶ The sequence of ideas here is not obvious, but the general meaning is that though God appears in different guises, sometimes as a destroying Power, and sometimes as a Power of peace and reconciliation, he is the same God in all his manifestations. This is contrasted with the erroneous doctrine of 'two Powers', or dualism, according to which a cosmic Power of destruction is in conflict with the Power of beneficence. The passage thus expounds the basic doctrine of Judaism, the unity of God, expressed in the *Shema*ʿ (see p. 205).

*'like an old man'*: it is not clear how this is deduced from the verse cited. The next verse cited (Dan. 7:9) does portray God in the guise of an old man ('ancient of days'), and perhaps it is meant that the vision of Exod. 24:10 was identical with the vision of Daniel.

*when they were redeemed*: this is an abbreviated form of a *haggadah* (see p. 19) found in a Talmudic *baraita* (see p. 35), which explains that the 'paved work of a sapphire stone' (Exod. 24:10) was a reminder to God of the brickwork constructed by the enslaved Israelites, while the 'like of the very heaven for clearness' only appeared when the Israelites were delivered. Our passage here adopts a truncated form of this *haggadah* to show that on this occasion, God revealed himself as a God of mercy. The Mekilta sometimes relies on the capability of readers to fill out the context of a remark through familiarity with haggadic ideas.

*to say that there are two Powers*: the rabbis considered that their chief ideological opponent was not so much polytheism (which they considered a weakened force) as dualism, which stemmed from the Persian religion of Zoroastrianism. Its adherents in the hellenistic world were the Gnostics, who are sometimes designated *minim* ('sectarians'), though it seems that this term can also mean Christians. The rabbis seem to have regarded Christians as believing in a doctrine of 'two Powers', probably because of the important role given in Christian thought to Satan. The dualism of the Qumran sect may also have been condemned as a doctrine of 'two Powers', though there is no clear reference to this sect in the rabbinic literature.

*'The Lord is a man of war, the Lord is his name'*: this verse is thus given the meaning 'Although the Lord sometimes appears in a destroying aspect, he is still the Lord, whose chief attribute is mercy'.

## Compensation to the injured

*Mekilta Neziqin 6 on Exodus 21:18–19*

And if men contend, and one smite the other with a stone, or with his fist, and he die not, but keep his bed; if he rise again, and walk abroad upon his staff, then shall he that smote him be quit; only he shall pay for the loss of his time, and shall cause him to be thoroughly healed.

Why is this passage said? Because it says, 'An eye for an eye!' (verse 24), but we have not heard about (compensation for) loss of work and healing-expenses . . .

'With a stone, or with his fist . . .' Telling that a stone and a fist are merely typical of instruments that can produce death. You say that this is the meaning, but perhaps it means that if he smites him with a stone or a fist he will be liable, but with anything else, he will not be liable? Another verse says, however, 'And if he smote him with a stone in the hand, whereby a man may die, and he died, he is a murderer' (Num. 35:17). This shows that he is not liable until he smites him with something that is capable of causing death. And whence do we know that it must also be in a part of the body where a blow could be fatal? This is taught by, 'And lie in wait for him and rise up against him, and smite him mortally that he die' (Deut. 19:11). This shows that he is not liable unless he smites him both with something capable of causing death and in a part of the body where a blow could be fatal.

'If he rise again and walk'. I might understand this to mean within the house; so it teaches, 'Abroad'. I might understand this to mean even if he was failing; so it teaches, 'If he rise again, and walk abroad upon his staff'. The phrase, 'upon his staff' means 'restored to health'. This is one of three things that Rabbi Ishmael used to interpret in the Torah as being metaphorical. One such interpretation was on the verse, 'If the sun be risen upon him . . .' (Exod. 22:2). But does the sun rise on him alone? Does it not rise upon the whole world? But it means: just as the sun represents peace in the world, so if it is known that he (the burglar) would have gone away from him in peace, and yet he killed him, he is guilty (of murder). The other example is, 'They shall spread the sheet' (Deut. 22:17): they shall make the matter as clear as a white sheet. So here, 'upon his staff' should be interpreted as 'restored to health'.

*'An eye for an eye'*: the rabbis take this to mean monetary compensation for the loss of an eye. Consequently, the present passage is taken to refer to additional forms of compensation. Two further heads of compensation not mentioned here, but included in rabbinic law, are for pain and for public embarrassment or humiliation caused by an injury. This makes five heads of compensation for an injury: for the injury itself, for pain, for healing, for loss of time and for indignity (see M. B.Q. 8:1).

*You say that this is the meaning*: this is a typical standardized dialogue-form for stating possible objections to a statement that has been made, and then answering them.

*with something that is capable of causing death*: this is shown by the phrase, 'whereby a man may die', and this also shows that any instrument that could be fatal is meant, not just a stone or a fist, which are merely examples.

*in a part of the body where a blow could be fatal*: this is shown by the phrase, 'smite him mortally', i.e. a blow from which death might be expected to ensue. This excludes liability for murder in cases where a light blow unexpectedly caused death.

*'restored to health'*: the Hebrew word *miš‘enet* ('staff') means literally 'support', so Rabbi Ishmael takes the whole phrase to mean 'by his own support', i.e. 'without help', which is almost the opposite of the plain meaning, 'with his staff'.

*one of three things that Rabbi Ishmael used to interpret in the Torah as being metaphorical*: Rabbi Ishmael was known to prefer a plain method of interpretation as a rule, on the principle enunciated by him (b. Ker. 11a). 'The Torah speaks in the language of men', so the three occasions on which he employed a symbolic method are regarded as noteworthy. On the other hand, many of Rabbi Ishmael's exegeses strike the modern mind as far from literal, being based on the hermeneutical methods associated with his name (see p. 172). The three exegeses mentioned here are evidently regarded as his greatest departures from literalism.

*the sun represents peace in the world*: deeds of violence are associated with darkness and the night.

*would have gone away from him in peace*: if it is clear that the burglar would have offered no violence, but would have run away on being disturbed by the householder, the latter is not entitled to kill him, even if it is still night. On a literal interpretation, however, all violence is permitted to the householder as long as day has not yet dawned. Rabbi Ishmael's abandonment of literalism is thus actuated by humanity.

*they shall make the matter as clear as a white sheet*: again Rabbi Ishmael departs from literalism in order to enact a reform of biblical law. The primitive custom of showing (on the morning after the wedding-night) the proofs of virginity (i.e. a blood-stained bed-sheet) is abolished, by being interpreted as a requirement of careful private investigation in case of doubt. Rabbi Ishmael's willingness to stretch interpretation in the interests of humane reform is in contrast to his unwillingness to do so in order to make the law more severe (see b. Sanh. 51b).

## An inductive reasoning

*Mekilta Neziqin 9 on Exodus 21:27*

And if he smite out his bondman's tooth.

I might understand this to apply even if he knocked out a milk-tooth. The text therefore teaches, 'Eye': just as an eye cannot grow back, so 'tooth' means the kind of tooth that cannot grow back.

So far I know only about a tooth or an eye, which are specifically mentioned. How do I know about all the other chief organs? You must build an induction from the two of them. The nature of a tooth is different from that of an eye, and the nature of an eye is different from that of a tooth, but the common characteristics of them are that their loss is permanent, they are chief organs which are visible, and if they are intentionally destroyed, the slave goes out a free man. Consider now the case that the master merely cut some flesh from him. The text mentions specifically the tooth and the eye, whose loss is permanent, and which are visible chief organs intentionally destroyed in such a way that they cannot grow again, and for these the slave goes free. So, I conclude, only when the part affected is one whose loss is permanent, and which is a visible chief organ, and has been intentionally destroyed in such a way that it cannot grow again, does the slave go free.

¶ This passage contains typical formal reasoning of the kind known as *middot* ('measures'). These are listed in the Thirteen *Middot* of Rabbi Ishmael, a simpler list being the Seven *Middot* of Hillel (see p. 172). These formal methods of reasoning (for which parallels can be found in other legal systems) enabled the laws of the Torah to be systematized. There are also many modes of reasoning in the rabbinic writings which were considered too straightforward and obvious to be given a technical name or included in a list of methodology.

*just as an eye cannot grow back*: the Babylonian Talmud (b. Qid. 24b) asks why the Torah did not then simply state 'eye', omitting mention of 'tooth'. The answer given is that, in that case, we might have thought that the law freeing the slave applied only to the loss of organs which were 'created with him', i.e. with which he was born, and this would have excluded 'tooth'.
*You must build an induction*: the Hebrew technical term is *binyan 'ab*, literally 'building a father', i.e. constructing a generalization. When the biblical text gives two or more specific instances, it is possible to arrive at the general law underlying these instances by considering what the instances have in common. This kind of reasoning from the particular to the general is similar to that known in modern science as 'induction'.
*The nature of a tooth is different from that of an eye, and the nature of an eye is different from that of a tooth*: this formula always introduces a *binyan 'ab* reasoning, because if the instances are too similar, nothing can be deduced. This is the principle called the Method of Agreement by John Stuart Mill in his analysis of inductive reasoning (*A System of Logic*, Longmans, Green & Co., 1947, pp. 253–264). The rabbinic formulation of the principle is 'Two instances which are identical teach nothing'. For a full discussion of the parallel between *binyan 'ab* and induction, see Louis Jacobs, *Studies in Talmudic Logic and Methodology* (London, Valentine Mitchell, 1961).

## The stranger

*Mekilta Neziqin 18 on Exodus 22:21*

And a stranger shalt thou not vex, neither shalt thou oppress him; for you were strangers in the land of Egypt.

You shall not vex him with words; and you shall not oppress him in money matters. You shall not say to him 'Yesterday you were a worshipper of Bel, Qores, Nebo, and up to now there was swine's flesh between your teeth, and you stand and speak against me!' And what proof is there that if you have vexed him, he is able to vex you? It is said, 'And a stranger shalt thou not vex, neither shalt thou oppress him; for you were strangers in the land of Egypt'. From this Rabbi Nathan used to say: a fault that is in you, do not cast up against your fellow.

Beloved are the strangers, for everywhere we find injunctions about them. 'And a stranger thou shalt not vex . . .' 'Love therefore the stranger . . .' (Deut. 10:19). 'For you know the heart of a stranger . . .' (Exod. 23:9). Rabbi Eliezer says: It is because the leaven of the stranger is evil that Scripture has so many injunctions about him. Rabbi Simeon ben Yoḥai says: Behold, it says, 'But they that love him be as the sun when he goeth forth in his might' (Judg. 5:31). Surely now, who is greater, he who loves the King, or he whom the King loves? You must say: He whom the King loves. And it is written, 'And loveth the stranger . . .' (Deut. 10:18).

Beloved are the strangers, for everywhere Scripture gives them the same description as Israel. Israel are called 'servants', as it is said, 'For to me the children of Israel are servants' (Lev. 25:55). And the strangers are called 'servants', as it is said, 'And to love the name of the Lord, and to be his servants' (Isa. 56:6). Israel are called 'ministers', as it is said, 'But you shall be named the priests of the Lord, men shall call you the ministers of our God' (Isa. 61:6). And the strangers are called 'ministers', as it is said, 'Also the aliens, that join themselves to the Lord, to minister to him' (Isa. 56:6).

. . . And so you find in the four groups who make response before him who spoke and the world came into being. 'One shall say: I am the Lord's' (Isa. 44:5), that is 'I am entirely the Lord's, and may no sin be mixed in me'. 'And another shall call himself by the name of Jacob' (*ibid.*), these are the righteous proselytes. 'And another shall subscribe with his hand to the Lord' (*ibid.*), these are the repentant. 'And surname himself by the name of Israel' (*ibid.*), these are the Heaven-fearers.

¶ The biblical word 'stranger' is usually taken by the rabbis to mean a proselyte, i.e. one who has been converted to Judaism, and has joined the Jewish nation. Having left his own family and nation, the proselyte, without kin in his adopted nation, could be isolated and friendless unless a special effort is made to welcome and befriend him.

*vex . . . oppress*: the two terms are regarded not as a mere parallelism, but as denoting two different modes of unfriendly behaviour.

*Bel, Qores, Nebo*: these three words appear in Isa. 46:1, but the second word *qores* is actually a verb meaning 'stoops' ('Bel has bowed, Nebo stoops'). Our passage, however, takes the three words to be names of deities, or possibly the triple name of one deity.

*a fault that is in you*: this is probably a folk-proverb; the rabbis were fond of finding authority for such proverbs in the Bible. The explanation given of, 'For you were strangers in the land of Egypt' is 'You too are vulnerable to taunts'. Scripture itself, however, gives the different and more morally sensitive reason, '. . . for you know the heart of a stranger, since you were strangers in the land of Egypt' (Exod. 23:9). It is probably because this reason is given in the next chapter that some other reason is sought here, since it was believed that there is no needless repetition in the Torah.

*Rabbi Eliezer says: It is because the leaven of the stranger is evil*: The contrasting attitudes of Rabbi Eliezer and Rabbi Simeon are found elsewhere in the rabbinic literature. Rabbi Eliezer regards proselytes as a necessary evil, while Rabbi Simeon thinks that they are more beloved than born Jews. This reflects the experience that proselytes tended to extremes; either they became utterly devoted to Judaism, or they failed to make the adjustment to Jewish life and lapsed into heathenism, or into dualistic heresy. The expression 'leaven', meaning inclination to evil, can be found in the New Testament (Mark 8:15; 1 Cor. 5:7–8).

*'And another shall call himself by the name of Jacob'*: this is ascribed to the proselytes, who were not born with the name of Jacob.

*'And surname himself by the name of Israel'*: this is ascribed to the 'Heaven-fearers' or 'God-fearers', who attach themselves to the God of Israel without becoming Jews, and therefore have the 'surname', or secondary name (or 'appellation', rather than 'name') of Israel. The God-fearers (often mentioned in the New Testament, e.g. Acts 10:22; 13:17), were given a respected status in Judaism as non-Jewish monotheists who adhered to the Noachian Covenant (see p. 144).

### Decision by a majority

*Mekilta Kaspa 2 on Exodus 23:2*

Thou shalt not follow a multitude to do evil; neither shalt thou bear witness in a cause to turn aside after a multitude to pervert justice.

'Thou shalt not follow a multitude to do evil'. A simple inference is that while you must not be with them to do evil, you may be with them to do good. How so? If twelve are for acquittal and eleven are for conviction, he is acquitted. If thirteen are for conviction and ten are for acquittal, he is convicted. But in case I should infer that he is convicted even if twelve are for conviction and eleven for acquittal, we are told, 'Neither shalt thou bear witness in a cause'. The Torah is telling us: sentence of death may be by the mouth of witnesses, and it may be by the mouth of judges making up a majority. Just as there must be two witnesses to produce a conviction, so there must be two judges making up a majority before there can be a conviction. If eleven are for acquittal and eleven are for conviction and one says 'I do not know', we have here an injunction to the juror not to swing the majority except for an acquittal, as it is said, 'Neither shalt thou bear witness in a cause'.

¶ The biblical moral injunction to follow one's principles irrespective of the pressure of public opinion is here given a forced interpretation in order to give biblical sanction to traditional juridical practice, by which capital cases were settled by a majority of a panel of judges. The moral injunction itself, of course, is not being denied: it is enshrined in such rabbinic sayings as: In a place where there is no man, strive to be a man (M. 'Ab. 2:5). But the effort to find biblical backing for laws of the Oral Torah which were, in fact, often based on tradition (see Part I, p. 28) sometimes leads to the wrenching of texts even when their plain meaning has moral majesty. The medieval commentator Rashi, however, warns against regarding this rabbinic interpretation of the verse as intended to be the literal meaning: he assigns it to the category of *deraša*, regarded as an additional meaning leaving intact the literal meaning (*pešat*), which, says Rashi, is simply that when acting as a member of a panel of judges, a man should not be influenced by the majority opinion, but should follow his own reading of the facts. The use of juridical words in the context ('witness' and 'cause') supports this interpretation, but the more general moral meaning of not being swayed by evil public opinion in any circumstances is also present.

*A simple inference*: this expression means that the reasoning does not involve one of the technical modes of deduction contained in the Thirteen *Middot*.

*to do evil*: since the word 'multitude' (*rabbim*) is here interpreted to mean simply 'majority' (i.e. the majority of a panel of judges trying a capital case), 'a multitude to do evil' is interpreted as 'a majority for declaring the accused guilty'. The meaning, therefore, is that a simple majority of one is not enough to convict, though it is enough to acquit.

*'Neither shalt thou bear witness in a cause'*: the use of an expression usually employed for the giving of evidence by a witness shows that there is a likeness between witnesses and members of a panel of judges: just as a conviction requires two witnesses, so it requires two judges (over and above the judges who cancel themselves out by their opposing judgements). In practice, in a panel of twenty-three (the minimum for a capital case), there must be a majority of three for a conviction, since a majority of two is impossible.

*an injunction to the juror not to swing the majority except for an acquittal*: commentators have puzzled over this remark, since even if the undecided juror made up his mind for conviction, this would not actually produce a conviction, since there would be a majority of only one. The explanation seems to be the following. In the case described, with eleven for acquittal, eleven for conviction and one undecided, the procedure is to add a minimum of two judges and try the case again (see M. Sanh. 5:5). What our present passage says is that these extra judges can only decide for acquittal, not for conviction. In that case, asks the Talmud, why not discharge the accused immediately without adding judges? One authority, Rabbi Yose, thinks that this is what should be done. Others, however, take the view that it is inconsistent with the dignity of a court to decide the matter by default, and that judges should be added until the requisite majority of one for an acquittal is obtained.

### Insufficient evidence

*Mekilta Kaspa 3 on Exodus 23:7*

And the innocent and righteous slay thou not.

Simeon ben Shetaḥ once sentenced to death a witness who had been proved to have given false evidence (in a capital case). Judah ben Tabbai said to him: May I not live to see the Consolation if you did not shed innocent blood! The Torah has said: execute by the mouth of witnesses; execute by the mouth of refuting witnesses. Just as witnesses are with two, so refuting witnesses are with two.

And once Judah ben Tabbai entered a ruin and found there a man who had been killed and was still writhing, and the sword was dripping blood in the hand of his slayer. Judah ben Tabbai said to him: May (a punishment) come upon me if it is not true that only you or I could have killed him. But what can I do, for the Torah has said, 'At the mouth of two witnesses . . . shall a matter be established' (Deut. 19:15)? But he who knows, and is the master of thoughts, will punish you. He had hardly come from there when a snake bit him and he died.

¶ The biblical injunction not to slay the innocent and righteous was regarded as too obvious to be taken literally, and was therefore taken to refer to cases where the guilt of the accused was not fully established, i.e. where the evidence was circumstantial, or where there was only one witness instead of the required two. In such cases, the judges were required to acquit the accused, however sure they might be about his guilt, and any fudging of the law in this context was regarded as a breach of the injunction not to slay the innocent. The early masters of the Pharisees were credited with the firm establishment of this principle.

*Simeon ben Shetaḥ*: he and Judah ben Tabbai formed one of the 'pairs' listed in the first chapter of *'Abot*, who headed the Pharisees in the generations leading up to the 'pair', Hillel and Shammai. The dates of Simeon and Judah may be estimated at 100–70 BC. There is some confusion in the sources about which of the two was the leader or *Nasi*, and which the subordinate, or *'Ab Bet Din*. In this version of the story, Judah is given the leading role, and Simeon is admonished, while in the Tosephta version of the story, the roles were reversed. Later legend tended to exalt Simeon over Judah, for reasons that are not clear.

*a witness who had been proved to have given false evidence*: literally, 'an intending witness', a technical term derived from the biblical verse, 'You shall treat him as he intended to treat his fellow' (Deut. 19:19). A witness proved to be false (by evidence showing him to have been elsewhere at the time of the alleged crime) had to undergo the same punishment that he had tried or intended to bring upon his fellow.

*May I not live to see the Consolation*: literally, 'May I live ...', a euphemistic expression. The Consolation means the restoration of Israel. This is a rather strange expression in the mouth of Judah ben Tabbai, in whose day Israel was independent under the rule of Queen Alexandra, and the Temple was still standing.

*if you did not shed innocent blood*: for Simeon had executed a single witness who had been proved false. Only if both witnesses had been proved false could the law of the 'intending witness' be invoked. The proof given here, however, lacks logical cogency. In the later version of the story found in b. Mak. 5b, it is omitted, and instead the principle that both witnesses must be proved false is simply stated as a tradition of the Sages, which had been overlooked on this occasion. The Talmud further embellishes the story by describing the lifelong penitence of the offending judge.

*Judah ben Tabbai entered a ruin*: other sources, too, make Simeon ben Shetaḥ the hero of this story.

*was still writhing*: Judah did not actually see the murder committed, though the circumstantial evidence was very strong. Later, however, Judah locates the inadequacy of his evidence in the fact that he is a single witness. There seems to be a conflation of two versions of the story, one of which concerned circumstantial evidence as its main point, and the other the inadequacy of one witness. A *baraita* in b. Sanh. 37b, explaining the legal inadequacy of circumstantial evidence, says 'Perhaps you saw him running after his fellow into a ruin, you pursued him, and found him sword in hand with blood dripping from it, whilst the murdered man was writhing. If this is what you saw, you saw nothing'. These words were to be addressed to witnesses in a murder case. A similar passage is found in the Mekilta immediately preceding our present passage.

## Saving life on the Sabbath

*Mekilta Šabbeta 1 on Exodus 31:13*
Above all you shall observe my Sabbaths.

Once Rabbi Ishmael, Rabbi Eleazar ben Azariah and Rabbi Akiba were walking along the road followed by Levi the Netmaker and Ishmael the son of Rabbi Eleazar ben Azariah. And this question was asked before them: Whence do we know that the duty of saving life annuls the Sabbath? . . . Rabbi Eleazar ben Azariah answered: If circumcision, which affects only one member of the body annuls the Sabbath, *a fortiori* for the rest of the whole body! . . . Rabbi Simeon ben Menasia says: Behold it says, 'And you shall keep the Sabbath for it is holy to you' (Exod. 31:14). To you the Sabbath is handed over, but you are not handed over to the Sabbath.

¶ (See b. Yoma 85b for another version, with Rabbi Simeon's saying attributed to Rabbi Jonathan ben Joseph, and another argument attributed to Rabbi Simeon ben Menasia.)
This passage is remarkable in that it shows rabbis of the second century using arguments about the Sabbath that were previously used by Jesus, as attested by the Gospels. The question may be asked, Did these rabbis derive their arguments, directly or indirectly, from Jesus, or were they drawing on a common stock of maxims, from which Jesus also drew?

The argument from circumcision, here attributed to Rabbi Eleazar ben Azariah, is found attributed to Jesus in John 7:23. The saying of Rabbi Simeon ben Menasia is very similar to the saying attributed to Jesus, 'The Sabbath was made for the sake of man, not man for the Sabbath' (Mark 2:27).

The likelihood is that these sayings preceded both Jesus and the rabbinic transmitters of traditions, and were part of the oral tradition of the Pharisees, who were concerned to humanize the laws, and especially to stress that the Sabbath was a gift from God, not a day of penance, and should therefore be observed with joy and ease.

It should be noted that Jesus' use of the saying, 'The Sabbath was given to man', shows that he had a positive attitude towards the Sabbath as a gift from God; his insistence on the Pharisaic view that healing was permitted on the Sabbath does not imply that he wished to abolish the Sabbath.

The Gospel allegations that the Pharisees opposed Jesus' healing on the Sabbath are impossible to reconcile with the actual teachings of the Pharisees. It has been suggested that these conflicts were actually between Jesus and the Sadducees, who had stricter views on Sabbath observance. Later, when the early Pauline Church was in conflict with the Pharisees, these stories were altered to make 'Sadducees' read 'Pharisees'. This would explain stories that have survived showing friendship between Jesus and the Pharisees (e.g. Luke 13:31), and between the Jerusalem Church and the Pharisees (e.g. Acts: 5:34–9), and also the strong affinity between Jesus' teachings and those of the Pharisees, suggesting that Jesus was himself a Pharisee.

Healing was not forbidden on the Sabbath by the Pharisees. It is not included among the thirty-nine kinds of work forbidden on the Sabbath (M. Šab. 7:2). A problem arose only when the *method* of healing contravened one of the thirty-nine rules; e.g. if lighting a fire were prescribed for the patient. In such a case, the ruling was that the Sabbath should be violated if the patient was in any serious danger (see b. Šab. 147). Jesus' method of healing did not involve any form of Sabbath-work (such as grinding herbs for medicines, lighting fires, or cutting up bandages). Consequently, the Pharisees would have had no objection to his healing on the Sabbath even in the case of trivial complaints that did not endanger life. Our present passage is concerned with violating the Sabbath in order to save life; but this issue would not even have been raised by Pharisees in relation to Jesus' healing on the Sabbath, which in Pharisaic eyes would not be regarded as involving any violation of the Sabbath at all. Jesus' use of stock Pharisaic arguments thus makes sense only if he is addressing an audience which believes that healing *per se* is forbidden on the Sabbath – possibly an audience of Sadducees or Essenes, who need to be persuaded that healing should not be regarded as a violation of the Sabbath. The author of the Gospel of John seems to have been aware that the Pharisees did not regard healing *per se* as a violation of the Sabbath, for he introduces an element of clay-making into a story of healing (John 9:6) which, in an earlier version (Mark 8:23) had not contained this element (clay-making would be a violation of the Sabbath). This is a late attempt to make Jesus' alleged conflict with the Pharisees over healing on the Sabbath more plausible (though, in fact, the Pharisees would have permitted any violation of the Sabbath in the case of so serious a complaint as blindness). See also John 5:9–10, where the author transfers to the Sabbath a healing story which, in an earlier version (Mark 2:1–12), had occurred on a weekday, so that the injunction, 'Take up your bed and walk' becomes a violation of the Sabbath. This shows also that the author of John was aware that healing *per se* was not regarded by the Pharisees as a violation of the Sabbath. Since he knew that carrying a bed *would* have been a violation (M. Šab. 7:2), he shifts the story to the Sabbath in order to provide *some* link between Jesus' healing on the Sabbath and alleged Pharisaic disapproval.

## *Sifra*

### The hermeneutic methods

*Sifra Introduction 7*

Hillel the Elder employed seven hermeneutic methods before the elders of Beteyra: *a fortiori* (*qal wa-ḥomer*); 'verbal similarity' (*gezerah šawah*); 'induction' (*binyan 'ab*); 'two verses' (*šeney ketubim*); 'the general and the particular' (*kelal uperaṭ*); 'the particular and the general' (*peraṭ ukelal*); 'something that is understood through its context' (*dabar ha-lamed me'inyano*).

¶ This is the earliest list of hermeneutic methods (*middot*). The text is somewhat faulty, and has been emended above in the light of the researches of A. Schwarz (whose work was partly anticipated by the medieval commentator, Rabbi Abraham ben David). The later list of Thirteen *Middot*, ascribed to Rabbi Ishmael, is an extension of the list ascribed to Hillel, in which Hillel's fifth and sixth methods are divided into eight. The *Middot* are essentially means of drawing logical inferences from biblical texts in such a way as to decide the scope and implications of the laws found in the Torah. The *Middot* of Hillel and of Rabbi Ishmael are thus used mainly in a halakic context; but they could be used also in a haggadic context, when their use was not such a seriously practical matter, and could therefore sometimes acquire an air of playfulness or *jeu d'esprit*. A list of thirty-two *Middot* intended especially for haggadic exegesis was elaborated and ascribed to the second-century Rabbi Eliezer ben Yose, the Galilean, though the compilation of these rules probably dates to as late as the eighth or ninth century.

*Hillel the Elder . . . before the elders of Beteyra*: a story exists in several versions in rabbinic literature about how Hillel, at that time a newcomer from Babylonia, argued before the 'sons of Beteyra' (the leading religious authorities of the time) that a disputed question (whether the Passover offering, the *ḥagigah*, could be slaughtered on the Sabbath) could be settled by hermeneutic methods or *middot* (see Tos. Pes. 4:12; y. Pes. 6:1; b. Pes. 66a). It was probably because of this story that the list of Seven *Middot* was ascribed to the authorship of Hillel. The list was probably compiled in the first or second century AD, though there is no need to deny that Hillel contributed to the development of such exegetical methods. The 'sons of Beteyra', or (as here) 'the elders of Beteyra' may be identical with the family of Zamaris the Babylonian, settled in Bathyra by Herod I (Josephus, *Ant.* xvii.2.2 (26)).

*a fortiori* (*qal wa-ḥomer*): the Hebrew term means literally 'light and heavy'. What is known about something 'light' can be known 'all the more so' about something 'heavy'. The *qal wa-ḥomer* argument was regarded as the basic logical tool of halakic reasoning, so much so that it is often called simply *din*, meaning 'argument'. The *qal wa-ḥomer* is a reasoning by analogy, a form of reasoning especially useful in legal argument, in which it is often necessary to compare cases. Thus rabbinic logic differs from Aristotelian logic: this is based on the syllogism, which is concerned with relations of inclusion and exclusion of classes or sets, and has its special usefulness in scientific, rather than legal, argument. Greek thinkers never developed a logic of analogy, which they regarded as a device of rhetoric, not of strict reasoning.

An example of *qal wa-ḥomer* reasoning is the following (b. B.M. 95a). It is stated in Exod. 22:14 that a borrower must pay the value of the borrowed article or animal to the owner if it is destroyed or dies. What about if the article or animal is stolen? Scripture does not tell us explicitly, but a *qal wa-ḥomer* argument yields the answer, by analogy with the case of a paid guardian:

1. A paid guardian is free from payment if the article is destroyed, but is liable if it is stolen (Exod. 22:10–12);
2. Therefore, *all the more so*, a borrower, who is liable if the article is destroyed, should be liable if it is stolen.

An important principle in the rabbinic use of the *qal wa-ḥomer* argument is called *dayo* (literally, 'it is enough for it'). This principle states that the conclusion of a *qal wa-ḥomer* argument can never contain more than its premises. Thus the following would be an invalid *qal wa-ḥomer* argument:

1. A moderately good child should be given a sweet;

2. Therefore, a very good child should be given two sweets.

The correct conclusion is:

2. Therefore, *all the more so*, a very good child should be given a sweet.

The latter is as far as one can go in strict logic, since any attempt to add to the premises must be arbitrary. The *a fortiori* arguments used by Paul in his Epistles are mostly invalid by the rule of *dayo* (e.g. Rom. 5:10), which shows that his style of argument is based on Greek rhetoric rather than rabbinic logic.

A biblical source was found both for the *qal wa-ḥomer* argument itself and for the rule of *dayo*. This was the incident of the punishment of Miriam by leprosy, when God argues as follows, 'If her father had but spit in her face, should she not be ashamed seven days? Let her be shut out from the camp seven days, and after that let her be received in again' (Num. 12:14). The argument may be paraphrased as follows: if offending a father (a relatively light thing) is punished with banishment for seven days, offending God (a relatively heavy thing) should be punished *all the more so* with banishment for seven days. The Bible here provides an impeccable *qal wa-ḥomer*, studiously refraining from adding any days to Miriam's punishment, beyond the number yielded by the principle of *dayo*.

The rabbinic theory of the *qal wa-ḥomer* also covered possible refutations of such an argument based on questioning the 'lightness' or 'heaviness' of the terms involved.

*gezerah šawah*: literally, 'similar expression'. This is a more artificial, or perhaps more literary, type of reasoning than *qal wa-ḥomer*. If a certain distinctive word or phrase is found in two different contexts in the Torah, it is assumed that the second occurrence of the word or phrase was deliberately inserted to recall the first occurrence, so that some connection should be looked for between the two contexts which would throw light on some doubtful point in one of them.

An example of *gezerah šawah* reasoning is the following (Mek. Neziqin 16). A paid guardian of goods (*šomer sakar*), who takes an oath that goods accidentally destroyed while in his care had been guarded without negligence, thereby absolves himself from paying compensation to the owner of the goods (Exod. 22:10f). In the case of an unpaid guardian, however (Exod. 22:6–8), it is not said explicitly that he must take an oath in order to indemnify himself from paying compensation. Must he then take an oath, or is a simple declaration by him (that he is not guilty of negligence) enough? The question is settled by a *gezerah šawah*. In both cases, the words are used '. . . that he has not stretched out his hand against his neighbour's property' (i.e. he has not been dishonest). This is taken as an indication that just as an oath is required in the case of the paid guardian (where it is explicitly mentioned), so it is required in the case of the unpaid guardian. (Note that the oath of a paid guardian indemnifies him against accident, but not against theft or loss, for which he is liable even if not negligent. The oath of the unpaid guardian indemnifies him against accident, theft or loss. This, indeed, is why Exod. 22:12, which makes the guardian liable for theft, is regarded as concerned with a paid guardian, even though this is not explicitly stated. Despite the overall difference in the scope of the two oaths, the *gezerah šawah* establishes that an oath must be taken in both cases.)

*binyan 'ab*: for an explanation of this method, and an example of its use, see p. 162.

*'two verses'* (*šeney ketubim*): this method concerns two verses which appear to contradict each other (Schwarz argues convincingly against other interpretations). The full statement of the method, or rule, is found in the Thirteen *Middot* of Rabbi Ishmael: When two verses contradict each other, (the solution can be found) only when a third verse comes to harmonize them.

An example of *šeney ketubim* reasoning is the following. One verse, Exod. 13:6, says, in connection with the Passover, 'Seven days shalt thou eat unleavened bread'. Another verse, Deut. 16:8, says, 'Six days thou shalt eat unleavened bread'. The third verse, which harmonizes the contradiction, is Lev. 23:14, 'And ye shall eat neither bread, nor parched corn, nor green ears, until the selfsame day that ye have brought an offering unto your God . . .' (NEB amends and changes the sense). This verse, according to rabbinic interpretation, prohibits the eating of new produce until after the offering of the *'Omer*, which took place on the morning after the first day of the festival of Passover (see p. 130). Consequently, the unleavened bread which was eaten on the first day of the festival had to be from the old produce, not from the new harvest. Thus there are two kinds of unleavened bread; that made from the old harvest, and that made from the new harvest. The first kind might be eaten all seven days of the festival, but the second might be eaten only during the last six days of the festival: one verse refers to one kind, and the other to the other kind. Harmonization of contradictory verses can, of course, be done in an infinite variety of ways, without necessarily citing a third verse, and it would be possible to point to many rabbinic examples of harmonization which do not utilize a third verse, but simply find an ingenious harmonizing idea. But the rabbis felt that it was best to find a third verse if possible, for this showed that God, in composing the Torah, had himself provided the means for harmonizing apparently contradictory passages.

*'the general and the particular'* (*kelal uperaṭ*): this principle, and the following one, refer to texts in which a general proposition is accompanied by particular instances. We are concerned, at present, with the case when the general proposition comes first, and the particular instances later. In this case, our hermeneutical rule states that the particular instances limit the scope of the general proposition.

An example of *kelal uperaṭ* reasoning is the following. '. . . you shall bring your offering of the cattle; of the herd and of the flock' (Lev. 1:2). The word 'cattle' (*behemah*) is a general word, which might be construed as including undomesticated as well as domesticated animals. The specifications 'of the herd' and 'of the flock', however, should not be regarded as mere instances, but as limiting the term 'cattle' to these particulars, i.e. to domesticated animals, which alone may be offered as sacrifices.

*'the particular and the general'* (*peraṭ ukelal*): on the other hand, when the particulars come first, and then the general term or proposition, the opposite rule holds: the general term is not limited to the scope of the particulars. An example of *peraṭ ukelal* reasoning is the following (given, like the previous example, by the Sifra). 'If a man delivereth to his neighbour an ass, or an ox, or a sheep, or any beast to keep, and it die . . .' (Exod. 22:10). Here we have first the particulars, 'ass', 'ox', 'sheep', and then the general term, 'any beast'; and the rule states that the general term must be regarded as including any animal whatever, not just those specified in the particulars.

The above two rules may be regarded as common-sense analysis of linguistic usage, in which the use of a general term, followed by particulars, is intended as a narrowing-down process, while the opposite procedure is intended as a widening process. In the Thirteen *Middot* of Rabbi Ishmael, these two rules are extended by considering the following cases: where a general term is followed by a particular term, and then by a general term; where either the general term or the particular term is ambiguous; where a special detail is appended to one particular already covered by a general term; where a particular is mentioned, apparently unnecessarily, without any special detail being involved; where a particular is to be regarded as an exception to the general rule.

*'something that is understood through its context'* (*dabar ha-lamed me'inyano*): an example found in the Babylonian Talmud (b. Ḥul. 63a) is as follows. Lev. 11:18, among a list of forbidden birds, includes the word *tinšemet*, and the same word is included in Lev. 11:30 among a list of 'creeping things'. We must not assume that the same creature is being mentioned in both cases, but must conclude from the context that in one case, the word is the name of a bird, and in the other, the name of a 'creeping thing'. The Talmud thus identifies the word as meaning in one context 'bat', and in the other 'mole'.

## *Sifre*

### The punishment of the beloved

*Sifre Deuteronomy 26 on Deuteronomy 3:23*
At that same time I pleaded with the Lord . . .

This is what is meant by the text, 'The poor man speaks in a tone of entreaty, and the rich man gives a harsh answer' (Prov. 18:23).

Two good leaders arose for Israel, Moses and David, King of Israel. Moses said before the Holy One, blessed be he, 'Lord of the Universe, let the transgression which I committed be written after me, so that people should not say "It seems that Moses falsified the Torah, or said something which was not commanded".'

This may be likened to a King who decreed 'Anyone who eats unripe figs of the Seventh Year shall be paraded in the campus'. A certain woman, of good family, gathered and ate unripe figs of the Seventh Year, and they paraded her in the campus. She said to him 'I pray you, my lord King, make known my fault, so that the people of the region may not say "It seems that some matter of adultery or witchcraft was found in her". If they see unripe figs hanging from my neck, they will know that it is because of them that I am paraded'. So Moses said before the Everpresent 'May the transgression which I committed be written after me'. Then the Holy One, blessed be he, said 'Behold I am writing that it was only the matter of the water, as it is said, "For you and Aaron disobeyed my command . . ." (Num. 27:14).'

Rabbi Simeon says: It may be likened to a King who was going on a journey, and his son was with him in his carriage. He came to a narrow place, and his carriage was overturned on his son, whose eye was blinded, his hand cut off and his leg broken. Whenever the King reached that place, he would say 'Here my son was injured: here his eye was blinded, here his hand was cut off, here his leg was broken'. Just so the Everpresent mentions three times, 'The waters of Meribah', 'The waters of Meribah,' 'The waters of Meribah' (Num. 20:13, 24; 27:14); as if to say 'Here I killed Miriam', 'Here I killed Aaron', 'Here I killed Moses'. And so he says, 'Their judges were overthrown through a rock' (Ps. 141:6).

David said before the Everpresent 'I have committed a transgression; let it not be written after me'. Said the Everpresent to him 'Is it not acceptable to you that people should say "Because he loved him, he forgave him?"' It may be likened to someone who borrowed from the King a thousand *kors* of wheat every year. All the people used to say 'Is it possible that this man can stand by a thousand *kors* of wheat every year?' And the King did not demand a pledge, but he wrote for him a promise to pay. Once he reserved (his goods) and did not pay him (the King) anything. The King then entered his house, and took his sons and daughters, and placed them on the selling-stone. In that hour, all knew that he had not (previously) reserved anything in his hand. So, indeed, all the punishments which came on David were redoubled, as it is said, 'He shall pay for the lamb four times over' (2 Sam. 12:6). Rabbi Ḥananiah says: The word *'arbaʿtayim* means sixteen times. So too the prophet Nathan came and reproved him over that deed which he did, and David said, 'I have sinned against the Lord' (2 Sam. 12:13). What did he say to him? 'The Lord has put away your sin; you shall not die.' And he says, 'Against thee, thee only, I have sinned, and done what displeases thee' (Ps. 51:4).

Two good leaders rose up for Israel, Moses and David, King of Israel, and they could have made the world depend on their good deeds, but when they sought a gift from the Everpresent, they asked for it as an undeserved gift. And is not this a case for an *a fortiori* argument? If these, who could have made the world depend on their good deeds, prayed to the Holy One, blessed be he, as for an undeserved gift, all the more so someone who is not reckoned as one of the many thousands and myriads of their disciples' disciples should pray to the Holy One, blessed be he, only as one praying for an undeserved gift.

¶ Here we have some examples of the rabbinic use of parables, which were characteristic of the Pharisaic style of preaching, as employed also by Jesus. The end of the passage is significant in relation to the rabbinic doctrine of merits and 'good works', while the passage as a whole throws light on the rabbinic attitude towards punishment, reward and forgiveness.

*and the rich man gives a harsh answer*: the 'rich man' of this proverb is interpreted as an allegory of God, refusing Moses' prayer to be allowed to enter the Promised Land (Deut. 3:25–8). This rather daring interpretation (implying some criticism of God's refusal) is found more explicitly in Deut. R. 2:4, but in b. Sanh. 44a, the 'rich man' is interpreted as Joshua.
*be written after me*: i.e. be written in the Torah, so that posterity will know it.
*Moses falsified the Torah*: Moses is represented as not concerned about his own good name, but only that doubt might be thrown on the authenticity of the Torah, if the nature of his transgression is unknown.
*unripe figs of the Seventh Year*: it was forbidden to cultivate crops in the Seventh Year (Exod. 23:10), but crops which grew without cultivation during that year were common property and could be gathered and eaten by anyone. The King might be concerned, however, that some growths of this kind were unhealthy, and forbid their use.
*shall be paraded in the campus*: the word here is *qanpon*, derived from the Latin *campus*, or more probably from its Greek form, *kampos*, meaning a public area.
*Rabbi Simeon says: It may be likened to a King*: Rabbi Simeon's parable

of the King and his son is not relevant to the previous one, but arises out of the verse quoted at the end of the previous paragraph. Such loose links are frequent in the Midrashim. Many rabbinic parables are about 'a King and his son'. For an example of the genre in the Gospels, see Matt. 22:1–14.

*the Everpresent mentions three times, 'The waters of Meribah'*: the repetition of this expression suggests that it stirred especial grief in God. Rabbi Simeon shows here a degree of literary sensitivity, for the repetition does seem significant in the narrative. The Hebrew for 'Everpresent' is *maqom*, which means literally 'place', and a *midrash* explains that God is called 'Place' because 'he is the place of the world, but his world is not his place', i.e. all things are situated in him, but he has no location (Gen. R. 68).

*'Their judges were overthrown through a rock'*: in the context, this does not refer to Moses, Aaron and Miriam, but Midrashic interpretation often takes a verse out of its context. The translation 'through a rock' depends on taking the Hebrew expression *biydey sela'* in a sense more appropriate to Mishnaic than to classical Hebrew.

*let it not be written after me*: David asked that his sin with Bathsheba should not be recorded in Scripture. Moses was anxious that his sin should not be exaggerated and so wished it to be recorded; but David's sin was heinous, involving both adultery and indirect murder (2 Sam. 11:6–17).

*'Is it not acceptable to you that people should say Because he loved him, he forgave him?'*: David is regarded in the rabbinic literature as the supreme exemplar of repentance. Thus David is adjured by God, in this remarkable Midrashic dialogue, to accept his role in the Bible as an example to all mankind of the power of repentance and of the mercy and forgiving love of God, even though this means that the baseness of David's sin will be made known to all future generations. The parable that follows seems, at first sight, not quite appropriate to the theme of God's love of the repentant sinner, but, in fact, it does pursue an aspect of this theme.

*'Is it possible that this man can stand by a thousand kors of wheat every year?'*: the people suspected that the man was failing to pay his dues to the King, who was allowing him to default. A *kor* (or *ḥomer*) was equivalent to about 12½ bushels.

*all knew that he had not (previously) reserved anything in his hand*: the point of the parable is that when a person receives a severe punishment from God, this shows that previously he had been blameless. The idea behind this is that those whom God especially loves should not expect their sins to be overlooked, but, on the contrary, that their sins will receive especially severe punishment. Biblical expressions of this idea are Deut. 8:5; 2 Sam. 7:14; Ps. 89:29–32; Amos 3:1–2; Prov. 3:12. The severity of God's punishment of David thus shows how much God loved him and how much was expected of him. Thus the parable pursues the topic of God's treatment of those whom he loves especially, and confirms the importance of the case of David as the chief biblical illustration of God's correction of his people. The parable, however, is not directly relevant to God's forgiveness as evidence of his love; it rather stresses that forgiveness is harder to attain for God's people than for those who have not been brought into his inner sanctuary. Further evidence is now given of the severity of David's punishment.

*redoubled*: the expression implies 'doubled and redoubled'. That David had to pay for his sin fourfold (in fulfilment of his unconscious prophecy, 2 Sam. 12:6) is further elaborated in the Babylonian Talmud, which enumerates the fourfold punishment as follows: the death of his child (2 Sam. 12:18), the death of Amnon, the death of Tamar, and the death of Absalom (b. Yoma 22b).

*sixteen times*: the Hebrew word *'arba'tayim* seems to be a dual form, which Rabbi Ḥananiah takes to imply the square of four. Rabbi Ḥanina is concerned to emphasise even more the severity of God's punishment for his favourites.

*'The Lord has put away your sin; you shall not die'*: the final movement of this episode is to return to the theme of David's repentance and God's forgiveness. The effect of David's punishment and suffering is reconciliation with God.

*they could have made the world depend on their good deeds*: they could have said rightly that without the merit of their good deeds the world would not have deserved to continue.

*they asked for it as an undeserved gift*: this is derived from the word used for Moses' act of prayer, *'etḥanan* ('pleaded'), which is derived from the same root as the word *ḥen* ('grace'). The same word is used for David's act of prayer in Ps. 30:8, while in verse 10 of the same psalm, David prays directly, '. . . be gracious to me'. For a similar exegesis of Num. 6:25, see Sifre Num. 41, which adduces also Ps. 123:2, 3 and Isa. 33:2. Such rabbinic passages as these should be set against any over-simplified account of the rabbinic 'doctrine of merits'. When Moses and David prayed to God, they claimed nothing as of right, but threw themselves on God's grace, and how much more should we, their unworthy descendants, do the same!

## TANNAITIC PASSAGES IN THE TALMUD (*BARAITAS*)

See Part I, p. 35, for a general characterization of the Tannaitic passages in the Talmud.

### Martyrdom

*Babylonian Talmud Sanhedrin 74a*

Rabbi Joḥanan said in the name of Rabbi Simeon ben Yehoṣadaq: They were counted and they decided in the upper chamber of the house of Nitzah in Lydda that in the case of all the transgressions in the Torah, if they said to a man 'Transgress that you may not be killed', he should transgress and not be killed, except idolatry, the 'uncovering of nakednesses', and the spilling of blood. But is idolatry excluded? Has it not been taught: Rabbi Ishmael said: Whence (do we know) that if they said to a man 'Serve an idol that you may not be killed', that he should serve and not be killed? From the verse, '. . . he shall live by them' (Lev. 18:5). And not that he should die by them. Does this mean even in public? (No), for Scripture teaches, 'Neither shall ye profane my Holy name; but I will be hallowed' (Lev. 22:32). They ruled according to the opinion of Rabbi Eliezer. For it has been taught: Rabbi Eliezer said, 'And thou shalt love the Lord thy God with all thy heart and with all thy soul and with all thy might' (Deut. 6:5). If it is said, 'with all thy soul', what need is there to say, 'with all thy might'? And if it is said, 'with all thy might', what need is there to say, 'with all thy soul'? If there is a man whose life is dearer to him than his money, for him it is said, 'with all thy soul'; and if there is a man whose money is dearer to him than his life, for him it is said, 'with all thy might'.

¶ The Babylonian Talmud was redacted in the sixth century AD, but, like all rabbinic compilations, it contains earlier material. The present passage contains two *baraitot*, i.e. traditions from the Tannaitic period, and these portions of the passage belong to our period and are quoted as they were first composed. The passage as a whole gives valuable evidence of a very important debate that took place in the period before the redaction of the Mishnah. Which precepts of the Torah were so important that a person should be prepared to undergo martyrdom to uphold them? This was a question of great practical urgency both at his period and at later periods of Jewish history.

*Rabbi Joḥanan*: the greatest of the Palestinian *'Amora'im*, who flourished in the third century. His full name was Rabbi Joḥanan bar Napaḥa, but he is usually referred to simply as Rabbi Joḥanan. His teachings comprise a great portion of the Palestinian Talmud.
*Rabbi Simeon ben Yehoṣadaq*: there is some doubt as to whether he was a *Tanna* or an *'Amora*. In b. Suk. 11b, he is quoted as a *Tanna*, but in b. Sanh. 26a, he appears in a story as a contemporary of Rabbi Joḥanan. On many occasions, Rabbi Joḥanan transmits his opinions, as here, which would be unlikely in the case of a minor contemporary. *Tosaphot* (a medieval commentary on the Babylonian Talmud, composed by the disciples of Rashi, and regarded as a supplement to Rashi's own commentary) therefore concludes (b. Suk. 11b) that there were two of this name, one a *Tanna* and the other an *'Amora*, and that when Rabbi Joḥanan quotes him, it is the *Tanna* who is concerned. This seems likely, and in that case, it is understandable that Rabbi Joḥanan should transmit in his name a historical recollection of a previous generation. Further, Rabbi Simeon ben Yehoṣadaq is twice referred to as the teacher of Rabbi Joḥanan (b. Yoma 43 and b. R.Š. 34).
*They were counted and they decided*: this is the usual phrase for a majority vote at a council of rabbis.
*in the upper chamber of the house of Nitzah in Lydda*: this same 'upper chamber' is mentioned in relation to other decisions and even other councils (e.g. b. Qid. 40), so it seems that it was a regular council-chamber provided by the family of Nitzah, probably a wealthy and pious family. Compare the 'upper room' used by the early Church (Acts 1:13). Lydda was a great centre of Jewish learning up to the time of the Bar Kokhba revolt (AD 132–5). There was an early Christian community there (Acts 9:32–5).
*the 'uncovering of nakednesses'*: this biblical phrase (Hebrew, *gilluy 'arayot*, Lev. 20:11–21) is used to include the sexual offences, of a major kind, forbidden in the Bible, i.e. incest and adultery. In a situation in which one is able to prevent violence, it is permitted to shed the blood of the aggressor to prevent a rape, as well as to prevent murder, though not to prevent bestiality (see M. Sanh. 8:7,

which also forbids killing a person to prevent him from engaging in idolatry or breaking the Sabbath). In such a context, the deciding issue is whether there is a victim to be protected.

*the spilling of blood*: i.e. murder.

*Has it not been taught*: this is one of the phrases that are used regularly to introduce a *baraita*, i.e. a tradition of Tannaitic authority that was not included in the Mishnah (*baraita* meaning 'outside').

*Rabbi Ishmael*: a *Tanna* of great authority, who was however overruled in this instance in favour of Rabbi Eliezer.

*he shall live by them*: the full verse is, 'And you shall keep my statutes and my judgements: which if a man do, he shall live by them; I am the Lord your God'. This verse was also used to prove that in all cases of danger to human life, the Sabbath-laws should be broken if rescue or healing required this.

*Does this mean even in public?*: Rabbi Ishmael's lenient ruling (that one need not die rather than perform an act of idolatry) is here qualified: only when the act of idolatry is performed in private is it permitted; if force is used to compel a person to perform an act of idolatry in public (i.e. in the presence of ten Jews), he should undergo martyrdom, since such public idolatry constitutes a profanation of God's name. It is not quite clear, however, whether the qualification is part of Rabbi Ishmael's original statement, or a later addition intended to expound his view. The biblical example of Shadrach, Meshach and Abednego (Dan. 3) makes the qualification essential.

*with all thy soul*: the Hebrew noun used here is *nefeš*, which can be taken to mean 'life', and is so understood here.

*with all thy might*: the Hebrew noun *me'od* is understood to mean 'resources'. The whole sentence therefore means that one should sacrifice one's life and/or all one's property rather than fail in love of God by committing an act of idolatry. Rabbi Eliezer is thus understood to be saying that there is an unequivocal duty to undergo martyrdom rather than serve idolatry, an opinion that differs from the qualified view of Rabbi Ishmael, who makes a distinction between an act performed in private and one performed in public. This distinction however, according to the Talmud, is valid in another way: for it is laid down that the pre-eminence of the three commandments for martyrdom holds only for acts performed in private, while in public, even less important commandments require martyrdom. There is some disagreement among later commentators whether martyrdom, when not required, is positively forbidden: Maimonides holds that it is suicide and therefore wrong, while others hold that it is an act of supererogatory virtue. The martyrdom of Eleazar in 2 Macc. 6, rather than eat forbidden meat in public, was not in contradiction to the rabbinic view; but the martyrdom of those who died by refusing to defend themselves when attacked by the Syrian–Greeks (1 Macc. 2) on the Sabbath was mistaken on rabbinic principles, by which the duty of self-preservation overrode all Sabbath prescriptions (see b. Šab. 19a); a principle which was in fact first laid down during the Maccabean revolt (same chapter).

*Martyrdom, known as 'sanctification of the Name' (*qidduš ha-šem*) was regarded as the highest expression of faith. It was held that the command to love God with 'all thy soul' was a call to martyrdom. It was this biblical command that was cited by Rabbi Akiba, the most famous of the martyrs, who was tortured to death by the Romans because of his refusal to obey the Hadrianic decrees against Judaism. At the same time, a strong distinction was made between genuine martyrdom and suicidal folly. In making this distinction, the rabbis made clear that the moral commandments had precedence over the ritual commandments, and the three greatest moral commandments were isolated for this purpose. To give up one's life for the sake of a ritual commandment was regarded as wrong unless a greater principle was at stake – the public profanation or renunciation of God.

## THE TARGUMS

See Part I, p. 29, for a general characterization of the Targums.

The Targums that can be assigned, or partly assigned, to our period are the following:

*The Official Targums* so-called because they were accepted into the service of the synagogue:

1. *Targum Onqelos.* On the Pentateuch, attributed to Onqelos the Proselyte, sometimes confused by the Talmud with Aquila, the translator of the Bible into Greek.
2. *Targum Jonathan.* On the Prophets (including Joshua, Judges, Samuel and Kings, regarded in Jewish tradition as the work of prophets). Attributed to Jonathan ben Uzziel, the greatest pupil of Hillel (see b. Meg. 3a).

The above two Targums show strong similarities in language and style.

*The Palestinian Targum.* On the Pentateuch, so-called because it was considered, by modern scholars, that it alone originated from Palestine, the Official Targums originating from Babylonia; this view, however, is now doubtful (see Part I, p. 30). The Palestinian Targum exists in various recensions:

1. *Targum Pseudo-Jonathan*. The ascription to Jonathan ben Uzziel was due to a misreading of an abbreviation for 'Jerusalem' (i.e. the original name was *Targum Yerušalmi*);
3. *The Fragmentary Targum*. About 1000 verses of this have survived.
3. *Neofiti I*. This is a manuscript of the Palestinian Targum discovered in the Vatican in 1956, covering the complete Pentateuch.

Fragments of various recensions of the Palestinian Targum have been found in the Cairo Genizah (a store-room of documents of ancient and medieval times, preserved by the dry climate of Egypt).

Fragments of an early Targum on Job were found at Qumran. It shows more linguistic affinity to the Official Targums than to the Palestinian Targum.

*Targum on Genesis 3:10*

*Hebrew*: I heard your voice in the garden.

*Onqelos*: I heard the voice of your word in the garden.

¶ The Targums often put 'word' (*memra*, *memar*, or, sometimes, *dibbur*) or 'word of God' where the Hebrew simply has 'God'. In most cases, this is a respectful circumlocution, used especially where there might seem to be a hint of anthropomorphism. Thus here, the anthropomorphic 'voice' of God, heard by Adam in the garden, is distanced from the unknowable essence of God by being attributed to a kind of emanation from God called God's 'word'. Sometimes, however, the 'word of God' means simply his revealed word in the Torah. The question has often been raised whether the Targumic 'word' has anything in common with the Logos, the hypostatized creative aspect of God, as found in Greek philosophy and in Philo, and whose incarnation Jesus is claimed to be in the Gospel of John. In some Targumic usages, the 'word' does seem to be more than a mere circumlocution for God. It is equivalent to the term *šekinah*, meaning the power of God as manifested on earth, or God in action among his creatures. In this conception, however, there is no tendency towards hypostatization, or plurality of persons in the Godhead.

*Targum on Genesis 3:21*

*Hebrew*: And the Lord God made for Adam and for his wife garments of skins, and clothed them.

*Onqelos*: And the Lord God made for Adam and for his wife garments of glory on the skin of their flesh, and clothed them.

*Pseudo-Jonathan*: And the Lord God made for Adam and for his wife garments of glory from the skin of the serpent which he had cast off, on the skin of their flesh instead of their nail-like skin which had been cast off; and he clothed them.

¶ Onqelos here, despite his general aim of complete literalness, cannot forbear to introduce an haggadic element into his translation, which, however, he makes so brief as to be cryptic. Pseudo-Jonathan gives the haggadic legend, on which Onqelos is drawing, in more detail, but the full legend has to be gathered from other rabbinic sources, Midrash and Talmud, of a later date. We have here, then, a good illustration of the continuity of haggadic ideas.

The legend is that when Adam and Eve were first created, their outer skin, attached to their bodies, was of a hard, translucent material like that of finger-nails. When they sinned, this outer skin was removed, leaving them with soft skin, and that is why they felt themselves to be 'naked' (Gen. 3:7). God then clothed them with glorious garments which had previously been the outer skin of the disgraced serpent. These 'garments of glory' were passed down through the generations, and later became the 'coat of many colours' given by Jacob to Joseph (Gen. 37:3; the word used for 'coat', *ketonet*, is the same as that used for 'garments' here).

Instead of translating 'garments of skins' (i.e. of animal skins), the Targums translate 'garments for their skins', now for the first time exposed. It was no doubt felt that it was a derogation from the dignity of God to suppose that he killed animals and processed their skins for garments for Adam and Eve.

The concept of primordial skin made of a nail-like substance may explain the transformation of the skin of Moses (Exod. 34:29), where the expression *qaran ʿor panaw*, should perhaps not be translated, 'the skin of his face sent out rays of light', but 'the skin of his face became horn-like', thus reverting to the condition of the unfallen Adam.

*Targum on Genesis 4:7*

*Hebrew* (AV): If thou doest well, shalt thou not be accepted? And if thou doest not well, sin lieth at the door. And unto thee shall be his desire, and thou shalt rule over him.

*Onqelos*: If you do your work well, will you not be forgiven? And if you do not do your work well, your sin is stored up for the Day of Judgement, when you will have to pay for it if you do not repent; but if you repent, you will be forgiven.

*Pseudo-Jonathan*: If you do your work well, will not your debt be forgiven you? And if you do not do your work well in this world, your sin is stored for the great Day of Judgement, lying at the doors of your heart. And to you I have handed over control over the evil inclination, and towards you shall be its desire, and you shall have rule over it, whether for merit or for sin.

¶ In this very difficult passage, Onqelos deserts his literalness, while retaining his brevity. Pseudo-Jonathan, however, by his expansiveness, throws light on how Onqelos arrived at his translation.

The Targums do not adopt the interpretation that comes so naturally to Christian commentators – that sin is being personified in the verse as a devil, lying in wait for the souls of humanity. Such an image is actually alien to the Hebrew Bible, as well as to the rabbinic mind, which thought of sin as an internal 'inclination' or psychological force, which could be controlled, and even integrated into the total personality. The Targums also note correctly that the expression 'his desire shall be unto you' does not mean 'he is your enemy who wishes to eat you up', but denotes subordination, as in Gen. 3:16. Thus both Targums take 'sin lieth at the door' to mean 'sin remains undealt with'; but they add that even so, God has given the human psyche the means to control it and so achieve a 'return' to the true way.

*Targum on Genesis 9:6*

*Hebrew*: Whoso sheddeth man's blood, by man shall his blood be shed.

*Onqelos*: Whoso sheddeth man's blood with witnesses, on the sentence of the judges shall his blood be shed.

*Pseudo-Jonathan*: Whoso sheddeth man's blood with witnesses, the judges shall condemn to death; but he who sheds it without witnesses, the Lord of the world will bring punishment on him in the Day of the great Judgement.

¶ The Targum is so concerned that the biblical verse should not be understood to imply that private justice may be exacted for murder, that even the literal Onqelos adds words about the necessity for witnesses and judges. Pseudo-Jonathan, as usual more expansive, adds that those murderers who are not subject to human judgement will not go without due punishment.

*the Day of the great Judgement*: the Targum, partly because of its closeness to the biblical text (see Isa. 2:12; Ezek. 30:3; Joel 1:15, etc.) lays far more stress on the concept of the eschatological Day of Judgement than is found in the rabbinic writings. Though the concept does exist in the Tannaitic and later literature, it does not occupy a dramatic doctrinal position, as in Islam and (somewhat less so) in Christianity. Rabbinic writings tend to say that God will punish undetected murderers by premature death, rather than by judgement in the Last Days (see, for example, p. 168). The term 'Day of Judgement', in rabbinic writings, refers more often to the annual Day of Atonement than to the Last Days. We see here a shift of emphasis within the rabbinic movement from the earlier Targumic stance grounded in apocalyptic expectations, to a later stance, grounded in acceptance of the natural sequence of the world.

*Targum on Genesis 22:14*

*Hebrew*: And Abraham called the name of that place *Adonai*-jireh; as it is said to this day, 'In the mount where the Lord is seen'.

*Onqelos*: And Abraham worshipped and prayed there in that place. He said 'Before the Lord here will generations worship. Therefore it will be said, On this day and on this mountain, Abraham before the Lord worshipped'.

¶ Onqelos here supplies a remarkably free and imaginative rendering. This abandonment of sober literalness tends to occur when he is faced with a difficult, obscure text. But it is surprising that he goes so far as to read the word *šem* ('name') as if it were vocalized as *šam* ('there'). He also takes other surprising liberties: inserting prepositions where none exist, breaking up the natural punctuation, and translating the verbs 'to call' and 'to see' as if they could mean 'to pray' or 'to worship'. The motivation for these intellectual acrobatics may be partly to avoid the apparent anthropomorphism in the text of a visible God.

The Targumist would no doubt defend his translation of the verbs 'to call' and 'to see' by pointing to the occasional use of these verbs with a meaning related to praying or worshipping: for example, 'calling' in the sense of praying is found in Ps. 4:1 and elsewhere; 'seeing' in the sense of 'praying' is found in Exod. 23:15 and Deut. 16:16 (where 'seeing the face of God' is equivalent to 'worshipping in the Temple').

*On this day*: rabbinic tradition regarded the festival of the New Year as the anniversary of the Binding of Isaac by Abraham, though there was an alternative tradition that the event took place at the time of Passover. At any rate, the Targumist portrays Abraham as foreseeing that his descendants would worship at the Temple (the site of which was traditionally identified with Mount Moriah where the Binding of Isaac took place, see 2 Chron. 3:1) at some festival-time which they would acknowledge as the anniversary of the Binding (*'Aqedah*).

*Targum on Genesis 24:47*

*Hebrew*: . . . and I put the ring (*nezem*) upon her nose . . .

*Onqelos*: . . . and I put the ring (*qadaša*) upon her nose . . .

¶ The Aramaic word for 'ring' or 'nose-ring', *qadaša*, may throw light on a saying of Jesus recorded in the Gospels, 'Give not that which is holy unto the dogs, neither cast ye your pearls before swine . . .' (AV) (Matt. 7:6). In Aramaic, the word for 'that which is holy' (Greek, *to hagion*) is *qudša*, which could have been misread for *qadaša*, 'ring'. If so, Jesus' actual saying was, 'Give not a ring to dogs, neither cast ye your pearls before swine . . .'. This makes much more sense, since there is a clear parallelism between 'ring' and 'pearls'. This suggestion was one of the earliest made in the attempt to apply a knowledge of Aramaic to the study of the New Testament. The implications are that Jesus' sayings were first written down in Aramaic form, and were then translated into Greek by someone whose knowledge of Aramaic was imperfect.

The above conjecture has been strengthened by the discovery of the word *qadaš* in the fragmentary Targum of Job found in Qumran: this proves that the word was in use in the required sense at the time of Jesus, for it is used to translate the word 'ring' in Job 42:11.

*Targum on Genesis 49:23–4*
*Hebrew* (JPS): The archers have dealt bitterly with him, and shot at him and hated him;
But his bow abode firm, and the arms of his hands were made supple, by the hands of the mighty one of Jacob, from thence, from the Shepherd, the Stone of Israel.
*Onqelos*: The mighty men were bitter against him and took their vengeance and oppressed him, those who took cause against him. And his prophecy was confirmed against them, because he kept the law in secret and put his trust in the Almighty. Therefore gold was placed on his arms, and he took possession of the kingdom and was strong. This was granted to him by the almighty God of Jacob, who by his word sustained the fathers and the children, the seed of Israel.

¶ This is an example of how the desire of Onqelos for a plain meaning can sometimes lead him far away from the text; for where the text is poetic and metaphorical, he tries to reduce it to plain prose by interpretations that may be remote from the intentions of the poet. Here, in Jacob's blessing on Joseph, Onqelos tries to relate the cryptic expressions to what he knows about the life-story of Joseph, and struggles to connect this passage with Joseph's difficulties with his brothers, and the history of Joseph's descendants.

*because he kept the law in secret*: the Targumist takes the Hebrew, *be'eitan*, to mean 'by standing firm', referring to Joseph's resistance to Potiphar's wife.
*gold was placed on his arms*: he regards the Hebrew, *vayapozu*, as derived from *paz* ('refined gold'). It is derived, in fact, from *pazaz*, meaning 'to be supple'.
*took possession of the kingdom*: Onqelos sees the verse as prophesying the Northern Kingdom, in which the tribe of Ephraim, son of Joseph, took the leading role. The 'gold', therefore, is the royal gold. Alternatively, as Rashi thinks, the reference is to Joseph's own elevation to rule over the kingdom of Pharaoh, though the expression *'aḥaseyn* ('took possession'), hardly fits this interpretation.
*the fathers and the children*: Onqelos takes the Hebrew *'eben* ('stone') to be an abbreviation for two words *'ab* and *ben* ('father' and 'son'), as Rashi ingeniously explains.

*Targum on Leviticus 11:32*

*Hebrew* (AV): And upon whatsoever any of them, when they are dead, doth fall, it shall be unclean; whether it be any vessel of wood, or raiment, or skin, or sack, whatsoever vessel it be, wherewith any work is done, it must be put into water, and it shall be unclean until the even; then it shall be clean.

*Pseudo-Jonathan*: And when they are dead, if one of their severed limbs falls on anything, it shall be unclean; any vessel of wood, or clothing, or skin, or sack, anything with which work may be done, shall be put into forty *se'ahs* of water, and shall be unclean for any use until the evening; then it shall be clean.

¶ The text refers to the dead bodies of 'creeping things' (a term covering eight animals enumerated in verses 29–30), which convey 'uncleanness' by contact with people or utensils. This does *not* mean that people are forbidden to touch the corpses of such animals, but that, knowing that they have done so, they must not eat or touch holy food or enter holy precincts until they have performed the prescribed ablution.

The Targum is interesting because it gives a different *halakah*, in one respect, from that found in the Tannaitic literature and in the Talmud. This shows that Pseudo-Jonathan, despite its late redaction, preserves some pre-Tannaitic legislation which escaped the processes of revision. The Targums are thus important for the study of the historical development of the *halakah*.

The dissident view expressed here is that a utensil, having been cleansed in the ritual pool after contamination by a 'creeping thing', is still unclean 'for any use' until the evening. The standard Tannaitic view (as found in Sifra 123, commenting on this verse) is that such a vessel may not, indeed, be used for 'holy' food (*terumah*), but may be used for 'common' food even when it is desired to keep such food free of uncleanness; for in the period between immersion in the pool and the evening, the vessel counts as being in a 'second-degree of uncleanness', which cannot affect 'common' food. The view expressed by the Targum is so remote from the standpoint of the Tannaitic literature that it is not found there even as a minority view (as sometimes happens with dissident views found in the Targums).

*one of their severed limbs*: this means that even a portion of the corpse may convey uncleanness. This is standard rabbinic doctrine.

*forty se'ahs*: the standard rabbinic measurement for a ritual pool. A *se'ah* is about $2\frac{3}{4}$ gallons.

*Targum on Numbers 10:31*

*Hebrew* (AV): And he said, 'Leave us not, I pray thee; forasmuch as thou knowest how we are to encamp in the wilderness, and thou shalt be to us instead of eyes'.

*Onqelos*: And he said 'Do not leave us now, since you know about when we were camping in the wilderness, and you saw with your own eyes the mighty things that were done for us'.

*Pseudo-Jonathan*: And he said 'Do not leave us now, since you know about when we were camping in the wilderness for judgement, and you taught us about judgement, and you were beloved to us like the apple of our eyes'.

¶ The Targums forsake here the plain meaning of the text, in which Moses, addressing his father-in-law, Jethro (Hobab), asks him to accompany the Israelites as a guide. The Targumists evidently see that this request is not consistent with the picture of the crossing of the wilderness by Divine guidance (Exod. 13:21–2). Onqelos translates (literally), 'you were to us for eyes' (past tense instead of future), i.e. 'you were a spectator of what happened to us'. Pseudo-Jonathan, however, relates the text to the incident of Jethro's advice to Moses (Exod. 18:13–27), for which Moses is expressing gratitude. For Pseudo-Jonathan, therefore, the phrase 'you were to us for eyes' means 'you were as beloved to us as our eyes'. The expression 'apple of our eyes' is derived from Zech. 2:8, though a related expression is found in Deut. 32:10; Ps. 17:8, and elsewhere.

*Targum on Numbers 12:1*

*Hebrew*: And Miriam and Aaron spoke against Moses because of the Ethiopian woman whom he had married: for he had married an Ethiopian woman.

*Onqelos*: And Miriam and Aaron spoke against Moses because of the beautiful woman whom he had married: for the beautiful woman whom he had married had been set apart.

*Pseudo-Jonathan*: And Miriam and Aaron spoke against Moses words that were not fitting about the Ethiopian woman whom the

Ethiopians had caused Moses to marry when he had fled from Pharaoh, but whom he had set apart; for they had caused him to take as wife the Queen of Ethiopia, and he had withdrawn from her.

*Fragmentary Targum*: And Miriam and Aaron spoke against Moses about the Ethiopian woman whom he had married. And behold, it was not really a Cushite woman, but Zipporah, the wife of Moses. But how so? Just as a Cushite woman differs physically from every other creature, so Zipporah, the wife of Moses, was graceful in form and beautiful in appearance, and different, in her good works, from all women of that generation.

¶ The Ethiopian wife of Moses gave rise to legends found in extra-biblical works about a sojourn of Moses in Ethiopia. These legends were suppressed by the rabbis, who preferred to identify the 'Ethiopian woman' with Zipporah, Moses' Midianite wife, explaining that 'Ethiopian' simply means 'extraordinary' (see Sifre, Lev. 11:32). Onqelos follows this line, and the Fragmentary Targum gives the argument by which Onqelos arrived at his translation 'beautiful' for the Hebrew word *kušit*, which really means 'Ethiopian'. Nevertheless, the legend of Moses' sojourn in Ethiopia, and his marriage to the Ethiopian Queen, could not be entirely suppressed in the rabbinic literature, and it surfaces in the Targum of Pseudo-Jonathan, as well as in the Midrash collection, *Yalqut Šimoni*. For a full version of the legend of Moses in Ethiopia, see Josephus, *Ant.* ii.10.1–2 (238–51), though here the Ethiopian episode takes place *before* Moses' flight from Pharaoh.

The reason for the rabbis' suppression of the marriage of Moses to an Ethiopian woman, in the literal sense, was not colour prejudice, which had no part in rabbinic thinking, but unwillingness to see Moses as slighting Zipporah (who saved his life, Exod. 4:25–6) by taking another wife. So far from regarding Moses as expanding his sexual life, the rabbis interpreted the present episode as arising from a decision of Moses to cease from sexual intercourse with Zipporah in order to devote himself to service of God. This decision was opposed by Miriam and Aaron, on behalf of Zipporah, but God endorsed Moses' decision. This is what Onqelos means by saying that she had been 'set apart', and Pseudo-Jonathan adopts the same idea. Usually, sexual intercourse was regarded as a duty owed by a husband to a wife (Exod. 21:10 and M. Ket. 5:6), but Moses was regarded as the one exception, because of his constant dialogue with God.

## Hanged on a tree

*Targum on Deuteronomy 21:22–3*

*Hebrew*: And if a man has committed a sin worthy of death, and he is put to death, and you hang him on a tree; his body shall not remain all night upon the tree, but you shall surely bury him the same day; for he that is hanged is the curse of God; that you may not defile your land which the Lord your God gives you for an inheritance.

*Onqelos*: When a man guilty of the judgement of death is put to death, and you hang him on a gibbet, his body shall not remain on the gibbet, but you shall surely bury him on that day; for he was hanged because he had sinned before the Lord; and your land which the Lord your God has given you shall not be defiled.

*Pseudo-Jonathan*: When a man has become guilty of the judgement of death, and is condemned to be stoned, and they afterwards hang him on a beam, his dead body shall not remain on the beam, but you shall surely bury him on the same day; for it is a disgrace before God to hang a man unless his guilty deeds bring this about; and because he was made in the image of God, you shall bury him at the setting of the sun, that wild animals may not abuse him, and that you may not pollute with the bodies of condemned people your land which the Lord your God gives you to possess.

¶ This passage is given a peculiar interpretation by Paul (Gal. 3:13), 'Christ bought us freedom from the curse of the law, by becoming for our sake an accursed thing: for Scripture says, Cursed is everyone who is hanged on a tree'. According to Paul's interpretation, Deut. 21:23 means that even an innocent person, when hanged on a tree, undergoes a curse. The rabbinic literature, however, from the Targum onwards, gives no support to such an interpretation. Many distinguished members of the rabbinic movement were crucified by the Romans, and such victims of oppression were never regarded as being under a curse, but rather as being martyrs. Even criminals who suffered capital punishment for their crimes were not regarded by the rabbis as thereby incurring a curse, but, on the contrary, as gaining expiation for their sin (see Tos. Sanh. 9:5: 'Those who are put to death by the court have a share in the world to come'). The rabbinic interpretations of Deut. 21:23 never regard the curse as applying to the hanged person. Rabbi Meir's explanation (b. Sanh. 46b) is that it is cursing God, or blasphemy, to allow the corpse of an executed criminal to hang overnight, since the human body was made in the image of God. Another interpretation (M. Sanh. 6:4) is that the corpse of an executed criminal is suspended only in a case of blasphemy, when the condemned person has 'cursed God's name' (the translation of Deut. 21:23 would then be, 'A case of cursing God leads to hanging on a tree', while Rabbi Meir's translation would be: It is cursing God to hang someone on a tree). Onqelos, above, takes the same view as the Mishnah. Pseudo-Jonathan gives a hint of Rabbi Meir's view, but also gives his own explanation: that the thought '. . . unless he is guilty' should be interpolated, with the resulting translation of Deut. 21:23, '. . . otherwise it would be a blasphemy against God to hang someone'. Paul's interpretation seems to be derived (though incorrectly) from the Septuagint rendering, 'Everyone that is hanged on a tree is cursed of God' (see also the Temple Scroll 64 'Cursed by God and men are those who are hanged on the wood'): these statements however do not refer to innocent people, but to condemned criminals, who, in pre-rabbinic thinking, were regarded as accursed, in the sense of suffering eternal disgrace for their crimes. Paul's understanding of Deut. 21:23 as referring to some kind of magical curse adhering even to an innocent person through hanging *per se*, should certainly not be adduced as evidence of Paul's alleged rabbinic training, or even as having any precedent at all in Judaism.

*and you hang him on a gibbet* (*Onq.*) . . . *and is condemned to be stoned, and they afterwards hang him on a beam* (*Ps.-J.*): here Pseudo-Jonathan reflects later rabbinic law as found in the Mishnah, while Onqelos seems to reflect an earlier form of Pharisaic law. In Mishnaic law, hanging is not a form of judicial execution at all. Its place has been taken by 'strangulation', a kind of garotting. It is only the *dead body* of an executed criminal that is suspended for a short time after execution and then taken down. Deut. 21:23 is taken to refer to this post-execution hanging. Earlier law, however, included 'hanging' as one of the four methods of execution. This should not be confused with crucifixion, which was never a Jewish punishment, and is referred to in Jewish sources as 'hanging a person alive, in the Roman manner'. This was regarded as barbarous (see Josephus, *Ant.* xiii. 14.2 (379–83), where Alexander Jannaeus is stigmatized for his imitation of non-Jewish cruelty when he crucified his enemies, thus acquiring the nickname 'the Thracian'). Some recent attempts to argue that crucifixion was practised officially by the Jews are without plausibility.

## Passing the love of women

*Targum on 2 Samuel 1:26*

*Hebrew*: Your love for me was wonderful, surpassing the love of women.

*Targum Jonathan*: Your love to me was distinguished from (or, more wonderful than) the love of two women.

¶ This verse is part of David's lament for Jonathan. The Targum surprisingly inserts the word 'two' into its translation, without warrant in the Hebrew. A medieval explanation of this is that, according to the Targum's interpretation of the verse, David was referring to his two wives, Abigail and Ahinoam. It has been suggested that the Targum's motive, in making this translation, is that this removes King David from the imputation of extensive, promiscuous acquaintance with 'the love of women'; instead, David is merely comparing Jonathan's love, to its advantage, with his own limited experience of married love.

This explanation of the Targum, however, is not completely satisfactory. One would have thought that the Targum, with its characteristic regard for the morals of biblical heroes, would have been more concerned about the possible imputation of homosexual love between David and Jonathan, arising out of the disparagement of heterosexual love.

I suggest, therefore, that what the Targum has in mind is a comparison of *friendship* between men and *friendship* between women. The purport of the Targum's translation is: the friendship between David and Jonathan was deeper than any friendship that could occur *between two women*. This relieves David's remark of unwanted sexual connotations, and reduces the relationship of David and Jonathan to the kind of warm friendship of which biblical examples relating to women can be found, e.g. Naomi and Ruth.

The original Hebrew text, however, almost certainly does not mean this. Without any conscious suggestion of homosexuality, it exalts the friendship of male warrior-friends above the more earthly love between the sexes, thus putting David and Jonathan on the same plane as hellenistic pairs such as Damon and Pythias or Aeneas and Achates. The Targum, however, perhaps because it belonged to an age, like our own, when homosexual motives were more readily imputed, and also because it does not share the warrior-ethic of David's lament, reduces the text ingeniously to a more humdrum meaning.

*Targum on Isaiah 40:6*

*Hebrew* (AV): . . . all flesh is grass, and all the goodliness thereof is as the flower of the field.

*Targum Jonathan*: . . . all flesh is grass, and all its strength is as the flower of the field.

¶ The Hebrew word translated by AV as 'goodliness' is *ḥesed*, which, however, usually means 'kindness', but can sometimes mean 'piety'. The Targum's translation 'strength' fits in with none of these meanings; we must conclude, therefore, that the text of the Hebrew Bible before the Targumist was not the same as the Masoretic text. The word in the Targumist's text was probably not *ḥesed* but *ḥosen*.

There are many such variations in the Targums, traceable to variations in the text before the Targumist (though care has to be taken in distinguishing these from variations due to other causes). In many cases, the same variation can be found in the Septuagint and the *Peshitta* (Syriac) as in the Targum, though the above is not one such case.

The fact that such textual variations are found more frequently in the Official Targums (Onqelos on the Pentateuch, and Jonathan on the Prophets) than in the Palestinian Targums is one of the indications that the Official Targums, contrary to a recent fashionable school of thought, are earlier than the Palestinian Targums.

*Targum on Isaiah 52:13–15; 53:1–12*

*Hebrew* (NEB):

13 Behold, my servant shall prosper, he shall be lifted up, exalted to the heights.

14 Time was when many were aghast at you, my people; his
form, disfigured, lost all the likeness of a man, his beauty
changed beyond human semblance,
15 so now many nations recoil at sight of him, and Kings curl
their lips in disgust. For they see what they had never been told
and things unheard before fill their thoughts.

1 Who could have believed what we have heard, and to whom
has the power of the Lord been revealed?
2 He grew up before the Lord like a young plant whose roots are
in parched ground; he had no beauty, no majesty to draw our
eyes, no grace to make us delight in him. (See below.)
3 He was despised, he shrank from the sight of men, tormented
and humbled by suffering; we despised him, we held him of no
account, a thing from which men turn away their eyes.
4 Yet on himself he bore our sufferings, our torments he
endured, while we counted him smitten by God, struck down
by disease and misery;
5 but he was pierced for our transgressions, tortured for our
iniquities; the chastisement he bore is health for us and by his
scourging we are healed.
6 We had all strayed like sheep, each of us had gone his own way;
but the Lord laid upon him the guilt of us all.
7 He was afflicted, he submitted to be struck down and did not
open his mouth; he was led like a sheep to the slaughter, like a
ewe that is dumb before the shearers.
8 Without protection, without justice, he was taken away; and
who gave a thought to his fate, how he was cut off from the
world of living men, stricken to the death for my people's
transgression?
9 He was assigned a grave with the wicked, a burial-place among
the refuse of mankind, though he had done no violence and
spoken no word of treachery.
10 Yet the Lord took thought for his tortured servant and healed
him who had made himself a sacrifice for sin; so shall he enjoy

long life and see his children's children, and in his hand the Lord's cause shall prosper.

11 After all his pains he shall be bathed in light, after his disgrace he shall be fully vindicated; so shall he, my servant, vindicate many, himself bearing the penalty of their guilt.

12 Therefore I will allot him a portion with the great, and he shall share the spoil with the mighty, because he exposed himself to face death and was reckoned among transgressors, because he bore the sin of many and interceded for their transgressions.

*Targum Jonathan*:

13 Behold, my servant, the Messiah, shall prosper; he shall be high, and grow great and be very strong.

14 Just as the house of Israel hoped for him for many days, during which their countenance was darkened among the peoples and their splendour removed from the sons of man,

15 so he will scatter great peoples; because of him Kings will be silent, putting their hands on their mouths, because they will have seen things never spoken to them, and gazed on things unheard by them.

1 Who has believed these good tidings of ours, and to whom has been revealed the strength of the mighty arm of the Lord such as this?

2 The righteous will grow up before him, behold, like blooming shoots, and like a tree that sends forth its roots to streams of water, so will they increase, a holy generation in the land which was in need of him; his countenance will be no common countenance, nor its awesomeness that of an ordinary person; his look will be a holy look, so that all who see him will gaze at him.

3 Then the glory of all the kingdoms will be despised and will cease; they will be weak and mourning, lo, like a man of pains and one prepared for evils, and as if the presence of the Šekinah had departed from us, being despised and not esteemed.

4 Then he will pray for our sins, and our iniquities will be forgiven for his sake, and we will be reckoned as crushed, smitten from before the Lord and afflicted.

5 And he will build the Temple, which has been profaned by our sins, and delivered over through our iniquities, and by his teaching, his peace will grow great over us, and, through the eagerness of his words, our sins will be forgiven to us.

6 All of us like sheep had been scattered; we had wandered each one on his own way; but it was the will of the Lord to forgive the sins of all of us for his sake.

7 He prayed, and he was answered, and before he had even opened his mouth he was accepted; the strong ones of the peoples he will deliver up like a sheep to the slaughter and like a lamb that is dumb before its shearer; and there will be none to open his mouth or say a word before him.

8 He will bring our exiles near, out of their chastisements and punishment. Who can express the wonders that will be done for us in his days? For he will remove the rule of the Gentiles from the Land of Israel; the sins, which they sinned, my people will bring home to them.

9 And he will hand over the wicked to Gehinnom, and those who are rich in possessions who have acted oppressively to death of destruction, in order that those who perform sin should not be established, nor speak deceits with their mouths.

10 And it is the will of the Lord to refine and purify the remnant of his people, in order to cleanse their soul from sins. They shall see the kingdom of their Messiah; their sons and daughters shall be multiplied; they shall prolong their days; and those who perform the Torah of the Lord shall prosper by his will.

11 From the subjection of the Gentiles he will deliver their souls; they shall see the punishment of those who hate them, and be filled with the spoil of their kings; in his wisdom, he will declare the innocence of the innocent in order to bring many into subjection to the Torah; and he will pray for their sins.

12 Then I will divide for him the spoil of many peoples, and the possessions of strong cities shall he divide as booty, because he handed over his soul to death, and made the rebellious subject to the Torah; and he shall intercede for many sins, and the rebellious shall be forgiven at his request.

¶ The much-disputed Suffering Servant passage of Isaiah is very obscure in the Hebrew. No translation can be given that can be claimed as certainly expounding the sense of the Hebrew, but the NEB rendering is cited here as an attempt which uses the resources of modern scholarship, including occasional emendation (though the NEB's transposition of part of 52:14 to the end of 53:2 has been abandoned here, in order to facilitate comparison with the Targumic rendering).

The Suffering Servant has featured much, through the centuries, in Jewish–Christian controversy. Christians have seen the passage as a prophecy of the vicarious suffering of the Christian Messiah, Jesus. Jewish exegesis has passed through various phases. In the earliest extant Jewish exegesis, that of the Targum here, the passage is indeed interpreted as referring to the coming Messiah, but not to a suffering Messiah. The suffering mentioned in the passage is all allotted either to the Jews, suffering exile and subjection, or to the Gentiles, suffering punishment at the hands of a triumphant Messiah. This exegesis dates from the decade before the Bar Kokhba revolt (i.e. AD 125–35), when hopes were high for the coming of the Messiah to liberate the Jews from Roman rule. There is no intention, in this exegesis, to combat Christian interpretations of the passage, for these had not yet impinged strongly on the Jewish consciousness. After the failure of the Bar Kokhba revolt, the Jews themselves began to interpret the passage as referring to a suffering Messiah, who would be afflicted with leprosy (see b. Sanh. 98a–b).

In the Middle Ages, however, the prevailing exegesis among the Jews regarded the Suffering Servant as being the Jewish people itself, whose sufferings were regarded as atoning for the sins of the world. This view is found in the late Midrash, *Numbers Rabbah*, and in the commentators Rashi, Naḥmanides, David Kimḥi and others. This line of exegesis was partly dictated by a need to combat Christian interpretation of the Suffering Servant as referring to Jesus, which had now become an insistent feature of Christian missionary activity. The Jewish exegesis, however, had much to recommend it on purely objective grounds, and some modern scholars have found it the key to the biblical passage (see, for example, A. Peake's *A Commentary on the Bible*, London, T. C. and E. C. Jack, Ltd., 1920). Moreover there is evidence that the interpretation of the Suffering Servant as the Jewish people was adopted even in ancient times by some Jews (see Origen, *Contra Celsum*, I,

55). In some Jewish exegesis, the Servant is regarded as both the Messiah and the Jewish people, of which he is the symbol.

Other interpretations of the passage have also been given by Jewish exegetes. One Talmudic passage (b. Soṭ. 14a) refers the passage to Moses, while Saʿadia Gaon regarded it as being about the sufferings of Jeremiah.

*Targum Jonathan*:
3. *Then the glory of all the kingdoms will be despised and will cease*: Neubauer's translation (S. R. Driver and A. Neubauer, *The 'Suffering Servant' of Isaiah according to the Jewish Interpreters*, Oxford, 1877) reads: 'Then he will become despised, and will cut off the glory of all the kingdoms'. This makes little sense in the context of the Messiah's triumph. The translation given here has good manuscript support.
8. *the sins, which they sinned, my people will bring home to them*: Neubauer translates: '. . . and transfer to them the sins which my people have committed'. The idea that the Gentiles are to suffer for the sins of the Jews is quite unparalleled in rabbinic literature, so this translation is most unlikely to be correct. The translation given here also has the grammatical advantage of supplying a singular verb for the noun 'people'.

*Targum on Ezekiel 44:22*
*Hebrew*: Neither shall they take for their wives a widow, nor her that is put away: but they shall take maidens of the seed of the house of Israel, or a widow who was widowed from a priest.
*Targum Jonathan*: . . . and a widow who has become widowed, the other priests may marry her (rendering of the last clause above).

¶ The Targum here attempts to reconcile a contradiction between the law applying to priests in Ezekiel and that outlined in Lev. 21:7–15. According to Leviticus, an ordinary priest is permitted to marry a widow, and only a High Priest is forbidden to do so. According to Ezekiel, however, even ordinary priests are forbidden to marry a widow unless her deceased husband was a priest. Rabbinic law is based on the Torah or Pentateuch, and any discrepant laws found in the rest of the Bible have to be given an interpretation consonant with that found in the Pentateuch. The Targum follows this procedure here, at the cost of plausibility. The first part of the verse is assumed to apply to High Priests only, and the final clause is translated in such a way that 'from a priest' becomes 'the other priests'. The rationale of this translation appears to be that 'from a priest' could mean 'a portion of the priesthood', i.e. that portion which does not contain High Priests. A similar interpretation is found in b. Qid. 78b.

*Targum on Hosea 6:5*

*Hebrew* (AV): Therefore have I hewed them by the prophets: I have slain them by the words of my mouth: and thy judgements are as the light that goeth forth.

*Targum Jonathan*: ... and my judgement is as light that goes forth.

¶ Here, again, is an interesting example of Targumic translation that implies an underlying Hebrew text different from that of the Masoretic tradition. Moreover, the Targum's text is clearly superior, since it makes much more sense: God's judgement is relevant, but a judgement attributed to Ephraim, the object of a bitter diatribe here, is most perplexing, especially as it is described in incongruently complimentary terms.

In this case, the Targum's translation is identical with that of the Septuagint and *Peshitta*, which were clearly working with the same Hebrew text of the verse as the Targumist. Further, the text presupposed by all three (*u-mispati ke-'or yeṣ'e*) differs from the consonantal Masoretic text only by the detachment of one letter from the end of the first word and its attachment to the beginning of the next: so that we can understand quite easily how the corruption crept into the Masoretic text.

## LITURGY

See Part I, p. 36, for a further characterization of the liturgy.

The abbreviation PB stands for *The Authorized Daily Prayer Book*, edited and translated by S. Singer. The page numbers given refer to the 1962 edition and (in brackets) the 1891 edition. The translations given here, however, are in many respects new, and contain some emendations based on early sources (see the notes). Readers are advised, nevertheless, to consult PB in order to grasp the context and continuity of the prayers.

For the Passover liturgy (*Seder* service), see p. 81.

## God's love

*PB p. 40 (39)*

With a great love have you loved us, Lord our God; with a great and extraordinary pity you have pitied us. Our Father, our King, for the sake of our ancestors who trusted in you, and whom you taught the statutes of life, so be gracious to us and teach us. Our Father, merciful Father, you who show continual mercy, have mercy on us and put it into our hearts to understand, to discern, to hear, to learn and teach, to guard and to perform and to fulfil all the words of the teaching of your Torah with love. And enlighten our eyes in your Torah, and cause our hearts to cleave to your commandments, and unify our hearts to love and to fear your name, and let us not be put to shame for all time. For in your great, holy, awesome name we have trusted: let us rejoice and be glad in your salvation. And bring us to peace from the four corners of the earth, and lead us upright to our land. For you are a God who works salvation, and you chose us from every people and tongue and brought us near to your great name for ever in truth, that we might give thanks to you and declare your oneness with love. Blessed are you, Lord, who chooses his people Israel with love.

· Hear, Israel, the Lord our God, the Lord is one.

Blessed be the name of the glory of his Kingdom for ever and ever.

And you shall love the Lord your God will all your heart, with all your soul and with all your might.

¶ This 'blessing' or prayer, leading up to the reciting of the *Shema*ʿ ('hear'), centres on the concept of 'love'. The fatherhood and loving mercy of God are stressed, shown in his giving of the Torah to his chosen people, in his help to them in the process of learning the lessons of the Torah, and in his eventual bringing of salvation to them from exile and humiliation.

*be gracious to us*: though rabbinic Judaism stresses the need for human effort, both in order to learn the precepts of the Torah and to perform them, God's grace is also regarded as involved at every step.

*Our Father, merciful Father*: the rabbinic prayers are full of the fatherhood of God, as is the Old Testament. Yet, surprisingly, Jesus' 'Our Father' is still widely regarded as a new departure in religion. One form this contention takes is that there was something new and unique in Jesus' use of the expression *'abba* in prayer, this being a diminutive, similar to 'daddy', showing a special intimacy in Jesus' attitude to God. Actually, *'abba* is not a diminutive but is simply the Aramaic equivalent of the Hebrew *'ab*, 'father'. Jesus may have been innovative in using the Aramaic rather than the Hebrew term, but even this is not certain. In a Talmudic passage (b. Taʿan 23a), the word *'abba* is used for God by the charismatic Ḥanan in the course of a prayer for rain, though God is not actually addressed here as *'abba*.

*unify our hearts*: the verb used here is the same as that used later to mean 'to declare the unity' of God. Thus the awareness of the oneness of God produces a unification of the human psyche, bringing it peace from warring tendencies.

*lead us upright to our land*: see Lev. 26:13, '... I broke the bars of your yoke, and enabled you to walk upright'.

*who works salvation*: in the Old Testament and rabbinic literature, 'salvation' always refers to political liberation, which was regarded as essential for full spiritual development. The Christian notion of 'salvation' is more often related to the *soteria* of hellenistic cults, meaning a non-political liberation from spiritual disaster.

*who chooses his people Israel*: as a chosen people, who have been 'brought near' to God, it is the task of Israel to learn and teach and declare the unity of God.

*the glory of his Kingdom*: the recitation of the *Shemaʿ* was called 'the acceptance of the yoke of the Kingdom of God'. Jesus also associated this verse, central in the liturgy, with the 'Kingdom of God' (Mark 12:34).

## The resurrection of the dead

*PB p. 46 (44)*

You are mighty for ever, Lord, bringing the dead to life; you are strong to save.

[(*in the rainy season*) You cause the wind to blow and the rain to fall.]

You sustain the living with loving-kindness, bring the dead to life with great mercy, support the fallen, and cure the sick, and loose those who are bound, and keep faith with those who sleep in the dust. Who is like you, Master of mighty deeds, and who is similar to you, King who kills and brings to life, and causes salvation to spring forth? And you are faithful to bring the dead to life. Blessed are you, Lord, who bring the dead to life.

¶ This the second of the Eighteen Benedictions which form the chief prayer (*tepillah*) of the Jewish liturgy on weekdays. On Sabbaths and festivals, the opening three benedictions and the closing three are retained, but are combined with other benedictions, suitable to the occasion, forming the central portion of the *tepillah*. The present section is concerned with the resurrection of the dead, a basic belief of the Pharisees, as Josephus and the New Testament testify. The Pharisaic belief was that all deserving human beings would be brought back to life in the Last Days, to share in the glory of the Kingdom of God. The body would be revivified in its normal form, not in a transmogrified form, as in Paul's scheme (I Cor. 15:43). In addition, there was held a doctrine of spiritual survival in non-bodily form, but this was never given doctrinal definition, as it was considered to be beyond our human understanding, in accordance with the verse, 'For since the beginning of the world men have not heard, nor perceived by the ear, neither hath the eye seen, O God, beside thee, what he hath prepared for him that waiteth for him' (Isa. 64:4 AV). See b. Sanh. 99a. The Sadducees did not accept the doctrine of the resurrection of the dead, since there is no obvious mention of it in Scripture. The Pharisees, accordingly, are sometimes found in controversy with the Sadducees, arguing that the doctrine of resurrection from the dead can indeed be deduced from Scripture. A typical controversy of this kind is Jesus' argument with the Sadducees, Matt. 22:23–33, one of the many features in the Synoptic Gospels which support the view that Jesus was a Pharisee.

*strong to save*: expressions of 'salvation', usually used in connection with liberation from slavery and foreign domination, are also found in connection with the doctrine of the resurrection of the dead (but never in connection with ideas of non-bodily survival). The resurrection of the dead was considered to be the ultimate salvation in every sense, since it would happen at the time when the people of Israel would be vindicated in the eyes of the world, and would be

freed of all subjection and oppression. Consequently, it is associated in this passage with the hope of freedom ('loose those who are bound') as well as of release from want and sickness.
*cause the wind to blow and the rain to fall*: the connection between the theme of resurrection and that of the renewal of the seasons and the crops is one that has existed in religion since prehistoric times. In rabbinic Judaism, the Last Days are thought of as a renewal of creation, paralleling, on the macro-historical plane, the renewal brought about in the course of every year by the renewal of nature. It was, therefore, thought appropriate to pray for rain during the prayer for the resurrection of the dead, but only during the rainy season, since at other times, rain was unwelcome.
*keep faith with those who sleep in the dust*: see Dan. 12:2. The whole passage is full of biblical echoes, like so much of the liturgy. See 1 Sam. 2:6; Pss. 145:14; 146:7f; Isa. 63:1.
*causes salvation to spring forth*: the use of the term *maṣmiaḥ* ('causing to sprout'), usually referring to vegetation, reinforces the link between the resurrection of the dead and the renewal of nature.

## Heretics

*PB p. 50 (48)*
(The Prayer Book version has been emended by reference to Tos. Ber. 3:25.)
And for the separatists and for the heretics let there be no hope; and let all wickedness perish as in an instant; and let all thy enemies be cut off quickly; and mayst thou uproot and break to pieces and cast down and humble the arrogant kingdom quickly and in our days. Blessed art thou, O Lord, who breakest enemies and humblest the arrogant.

¶ This 'blessing' (so-called because it concludes with a blessing of God) forms the twelfth of the Eighteen Benedictions which form the basic prayer of the Jewish liturgy. It is, in essence, a prayer for the quick coming of the Last Days and the Judgement. This blessing was held against the Jews by Christian detractors in the Middle Ages and modern times, and has been very often described as 'a curse against Christians'. The prayer, however, dates from pre-Christian times, and its wording has differed at different times, in accordance with various internal threats from dissidents and heretics. At one time, mention of the Sadducees was included, and the prayer was known as 'the blessing of the Sadducees' (*birkat ha-ṣeduqim*). At another time, it was known as *birkat ha-minim*, when the chief internal threat came from heretics known as *minim*, perhaps Gnostics, or possibly Jewish–Christians (called by Jerome, 'Minaeans'). Some versions have been found, not earlier than the fourth century AD, in which mention of the 'Nazoreans' is included (*noṣerim*), and some scholars have held that this means simply 'Christians', whether Jewish–Christians or Gentile–Christians. The weight of evidence, however, is that the term 'Nazoreans' referred only to Jewish–Christians, who were regarded as heretical Jews, and that the twelfth blessing was never directed against Gentile–Christians, who were regarded as forming a separate religion, not as constituting an internal threat to Judaism.

*And for the separatists and for the heretics*: the Tosephta shows that this is how the blessing originally began. The word for 'separatists' is *perušim*, which shows how careful one has to be when translating this word as 'Pharisees' (see p. 139).
*the arrogant kingdom*: this refers to Rome, or to militaristic empires in general, as opposed to 'the kingdom of God' (*malkut šamayim*) for which Jews look in hope.

## The Kingdom of God

*PB p. 79 (76) ('Alenu)*
It is our duty to praise the Lord of all things, to assign greatness to him who formed the creation, who did not make us like the nations of the lands, and did not place us like the families of the earth, who did not set our portion like theirs, or our lot like that of the multitude of them. For they bow down to vanity and emptiness, and pray to a god who cannot save. But we kneel and bow down and give thanks before the King of Kings of Kings, the Holy One, blessed be he, who stretched out the heavens and laid the foundations of the earth, the seat of whose glory is in the heavens above and the dwelling of whose might is in the loftiest heights. He is our God: there is no other. Our King is truth; there is nothing besides him; as it is written in his Torah, 'You shall know this day, and reflect in your heart, that the Lord is God in the

heavens above and on the earth beneath; there is no other' (Deut. 4:39).

Therefore we look to you in hope, Lord our God, to see soon the glory of your might, when idols will be removed from the earth, and false gods will be cut off entirely; when the world will be perfected under the reign of Shaddai, and all the children of flesh will call on your name, and all the wicked of the earth will be turned to you. All the dwellers of the world will recognize and know that to you must bend every knee, and every tongue swear loyalty. Before you, Lord our God, they will kneel and prostrate themselves, and give honour to the glory of your name, and all of them will accept the yoke of your Kingdom, and you will reign over them (may it be soon) for ever. For the Kingdom is yours, and for all eternity you will reign in glory, as it is written in your Torah, 'The Lord will reign for ever and ever' (Exod. 15:18). And it is said, 'And the Lord will be King over all the earth; on that day the Lord will be one, and his name one' (Zech. 14:9).

¶ This prayer (known as *'Alenu*, from its first word meaning 'It is our duty') is probably first-century in its earliest version, but received some editing in the third century AD. Originally it formed part of the Day of Atonement liturgy, introducing the section devoted to the conception of God as King. Much later, in the Middle Ages, the prayer was added to the daily services as a finale to each service, a suitable position in view of its summing up of Judaism's combination of particularism and universalism. Present-day prayer books omit the sentence 'For they bow down to vanity and emptiness, and pray to a god who cannot save', since this sentence was the cause of persecution by Christians, who took it to be an attack on Christianity. In fact, it is an echo of Isa. 30:7 and 45:20 and existed in the Jewish liturgy in times and places remote from Christianity. The operation of Christian censorship, which insisted on the removal of many harmless passages from Jewish literature, is only now beginning to be counteracted in recent editions of Talmud and liturgy. In fact, the removal of this sentence spoils the point of the prayer, which is that the special position of the Jews is due entirely to their mission as the propagators of monotheism – a mission for which they are to thank God, despite the suffering involved.

*King of Kings of Kings*: the conception of God as supreme King is different from, but by no means incompatible with, the conception of God as Father, also prominent in the liturgy (see p. 206). Similarly, Jesus found no difficulty in reconciling God's fatherhood with his kingship (as in the much-repeated phrase 'the Kingdom of God').

*who stretched out the heavens and laid the foundations of the earth*: see Isa. 51:13 and Zech. 12:1. The Jewish liturgists (like the Christian liturgists) were steeped in Scripture and used its language as a natural part of their own forms.

*the world will be perfected*: the term 'perfecting' (*tiqqun*) is used in rabbinic and later mysticism to refer to the correction of the flaw in the universe caused by the fall of Adam. The *'Alenu* prayer, like some other parts of the rabbinic liturgy, thus shows the influence of mysticism, though this influence is always unobtrusive.

*Shaddai*: the name by which, according to Exod. 6:3, God was known to the Patriarchs; its use here thus reinforces the notion of a world returned to a state of primeval innocence.

*all the wicked of the earth will be turned to you*: this humane prayer says nothing about the judgement or punishment of the wicked in the Last Days, but dwells instead on their repentance and acceptance by God, in accordance with the text, 'Have I any desire, says the Lord God, for the death of the wicked man? Would I not rather that he should mend his ways and live?' (Ezek. 18:23); a text prominently featured in the liturgy of the Day of Atonement.

*the Lord will be one and his name one*: this universalistic text was understood by the rabbis (and indeed by Zechariah) as implying the conversion of the whole world eventually, not to Judaism, but to monotheism, of which Judaism was only one variety, that prescribed for the priest-nation, the Jewish people (which could, however, be joined by proselytes with a vocation for priesthood).

## Qidduš

*PB p. 169 (124)*

Blessed are you, Lord our God, King of the Universe, who create the fruit of the vine.

Blessed are you, Lord our God, King of the Universe, who sanctified us with his commandments and was pleased with us, and gave us his holy Sabbath as an inheritance, a remembrance of the work of creation. For it is the first of the holy convocations, a remembrance of the Exodus from Egypt. For you have chosen us and sanctified us from all the peoples, and you have given us as an inheritance your holy Sabbath, in love and favour. Blessed are you, Lord, who sanctify the Sabbath.

Blessed are you, Lord our God, King of the Universe, who bring forth bread from the earth.

¶ The basic structure of this Sanctification ceremony (*qidduš*) is mentioned in the Mishnah (M. Ber. 8:1), i.e. a blessing 'over the wine' and a blessing 'over the day', though there is disagreement between the House of Hillel and the House of Shammai about the order in which these two blessings are said (see p. 55). It is clear, too, from the Mishnah, that the Sanctification ceremony was performed in the home on the Sabbath eve by the master of the house. The third blessing, on the bread, is not, strictly speaking, part of the Sanctification ceremony, but simply the initiation of the meal, as on any weekday. A sip of wine is taken by each person present, after the Sanctification, and after the blessing on the bread, each person is given a piece of bread. The actual wording of the second paragraph above is not attested for our period, and may have reached its present form in the third century. It should be noted that this Sanctification ceremony has no mystical significance, but is simply a ceremony of thanksgiving for the Sabbath day, marking its sanctity and inaugurating its celebration in the home. (For the switches between second person ('you') and third person ('his'), see p. 216.)

A similarly structured *qidduš* was performed in the home for each of the festivals (PB p. 313 (230) and p. 334 (243)). It is not clear whether the bread and wine used by Jesus at the Last Supper represented a *qidduš* ceremony, since here the bread preceded the wine. Only Luke (Luke 22:17–20) appears to portray a *qidduš*, distinguishing the cup at the beginning of the meal from the cup at the end 'after supper', which was drunk as part of the Grace after Meals. In John's account (John 13:1), the Last Supper took place *before* Passover, in which case there was no *qidduš*.

*the fruit of the vine*: wine was held in high regard by the rabbis, as the essential accompaniment of all glad celebration and thanksgiving.

*his holy Sabbath as an inheritance*: although observance of the Sabbath is enjoined in the Ten Commandments, the rabbis did not regard it as an obligation on non-Jews, and therefore did not include it among the Noachian Laws incumbent on all mankind. Since the Sabbath was regarded as a gift rather than as a burden (see p. 170), God was thanked for giving his people this 'inheritance'. Nevertheless, a certain universality clings to the concept of the Sabbath, since in Genesis and Exodus it is regarded as commemorating God's creation of the world (Gen. 2:3; Exod. 20:11). In Deuteronomy, however, the Sabbath is linked to the history of Israel, being described as recalling the Israelites' slavery in Egypt (Deut. 5:14–15). This uncertainty, or ambivalence, is reflected in this blessing, which calls the Sabbath both 'a remembrance of the work of Creation' and 'a remembrance of the Exodus from Egypt'. Even the Deuteronomic conception, though it anchors the institution in Israelite history, relates the Sabbath to universal moral principles of freedom. The Sabbath thus cannot be divested of universality. Yet it is, after all, a rite or symbol, not a moral principle, and therefore its observance, the rabbis think, cannot be regarded as a universal precept. Some Jewish thinkers (e.g. Philo, and, in modern times, Hermann Cohen) have disputed this reasoning, and have argued that the Sabbath was instituted for all mankind.

*who bring forth bread from the earth*: an echo of Ps. 104:14.

## The Praise of God

*PB p. 173 (125) (Nišmat)*

The breath of every living being shall bless your name, Lord our God, and the spirit of all flesh shall glorify and exalt your mention continually. From everlasting to everlasting you are God, and apart from you we have no King, redeemer or saviour, setting free, and rescuing, and feeding, and having mercy at every time of trouble and distress. We have no King but you. God of the first and the last, Deity of all creatures, Lord of all generations, who is extolled with many praises, who guides his world with loving-kindness and his creatures with mercy. And the Lord does not slumber or sleep; he awakes sleepers and arouses slumberers, and causes the dumb to speak, and looses the bound, and supports the falling, and raises the bowed. To you alone we give thanks. If our mouth were full of song like the sea, and our tongue of exultant chant like the multitude of its waves, and our lips of praise like the expanse of the firmament, and our eyes shining like the sun and the moon, and our hands spread out like the eagles of the heavens, and our feet swift as deer, we would not be able to thank you, Lord our God of our fathers, and to bless your name for one thousandth of the many thousands and myriads of times you have benefited us and our ancestors. You redeemed us from Egypt, Lord our God, and released us from the house of bondage; in famine you fed us, and in plenty sustained us; from the sword you saved us, and from pestilence rescued us, and from evil and lasting diseases delivered us. Up to now your mercies have helped us, and your loving-kindnesses have not forsaken us; may you never abandon us, Lord our God. Therefore the limbs which you have separated in us, and the spirit and soul which you breathed into our nostrils, and the tongue which you put into our mouth, they indeed shall thank and bless and praise, and glorify, and exalt, and reverence and hallow and declare the Kingship of your name, our King. For every mouth shall give thanks to you, and every tongue shall swear to you, and every knee shall bow to you, and every height shall prostrate itself before you; and all hearts shall fear you, and all inward parts and kidneys shall sing to your name, according to the word that is written, 'All my bones shall say, Lord, who is like you?'

¶ This prayer is first attested (b. Pes. 118a) by Rabbi Joḥanan ben Napaḥa (see p. 183), who lived from *c.*180 to *c.* 280, but since he mentions it by its opening words as a well-known prayer, we can safely assign it to our period. It seems that the prayer was first used as a conclusion to the *Hallel* (recitation of the psalms of praise, i.e. Pss. 113–18) in the *Seder* service performed in the home on Passover (see p. 81). Later, the prayer was attached, in addition, to the psalms of praise (*pesuqey de-zimrah*) recited every Sabbath morning, concluding with the psalms of universalistic praise, Pss. 148–50, of which this prayer contains echoes. Part of the prayer was also used among prayers for rain. A Jewish tradition of uncertain antiquity attributes the composition of this prayer (known as *Nišmat*, from its first word) to none other than St Peter (regarded in Jewish tradition as always having been loyal to Judaism).

*The breath of every living being*: this recalls the last words of the Psalter 'Let everything that has breath praise the Lord'. The idea of a universal chorus of all living beings, from angels to animals, uniting in thankful praise of God, here achieves rabbinic expression; and this idea, as in the Psalms, is not felt to be inconsistent with the idea of the special historical mission of Israel as the chosen people of God, who owe special thanks for God's bounty, especially for the deliverance from Egypt. The word 'breath' (*nešamah*) also means 'soul', particularly when in parallel, as here, with 'spirit' (*ruaḥ*). This double meaning of *nešamah* exists already in the Bible (e.g. Prov. 20:27). The mediating idea is that God breathed his own breath into Adam (Gen. 2:7), so that the 'breath of life' is part of the Divine substance.

## Grace after Meals

*PB p. 378 (280)*

Blessed are you, Lord our God, King of the Universe, who feed the whole world with your goodness, with grace, with loving-kindness and with mercy. He 'gives food to all flesh, for his mercy endures for ever' (Ps. 136:25). And through his great goodness continually food has not failed us, and may it not fail us for ever and ever, for the sake of his great name. For he feeds and sustains all, and does good to all, and prepares food for all his creatures whom he created. Blessed are you, Lord, who feed all.

We thank you, Lord our God, because you caused our ancestors to inherit a Land, desirable, good and broad; and because you brought us out of the land of Egypt, Lord our God; and redeemed us from the house of slaves; and for your Covenant which you sealed in our flesh; and for your Torah which you taught us; and for your statutes which you made known to us; and for the life, grace and loving-kindness which you bestowed on us; and for the eating of food with which you constantly feed and sustain us every day, in every season and in every hour. For everything, Lord our God, we thank you and bless you, may your name be blessed in the mouth of all living continually for ever and ever. As it is written, 'And you shall eat and be satisfied, and you shall bless the Lord your God for the good land which he has given you' (Deut. 8:10). Blessed are you, Lord, for the Land and for the food.

¶ These first two blessings of the Grace after Meals are its most ancient elements. The Mishnah takes it for granted that these blessings are said, though it does not quote them in full (see M. Ber. 7). The first paragraph of the Grace is universalistic in its portrayal of God as provider for all living beings; the second paragraph thanks God for his particular mercies to Israel.

*and you shall bless*: this quotation from Deuteronomy was regarded by the rabbis as an actual injunction to say Grace after Meals. Thus Grace after Meals and the saying of the *Shema'* are the only elements of the liturgy which were regarded as having biblical authority (see p. 205). Petitionary prayer was regarded as having a subordinate status, being rabbinical in origin (b. Ber. 21a, as interpreted by Naḥmanides); the declaration of God's unity and of gratitude for his mercies were regarded as primary.

*The switches from second person ('Blessed are you') to third person ('... he feeds and sustains all ...') and back again are quite characteristic of the rabbinic liturgy, as of the biblical Psalms, for the attitude of the worshipper keeps changing from intimate address to contemplation of God's qualities.

## The Marriage Blessings

*PB p. 397 (299)*

Blessed are you, Lord our God, King of the Universe, who create the fruit of the vine.

Blessed are you, Lord our God, King of the Universe, who created all things for your glory.

Blessed are you, Lord our God, King of the Universe, Creator of man.

Blessed are you, Lord our God, King of the Universe, who created man in your image; and, in the image of the likeness of his (Adam's) shape, set up for him, out of himself, an eternal fabric. Blessed are you, Lord, Creator of man.

May she who was barren rejoice with all her heart and exult when her children are gathered within her in joy. Blessed are you, Lord, who make Zion rejoice with her children.

Make these loved companions rejoice greatly, as you made rejoice those whom you created in Eden of old. Blessed are you, Lord, who gladden bridegroom and bride.
Blessed are you, Lord our God, King of the Universe, who created joy and gladness, bridegroom and bride, merriment and song, dancing and rejoicing, love, brotherhood, peace and fellowship. Soon, Lord our God, may there be heard in the cities of Judah and in the streets of Jerusalem the voice of joy and gladness, the voice of bridegroom and bride, the jubilant voice of bridegrooms from their canopies, and of youths from their feasts of song.
Blessed are you, Lord, who make the bridegroom to rejoice with the bride.

¶ The Seven Blessings, as they are called, which are sung at the wedding and at the marriage feast, are first found cited by Rab Judah (third century AD) in b. Ket. 7b–8a, but are clearly older than this date. The apex of human joy recalls the bliss of Eden, but also, in contrast, calls to mind the desolation of Jerusalem.

*the fruit of the vine*: the blessings are said over a cup of wine, the accompaniment of all celebration and rejoicing.
*and, in the image of the likeness of his (Adam's) shape*: transferring the word 'and' from the beginning of the next clause to here, in accordance with the emendation of A. Berliner (based on an early source). This eliminates the improbably explicit anthropomorphism 'who created man in your image, in the image of the likeness of your shape'. Instead the idea is that Eve was made in the likeness of Adam's shape.
*an eternal fabric*: this refers to the human species, an eternal 'fabric' (*binyan*) set up by God through his creation of the two sexes.
*make Zion rejoice*: it was obligatory, on all occasions of rejoicing, to devote some thought to the desolation of Jerusalem and its future restoration, though this sadness was not to be carried to excess (see p. 141).
*who created joy and gladness*: this great blessing gathers together all the themes of the previous blessings, and asserts the fundamental mood of rabbinic Judaism as one of joy, despite the tragedy of the Destruction. The culmination is a reminiscence of Jer. 33:10–11.

## HISTORY

### *Megillat Ta'anit*

See Part I, p. 36.

*Megillat Ta'anit* (literally, 'Scroll of Fasting') is a halakic, not a historical, work, but it throws light on historical matters. It ranks as a *baraita*, and is probably the earliest extant rabbinic work, dating from the period of the last days of the Temple. It gives a list, in Aramaic, of thirty-six days on which fasting or other mourning ceremonies were forbidden, briefly giving the reason in each case, i.e. that some victory or happy event had taken place on that date. The work is attributed to Eliezer ben Ḥananiah, who is probably identical with Eleazar the son of Ananias, mentioned by Josephus, who initiated the war against the Romans by persuading the priests to refuse to sacrifice the offering of the Emperor in the Temple (*War* ii.17.2 (409)). Fuller explanations of the events mentioned are contained in a scholium in Hebrew attached to the work, but this scholium is of much later date (*c.* AD 450), though it is sometimes based on early sources.

*Megillat Ta'anit* itself contains no reference to the destruction of the Temple, and its tone is one of celebration, not of mourning. This, together with linguistic considerations, indicates that this work was composed before the destruction of the Temple in AD 70.

*Megillat Ta'anit* should not be confused with the tractate *Ta'anit* in the Mishnah.

#### Happy days

*Megillat Ta'anit 18*

*Marḥešwan*: the twenty-fifth: the capture of the wall of Samaria.

¶ This refers to the capture of Samaria by John Hyrcanus and his sons in 129 BC (see Josephus, *War* i.2.7 (64) and *Ant.* xiii.10.2 (275)). The account in Josephus of this event represents it realistically as motivated by political considerations, but the authors of *Megillat Ta'anit* include it as a religious victory over the heretical Samaritans, deserving of commemoration as a semi-festival on which fasting was forbidden.

*Megillat Ta'anit 23*

*Kislev* the twenty-fifth: *Ḥanukkah*, for eight days. No mourning in them.

¶ The feast of *Ḥanukkah* ('Dedication') commemorates the re-dedication of the Temple after the victory of Judas Maccabaeus (see 1 Macc. 4:36–59; 2 Macc. 1:8; 10:1–5; Josephus, *Ant.* xii.7.6–7 (316–25)). For a reference to this festival in the New Testament, see John 10:22. Of all the special days mentioned in *Megillat Ta'anit* in connection with the victories of the Hasmoneans, this is the only one which entered permanently into the Jewish religious year. It is celebrated in the home by the lighting of an eight-branched candlestick, one light being added on each day of the festival. This commemorates the resumption of the Temple service, especially the lighting of the seven-branched Temple Menorah (see p. 139), which, it was believed, was attended by a miracle (see b. Šab. 21b), though the earlier sources do not mention this miracle. The dropping of the other dates from the religious calendar was no doubt due to a longer perspective, in which the joyful events of the Hasmonean era were seen as less important. Both the Palestinian and the Babylonian Talmuds record that the special days of *Megillat Ta'anit* were 'rescinded' (y. Ta'an. 2:13; b. R.Š. 18b). This is a good example of the power of the rabbis to repeal earlier rabbinic legislation (see Part I, p. 4).

*Megillat Ta'anit 26*

On the twenty-second of it (*Šebat*), was abolished the worship that the enemy intended to bring into the Temple. No funeral orations.

¶ Most of the days singled out in *Megillat Ta'anit* as semi-holidays commemorate events in the Hasmonean period, but a few seem to be references to events in the period of Roman rule before the destruction of the Temple. The present laconic entry refers almost certainly to the attempt of Gaius Caligula to introduce his own worship into the Temple in AD 41, an incident of which we know a great deal from Philo and Josephus. Caligula's mad project, which he knew would provoke full-scale revolt, was delayed by Petronius, the Governor of Syria, and finally prevented only by Caligula's death. (See Josephus, *War* ii.10.1 (184–5).)

*Šebat*: the eleventh month of the Hebrew calendar, roughly equivalent to February. Caligula was murdered on 24 January, so the

rescinding of his decree, which took place shortly after his death, may well have occurred in the month of *Šebat*.
*No funeral orations*: the Hebrew word, *hesped*, can refer also to other ceremonies performed in honour of the departed. Such sadness was not permitted on a joyful day.

## *Seder ʿOlam Rabbah*

See Part I, p. 38.

### From Adam to Rebecca

*Seder ʿOlam Rabbah 1*
From Adam to the Flood, 1,656 years. And this is a detailed account of them: Adam, 130; Seth, 105; Enosh, 90; Kenan, 70; Mehalalel, 65; Jered, 162; Enoch, 65; Methuselah, 187; Lamech, 182; and Noah 'was 600 years old' (Gen. 7:6). Enoch buried Adam, and lived after him fifty-seven years. Methuselah stretched his days until the Flood. From the Flood to the Separation (Gen. 11:8–9), 340 years. It follows that Noah lived for ten years after the Separation; our father, Abraham, was 48 years old at the time of the Separation.

Said Rabbi Yose: Eber was a great prophet, for he called his son 'Peleg' through the Holy Spirit, as it is said, '. . . because in his days the earth was divided' (Gen. 10:25). If at the beginning of his days, was not his brother Joktan younger than he, yet he begot thirteen tribes before the Separation? And if in the middle of his days, does not the verse come to make plain, not to conceal? Therefore, when the verse says, '. . . because in his days the earth was divided', this must mean at the end of his days.

Abraham, our father, was 70 years old at the time when God communicated with him, 'between the pieces' (Gen. 15:13–21), as it is said, 'At the end of 430 years . . .' (Exod. 12:41). After he communicated with him, he (Abraham) went down to Haran, and spent there five years, as it is said, 'And Abraham was 75 years old when he left Haran' (Gen. 12:4). It follows that from the Separation to the departure of Abraham from Haran was twenty-seven years.

'They had been subject to Kedorlaomer for twelve years, but for thirteen years they rebelled, and in the fourteenth year Kedorlaomer came . . .' (Gen. 14:4–5). That was the same year that Abraham our father departed from Haran. That was the year of the famine, when he 'went down to Egypt' (Gen. 12:10), and he spent three months there, and went up and came and dwelt 'by the terebinths of Mamre at Hebron' (Gen. 13:18), and that is the year in which he conquered the kings (Gen. 14:14–24). And he spent there ten years before he married Hagar, as it is said, 'So Sarai, Abram's wife, brought Hagar the Egyptian, . . .' (Gen. 16:3); and it is written, 'Abram was 86 years old when Hagar bore Ishmael' (Gen. 16:16). It follows that Ishmael was fourteen years older than Isaac. It follows that from the Separation to the birth of Isaac, our father, was fifty-two years. The settlement of Sodom was for fifty-one years; for twenty-six of them, there was 'comfort and ease for her and her daughters' (Ezek. 16:49). And from the Flood until the birth of Isaac was 392 years. And this is a detailed account of them, 'These are the generations of Shem. Shem was 100-years-old when he begot Arphaxad, two years after the Flood' (Gen. 11:10). Arphaxad, 35; Shela, 30; Eber 34; Peleg, 30; Reu, 32; Serug, 30; Nahor, 29; Terah, 70; and 'Abraham was 100-years-old when his son Isaac was born' (Gen. 21:5). Our father, Isaac, was 37 years old when he was bound on the altar. 'And Abraham sojourned in the land of the Philistines many days' (Gen. 21:34); (this means that) those days were more numerous than those spent at Hebron, which were twenty-five years, and these were twenty-six years. At that very time, Rebecca was born; it follows that our father, Isaac, married Rebecca when she was three years old.

Our father, Abraham, buried Terah his father two years before the death of Sarah. Jacob served our father, Abraham, for fifteen years, and Shem for fifty years. The upshot is: our father Jacob served Shem for fifty years, and Shem served Methuselah for ninety-eight years, and Methuselah served Adam for 243 years; so that four people formed the basis of twenty-two generations; and seven people overlapped the whole world, and these are they: Adam, and Methuselah, and Shem, and Jacob, and Amram, and Ahijah the Shilonite, and Elijah, who is still alive.

¶ This first chapter of *Seder ʿOlam Rabbah* shows the method of the book. The attempt to work out a coherent chronology for the Bible sometimes leads to some surprising conclusions, and also uncovers a kind of secret history of biblical personalities. Where data seem to be lacking, rabbinical hermeneutic methods sometimes fill the gap. The calculations of *Seder ʿOlam* place the creation of the world at 3760 BC. It was not until the Middle Ages in Europe, however, that Jews began to date documents regularly by the *anno mundi* date. In Talmudic and even post-Talmudic times, up to the eleventh century, the usual method of dating was by the Seleucid era, beginning with 312 BC. The shift of the Jewish centre from Babylonia to Europe eventually made the Seleucid era meaningless.

*Adam, 130; Seth, 105*: the figures given are those for the age at which each person mentioned 'begot' his heir, his remaining years being irrelevant for the calculation of a continuous chronology. The final figure is Noah's age at the time of the Flood.
*Enoch buried Adam*: since Enoch was the most prominent person living at the time of Adam's death, he is considered as having taken the leading part in his burial.
*and lived after him fifty-seven years*: Enoch was born in 622 AM, and lived 365 years before his translation (Gen. 5:23–4). Adam died in 930 AM (Gen. 5:3), when Enoch still had fifty-seven years on earth.
*Methuselah stretched his days until the Flood*: since Methuselah lived to be 969, the year of his death, 1565 AM, coincides with the year of the Flood. This coincidence gave rise to the haggadic idea that God postponed the Flood as long as Methuselah, a saint, was alive. See b. Sanh. 108a–b where the lull of seven days before the onset of the Flood (Gen. 7:10) is construed as 'the days of mourning for Methuselah'. Noah's father, Lamech, it may be added, died five years before the Flood (Gen. 5:31).
*From the Flood to the Separation, 340 years*: the 'Separation' (*haplagah*) means the separation of the nations after the incident of the Tower of Babel (Gen. 11:8–9). For the figure of 340 years, see below.
*Noah lived for ten years after the Separation*: since Noah lived for 350 years after the Flood (Gen. 9:28). The calculation has thus uncovered a poignant picture of Noah living to see the dispersal of his descendants.
*Abraham, was 48-years-old at the time of the Separation*: the date of Abraham's birth can be calculated from Gen. 11:10–26 as 1948 AM, while the date of the Separation was 1996 AM. This calculation is

probably the basis for the *haggadah* that Abraham was 48-years-old when 'he recognized his Maker' (*Pesiqta Rabbati* 21:12; *Midrash ha-Gadol*; Gen. 11:13). Thus a by-product of the chronology is the picture of Israelite monotheism as stemming from Abraham's reaction to the Tower of Babel incident. There is even a *haggadah* that it was Abraham who prayed to God to divide the nations by diverse languages, in order to frustrate the plan to build the Tower of Babel.

*yet he begot thirteen tribes before the Separation?*: the thirteen tribes begotten by Joktan (Gen. 10:26–9) are included among the 'families' from whom 'the nations were separated in the earth after the Flood' (Gen. 10:32).

*does not the verse come to make plain, not to conceal?*: this is a rabbinic hermeneutic principle, used to extract precise information from a text that is apparently vague. If the text says that the Separation took place 'in the days' of Peleg, this must be at some precise moment in his days, i.e. at the beginning or the end, not indeterminately in the middle. Since our argument has ruled out the beginning, it must be at the end; consequently, the Separation can be dated precisely at 1996 AM, the last year of Peleg's life.

*Abraham, our father, was 70 years old*: the argument here is very succinct, but may be filled out from other rabbinic sources. Abraham was 100 years old when Isaac was born (Gen. 21:5). Now in order to reconcile the contradiction between Gen. 15:13, which says that the Egyptian exile would be 400 years, and Exod. 12:40, which says that the exile actually lasted 430 years, it was argued that the 430 years dated from the 'Covenant between the pieces', while the 400 years dated from the birth of Isaac (for the argument that neither figure could refer to the length of actual residence of the Israelites in Egypt, see p. 151). Since Abraham, at the birth of Isaac, was 100-years-old, it followed that at the time of the 'Covenant between the pieces', he was 70 years old.

*he (Abraham) went down to Haran*: the difficulty generated by the above argument is that the Bible states distinctly that Abraham was 75 years old when he left Haran at the behest of God to begin his mission (Gen. 12:4). Yet, according to the preceding argument, Abraham was only 70 years old at the time of the 'Covenant between the pieces', which, in the biblical narrative, takes place in chapter 15 of Genesis, after Abraham's departure from Haran, first sojourn in Canaan, descent to Egypt, return to Canaan, and defeat of the 'four kings'. This necessitates a radical shift of the order of events, by which the 'Covenant between the pieces' took place on an earlier visit to Canaan, before Abraham's Divine call (Gen. 12:1) was received. This kind of reordering of biblical events was validated by the rabbinic principle: there is no before or after in the Torah; i.e. the order of events in the Torah is not necessarily the order in which those events actually occurred (see b. Pes. 6b). Thus, Abraham, after the early visit to Canaan during which the 'Covenant between the pieces' took place, returned to Haran, and stayed there for five years before he received the call that took him back to Canaan.

*from the Separation to the departure of Abraham from Haran was twenty-seven years*: since, as previously calculated, Abraham was 48 years old at the time of the Separation, and was 75 years old at his departure from Haran.

*for twelve years, but for thirteen years they rebelled*: the twenty-seven years between the Separation and Abraham's departure from Haran are now neatly dovetailed with the history of the Cities of the Plain. Gen. 14:4 is translated to cover a period of twenty-five years (not, as in modern translations, '... in the thirteenth year they rebelled'; actually the translation given by *Seder 'Olam* is a more literal rendering of the Hebrew). It is assumed that the Cities of the Plain were founded at the time of the Separation. Thus the period when Kedorlaomer and his associate kings made their (two-year) expedition to subdue their rebellious subjects was the period when Abraham left Haran (for the second time), and after a brief sojourn in Egypt, he returned to Canaan where he defeated the four kings and rescued Lot.

*The settlement of Sodom was for fifty-one years; for twenty-six of them there was 'comfort ...'*: the destruction of Sodom took place shortly before the birth of Isaac, when Abraham was 99 years old, i.e. fifty-one years after the Separation, when Sodom was founded. For the first twenty-five years, Sodom and the other Cities of the Plain were subject to Kedorlaomer or in rebellion against him; thus their period of tranquillity, before their destruction, was twenty-six years. This does not seem to take into account the two years of the punitive expedition of Kedorlaomer, which were hardly years of 'comfort and ease'. Possibly the text here needs emendation, as parallel passages in Talmud and Midrash do show variations (see Gen. R. 49:6; b. Šab. 10b).

*Our father, Isaac, was 37 years old when he was bound on the altar*: the reasoning behind this is found in other rabbinic writings: the death of Sarah took place when Isaac was 37 years old (since Sarah was ninety when Isaac was born, and died at 127). But the death of Sarah is reported immediately after the account of the *ʿAqedah* of Isaac, which gives rise to the *haggadah* (based on the hermeneutic method of *semukin*, or juxtaposition) that Sarah's death was caused by the shock of hearing about Isaac's near escape from death. This calculation was not universally accepted, however, since Isaac is called a 'lad' at the time of the *ʿAqedah* (Gen. 22:12), and reasoning by *semukin* was regarded by some as doubtful.

*At that very time, Rebecca was born*: this means at the time of the *ʿAqedah*. This depends on reading Gen. 22:20–4 as an announcement of the birth of Rebecca, rather than as a report of births that had taken place some time before.

*Isaac married Rebecca when she was three years old*: this startling conclusion follows from the previous chain of reasoning; for we are told that Isaac married Rebecca when he was 40 years old (Gen. 25:20), and if Rebecca was born at the time of the *ʿAqedah*, when Isaac was thirty-seven, Rebecca must have been three at the time of her marriage. Since Rebecca certainly does not behave like a child of three, she has to be regarded as unnaturally precocious, and this chronological reasoning, containing several doubtful links, was regarded as little more than a *jeu d'esprit*.

*Jacob served Abraham for fifteen years, and Shem for fifty years*: the word 'served' (*šimeš*) is used in rabbinic literature to express the relationship between disciple and teacher. It is assumed that Jacob, from his birth, imbibed wisdom not only from his father, Isaac, but also from his grandfather, Abraham, who lived for fifteen years after Jacob's birth, and also from his long-lived ancestor, Shem, who survived until Jacob was fifty.

*seven people overlapped the whole world*: i.e. personal links existed between only seven people covering the whole of history from the creation of Adam until the coming of the Messiah, who would be accompanied by Elijah (Mal. 4:5).

*Ahijah the Shilonite*: the prophet who announced the splitting off of the Northern Kingdom (I Kings 11:29) and advised Jeroboam. According to rabbinic tradition, he was among the Israelites of the Exodus, and, like Seraḥ (see p. 155) survived into the age of the monarchy. He was held to have been the teacher of Elijah, who never died, being taken into heaven alive.

## HAGGADIC MIDRASHIM

See Part I, p. 37.

### Ben Zoma's trance

*Berešit Rabbah 2:4*

¶ The next passage illustrates the complexities of the dating of rabbinic materials. It comes from a haggadic work compiled about AD 425 which, however, contains much material deriving from the period before AD 200. There is a version of our passage in the Tosephta (Tos. Ḥag. 2:6). The Tosephta was probably compiled in the fourth century, but its version of this particular story has been shown by Saul Liebermann (*Texts and Studies*, New York, Ktav, 1974, pp. 230–3) to be later than that of *Berešit Rabbah*. There are also versions of the story in the Palestinian Talmud (y. Ḥag. 2:1) and the Babylonian Talmud, (b. Ḥag. 15a), but these too are later than the Midrashic version, which alone gives us an authentic glimpse into a type of mystical contemplation practised in the second century AD. Since rabbinic writings are all compilations, the date of redaction of a work gives little indication of the date of the materials included, and dating must be based on internal considerations of style and content in each individual case, while an assessment has to be made of the extent to which the passage has been subjected to editorial revision. The existence of parallel versions in many instances is very helpful in this kind of enquiry.

Once Simeon ben Zoma was sitting and meditating when Rabbi Joshua passed by and greeted him once and twice but received no reply. The third time he answered hurriedly. Said he (Rabbi Joshua) to him: Ben Zoma, from where are the feet? He replied: Not 'from where?' He (Rabbi Joshua) said to him: I call upon heaven and earth as my witnesses that I will not budge from here until you tell me from where are the feet. He said to him: I have been gazing at the work of Creation and there was only a space of two or three fingers between the upper and lower waters; for it is not written, 'And the wind of God blew', but 'hovered', like a bird flying and flapping its wings, which barely touch (the nest). Rabbi Joshua turned and said to his disciples: Ben Zoma has gone. Only a few days passed that Ben Zoma was in the world.

¶ Rabbi Joshua finds Ben Zoma rapt in a mystical trance and is alarmed at the depth of the trance, fearing for Ben Zoma's sanity or life. With a solemn adjuration, he endeavours to bring back Ben Zoma to a normal waking state, but succeeds only partially. Sadly he tells his disciples that Ben Zoma is doomed. The story supplements the rabbinic account of how four men entered the Garden (*pardes*) of mystical contemplation, and only one, Rabbi Akiba, was unharmed; of the other three, Elisha ben Abuyah became a renegade, Ben Azzai died and Ben Zoma went mad (see p. 136). The story expresses the mixed attitude of the rabbis towards mysticism: they regarded it with reverence as the apex of the religious life, but warned against its danger for all but a few gifted souls. The passage is also interesting in that it deals with a particular kind of rabbinic mysticism about which we have little information: that of the Work of Creation, based on the first chapter of Genesis.

*Simeon ben Zoma*: he was in the generation of *Tanna'im* that flourished from about AD 120 to about AD 139. He is generally called simply Ben Zoma, since, despite his high status as a scholar, he never became an ordained rabbi.

*from where are the feet?*: the general meaning of this strange enquiry is 'Where have you been?' Rabbi Joshua wishes Ben Zoma to report to him where he has been while in his trance. The early mystics, as the *Heykalot* literature shows (see p. 229) performed astral journeys while in the trance state. Those whose meditation was focused on the 'work of the Chariot' (*ma'aseh merkabah*) journeyed through the seven heavens to the throne-room of God. This kind of meditation was based on the first chapter of Ezekiel (for the restrictions on this study, see M. Ḥag. 2:1). Those, like Ben Zoma, whose interest was in the 'work of the Creation' (*ma'aseh berešit*), journeyed through space to the secret places of the universe, where God's creative power was most concentrated. At any rate, the present passage seems to point to such a journey. The form of Rabbi Joshua's enquiry ('From where are the feet?') may have been a usual formula for recalling ecstatics to the waking state. The explanation of it may lie in the fact that '. . . standing without feet in bottomless space is a characteristic experience of many ecstatics' (Scholem, *Major Trends*, p. 52). Thus to draw the ecstatic's attention to his feet may have been a way to bring him back to earth.

*He replied: Not 'from where?'*: the Hebrew is *lo' me-'ayin*, and this reading is found in certain codices and in a Genizah manuscript, instead of the banal *me'ayyen hayiti* ('I was meditating'). The meaning may be: Do not ask me, 'From where?', because I have not returned, and am still engaged in my journey. Rabbi Joshua, trying to induce Ben Zoma to return from his astral journey which has become dangerous, succeeds only in inducing a partial return, in which Ben Zoma is answering his questions in the manner of a medium, or one in a deep hypnotic trance, who can answer questions put to him but is far from being in a normal state.

*I call upon heaven and earth*: the solemn intensity of this adjuration shows that Rabbi Joshua is alarmed about Ben Zoma and is using all his authority as Ben Zoma's elder and teacher to counteract the fatal hold of the trance.

*I have been gazing*: Hebrew, *mistakel*, which signifies not mere musing, but actual visual experience of a mystical kind.

*a space of two or three fingers between the upper and lower waters*: this does not refer to the upper and lower waters that were separated by the 'firmament' on the second day of Creation; there was no mystery about how these were held apart, since the firmament itself acted as a partition. The reference is to the waters of the Deep (*tehom*), which were thought to have been repelled by God and were held back by a continuous miracle (see Job 38:8–11 and b. Ḥag. 15a, opinions of Rav Aḥa bar Jacob, the Sages and Mar Zutra). The myth behind this concept is that of the Babylonian god, Marduk, who conquered Tiamat, the goddess of the Deep, held her at bay, and set bars to keep her domain, the Deep, from flowing into earth and sky. The Talmud and the *Heykal* hymns preserve the idea that the lower waters are female and the upper waters of the earth and sky male (1 En. 54:7–10). The motif that there is a very small space separating these mighty forces, held apart only by the power of God, is a common one in rabbinic literature, and does not point to any heretical ideas on the part of Ben Zoma, as some have argued. This point of cosmic super-tension was the object of contemplation of the 'work of Creation' mystics, and one can understand that such contemplation could be disturbing to the balance of the mind.

*the wind of God*: the Hebrew word *ruaḥ* should be translated here as 'wind', not as 'spirit'. Ben Zoma has in mind the Targum translation which speaks of a wind blowing. Ben Zoma disagrees with the Targum's translation of the Hebrew word *meraḥefet* as 'blowing', and says that the correct translation is 'hovering'. This proves, he says, that the space between the upper and lower waters was very small, since there was no room for the wind to blow, but only to hover. The translation 'spirit of God' would foist on Ben Zoma a crude anthropomorphism: that the spirit of God had to contract itself to find its way between the upper and lower waters. Such an anthropomorphism would be quite uncharacteristic, and is here unnecessary.

*Ben Zoma has gone*: the Babylonian Talmud's version says: Ben Zoma is still outside; a version which points to Ben Zoma's state as one of ecstasy.

*was in the world*: to be 'out of the world' can mean to be mad, or to be dead. While the Babylonian Talmud says that Ben Zoma went mad and Ben Azzai died, the Palestinian Talmud transposes this, and has Ben Zoma die and Ben Azzai go mad.

## MYSTICAL LITERATURE

See Part I, p. 38. For other passages in rabbinic literature throwing light on rabbinic mysticism, see pp. 136 and 137.

### At the seventh gate

*Heykalot Rabbati 15:8–16:2*

And at the gate of the seventh palace stand upright all the warriors, powerful, strong and harsh, awesome and bewildering, taller than mountains and sharper than peaks; their bows are strung and stand before them; their swords are sharpened and are in their hands. And lightnings flash, issuing from the globes of their eyes, and balls of fire from their nostrils, and torches of fiery coals from their mouths. And they are adorned with helmets and coats of mail, and javelins and spears are hung upon their arms.

Their horses are horses of darkness, horses of the shadow of death, horses of deep darkness, horses of fire, horses of blood, horses of hail, horses of iron, horses of cloud. The horses, on which they ride, stand beside mangers of fire, full of coals of juniper, and eat fiery coals from their mangers, according to a measure of forty *se'ahs* of fiery coals in one mouthful. And the measure of the mouth of each horse is three mangers of the mangers of Caesarea, and the measure of each manger is according to the measure of the gate of Caesarea. And there are rivers of fire beside their mangers, and each of their horses drinks according to the measure of the fullness of the water-pipe which is in the Valley of Kidron which brings and contains all the rain water of all Jerusalem.

¶ This is one of the earliest passages of *Heykalot Rabbati*, dating from the first or second century AD, as is shown by the references to Caesarea and the Valley of Kidron, which are 'not based on a literary source, but on a concrete Palestinian reality known to the writer' (Scholem, *Jewish Gnosticism*, p. 32). The passage forms part of an account of the progress of the mystic through the seven heavens, facing fearsome dangers. In the seventh heaven, the mystic must pass through seven palaces (*heykalot*) before arriving at the throne of God, where he attains a vision of the figure seated on the throne of glory, as in the vision of Ezekiel. This man-like figure (Ezek. 1:26) is not the inmost essence of God, but is the highest manifestation of God attainable by man – so high, indeed, that it is hidden even from the angels. The journey of the mystic was not a bodily transportation, but a progress of the soul, while the mystic was in a deep trance. This conception of a spiritual journey, fraught with great dangers, was at least partly derived from hellenistic mysticism of the Hermetic type. Jewish mysticism was not derived from Christian Gnosticism, which indeed shows great evidence of having been influenced by Jewish mysticism, as well as by Hermeticism and proto-Gnosticism. For Talmudic and Midrashic evidence of the rabbinic practice of mysticism, see pp. 136 and 226. There are strong affinities between rabbinic mysticism and that found in the Qumran sect and in apocalyptic circles (see especially, the Apocalypse of Abraham). The great difference is that in rabbinic Judaism such mystical experience is regarded as peripheral. There is a remarkable contrast, in fact, between the sense of the nearness of God found in the rabbinic everyday liturgy, and the sense of God's remoteness found in the mystical literature. It would seem that as long as God is regarded as unpicturable, it is possible to have an intimate, loving relationship with him as Father; but when an actual vision of God's glory is sought, an atmosphere of terror arises, requiring a journey over immeasurable distances in order to view a God conceived not as Father, but as all-powerful King.

*the seventh palace*: of the seventh heaven. For the names of the seven heavens, see b. Ḥag. 12b. An alternative view in rabbinic sources is that there are only three heavens (Deut. R. 2:32), and this view is reflected in 2 Cor. 12:2. The earliest Jewish source for seven heavens is 2 En. 3–21 (see also 3 Bar, T Levi 2:7–38). In Mesopotamian myth, there are three heavens, but seven stages in the descent to hell. Philo explains the mystical character of the number seven as derived from the seven determinations of everything physical: above, below, right, left, before, behind, and the individual centre (Leg. All. 1.2). Sevenfold themes are frequent in Revelation (Rev. 8:1; 10:7; 17:9–10).

*the warriors*: the angels guarding the gate of the seventh palace. Their names are not given, though in the account of the first six palaces, the strange compound names of the angels of the gate are given: such as Dehabiel, Qasriel, Sataqiel, Garpiel.

*horses of darkness*: there are echoes here of Ps. 18:8–13. See also Rev. 6:1–8; 9:7–10, 17. The horses and their riders are evidently projections of God's anger: the last obstacles to the progress of the mystic to the throne-room of God.

*coals of juniper*: See Ps. 120:4.

*forty seahs*: this is the measure of a ritual bath, equivalent to about 110 gallons.

*the mangers of Caesarea*: this is a reference to the Hippodrome of Caesarea, mentioned by Josephus (*Ant.* xvi.5.1 (137)), but never mentioned elsewhere in the rabbinic literature.

*Heykalot Rabbati: Hymns*

1. *Song of the Ministering Angels* (2:4)

The beginning of praise and the first of song,
The beginning of rejoicing and the first of jubilation
Sing the princes, who serve each day,
To YHWH, the God of Israel and to his throne of glory;
They lift up the wheel of his throne of glory, singing:
'Rejoice, rejoice, throne of glory,
Sing, sing for joy, heavenly seat!
Shout, shout for joy, vessel of delight,
Fashioned with marvel upon marvel!
May you gladden the King who sits on you,
As a bridegroom rejoices in his bridal chamber!'

2. *The Song of the Throne* (3:2)

King of miracles, King of mighty deeds,
King of wonders, King of marvels,
Your throne hovers and remains stationary,
From the hour when you fixed the peg of the weaving-loom
Upon which the perfection and course of the world depends,
For so many years, generations without end.
And it has never touched the floor of the Seventh Heaven,
But like a bird it hovers and remains stationary.
The proudest of the proud, bound with crowns,
And all the Kings of the highest qualities whom you have created,
Stand crowded under your throne of glory,
And they continually bear it with strength, might and power.
And they too have never set foot on the floor of the Seventh Heaven,
But like a bird hover and remain stationary.
And three times every day,
Your throne of glory stretches itself before you and says to you:
Zohorariel, YHWH, God of Israel,
Assume your glory and sit upon me, King of Splendour,
For your burden is beloved and dear to me and is not heavy upon me.
As it is said,
'Holy, holy, holy is the Lord of Hosts. All the earth is full of his glory'.

¶ The hymns included in *Heykalot Rabbati* cannot be positively dated before the third century, but prototypes of them can be found at an earlier date in the writings of the Qumran sect and in the apocalyptic writings. They are hymns attributed to the angels, performing their duties of praise and service in the heavens; but they are also hymns to be sung by the mystic in the course of his spiritual journey through the seven heavens and the seven palaces. The throne of God is itself regarded as an angel – a living being who sings praise to God. This conception is derived from the visions of Isaiah and Ezekiel, and each hymn concludes with the Trisagion, 'Holy, holy, holy ...' (Isa. 6:3). This chorus of the angels is echoed on earth in the section of the liturgy known as the *Kedushah* (see PB (1962), pp. 47, 187, 212; PB (1891), pp. 45, 137, 160, for various forms of this). The *Kedushah* thus forms a link between normative, everyday rabbinic Judaism and the practice of the rabbinic mystics (this is true also of the *ʿAlenu* prayer, to some extent, see p. 209).

*Stand crowded under your throne of glory*: according to Talmudic *haggadah*, the souls of the unborn, including the Messiah, also dwell under the throne of God.

*Zohorariel*: this is one of the special names of God found in the mystical literature. Many of them contain doubling of letters, in the manner characteristic of 'speaking with tongues' and other forms of mystical linguistic afflatus. This name means 'the splendour (or radiance) of God', with a doubling of the 'r'. A name of God frequently found is *totrossiyah*, which may be derived from the Greek *tetras* ('four') with an allusion to the fourfoldness of the letters of the Tetragrammaton.

# Further reading


## TRANSLATIONS AND ANTHOLOGIES

H. Danby, *The Mishnah*, Oxford University Press, 1933.

J. Z. Lauterbach, *Mekilta de-Rabbi Ishmael*, 3 vols., Jewish Publication Society of America, 1933–5.

J. Goldin, *The Song at the Sea* (translation and commentary on part of Mekilta), Yale University Press, 1971.

W. G. Braude, *Pesikta Rabbati*, 2 vols., Yale University Press, 1968.

S. Singer, *The Authorized Daily Prayer Book*, Eyre & Spottiswoode, London, 1918 and 1962.

J. H. Hertz, *The Authorized Daily Prayer Book*, revised edition with commentary, National Council for Jewish Religious Education, London, 1942.

I. Abrahams, *A Companion to the Authorised Daily Prayer Book*, 2nd edn, Eyre & Spottiswoode, London, 1922.

J. Bowker, *The Targums and Rabbinic Literature*, Cambridge University Press, 1969.

C. G. Montefiore and H. Loewe, *A Rabbinic Anthology*, Meridian Books, New York, 1963.

L. Ginzberg, *The Legends of the Jews*, 7 vols., Jewish Publication Society of America, 1947.

H. Freedman and M. Simon, *Midrash Rabbah*, 11 vols., Soncino Press, London, 1951.

I. Epstein, *The Babylonian Talmud*, 34 vols., Soncino Press, London, 1952.

## BACKGROUND READING

J. R. Bartlett, *Jews in the Hellenistic World*, Cambridge University Press, 1985.

D. Daube, *The New Testament and Rabbinic Judaism*, Athlone Press, London, 1956.

R. Gordis, 'A basis for morals', *Judaism*, no. 97, Winter, 1976.

R. T. Herford, *The Pharisees*, George Allen & Unwin, London, 1924.

M. Kadushin, *The Rabbinic Mind*, Blaisdell, New York, 1965.

K. Kahana, *The Theory of Marriage in Jewish Law*, E. J. Brill, New York, 1966.

P. Kahle, *The Cairo Geniza*, 2nd edn, Oxford, 1959.

S. A. Kaufman, 'The Job Targum from Qumran', *Journal of American Oriental Studies*, no. 93, 1973.

E. Y. Kutscher, 'The Language of the Genesis Apocryphon', *Scripta Hierosolymitana*, vol. iv, ed. C. Rabin and Y. Yadin, 1965.

A. R. C. Leaney, *The Jewish and Christian World, 200 BC to AD 200*, Cambridge University Press, 1984.

S. Lieberman, *Hellenism in Jewish Palestine*, Jewish Theological Seminary of America, 1950.

H. Maccoby, *Revolution in Judaea*, Taplinger, New York, 1980.

H. Mantel, *Studies in the History of the Sanhedrin*, Harvard University Press, 1965.

M. Mielziner, *Introduction to the Talmud*, Bloch Publishing Co., New York, 1925.
G. F. Moore, *Judaism in the First Centuries of the Christian Era: the Age of the Tannaim*, 3 vols., Harvard University Press, 1927–30.
J. Neusner, *Judaism: the Evidence of the Mishnah*, University of Chicago Press, 1981.
J. Parkes, *The Foundations of Judaism and Christianity*, Valentine Mitchell, London, 1960.
E. Rivkin, *The Hidden Revolution: the Pharisees' Search for the Kingdom Within*, Abingdon, Nashville, 1975.
E. P. Sanders, *Paul and Palestinian Judaism*, SCM Press, London, 1977.
S. Sandmel, *The First Christian Century in Judaism and Christianity: Certainties and Uncertainties*, Oxford University Press, 1969.
G. Scholem, *Jewish Gnosticism, Merkabah Mysticism and Talmudic Tradition*, Jewish Theological Seminary of America, 1960.
*Major Trends in Jewish Mysticism*, Thames & Hudson, London, 1961.
L. Smolar and M. Aberbach, *Studies in Targum Jonathan to the Prophets*, Ktav, New York, 1983.
H. L. Strack, *Introduction to the Talmud and Midrash*, Meridian Books, New York, 1959.
A. Tal, *The Language of the Targum of the Former Prophets and its Position within the Aramaic Dialects*, Tel Aviv, 1975 (Hebrew).
E. E. Urbach, *The Sages: their Concepts and Beliefs*, Magnes Press, Jerusalem, 1975.
G. Vermes, *Scripture and Tradition in Judaism*, E. J. Brill, New York, 1961.

# Index